Spin Wars
and
Spy Games

Spin Wars and Spy Games

Global Media and Intelligence Gathering

MARKOS KOUNALAKIS

HOOVER INSTITUTION PRESS
Stanford University
Stanford, California

With its eminent scholars and world-renowned library and archives, the Hoover Institution seeks to improve the human condition by advancing ideas that promote economic opportunity and prosperity, while securing and safeguarding peace for America and all mankind. The views expressed in its publications are entirely those of the authors and do not necessarily reflect the views of the staff, officers, or Board of Overseers of the Hoover Institution.

www.hoover.org

Hoover Institution Press Publication No. 693

Hoover Institution at Leland Stanford Junior University,
Stanford, California 94305-6003

Efforts have been made to locate original sources, determine the current rights holders, and, if needed, obtain reproduction permissions. On verification of any such claims to rights in the articles reproduced in this book, any required corrections or clarifications will be made in subsequent printings/editions.

Hoover Institution Press assumes no responsibility for the persistence or accuracy of URLs for external or third-party Internet websites referred to in this publication, and does not guarantee that any content on such websites is, or will remain, accurate or appropriate.

First printing 2018
26 25 24 23 22 21 20 19 18   9 8 7 6 5 4 3 2 1

Manufactured in the United States of America

The paper used in this publication meets the minimum requirements of the American National Standard for Information Sciences—Permanence of Paper for Printed Library Materials, ANSI/NISO Z39.48-1992.♾

Cataloging-in-Publication Data is available from the Library of Congress.
ISBN-13: 978-0-8179-2195-8 (paperback)
ISBN-13: 978-0-8179-2196-5 (EPUB)
ISBN-13: 978-0-8179-2197-2 (Mobipocket)
ISBN-13: 978-0-8179-2198-9 (PDF)

CONTENTS

Foreword *by Peter Laufer*   ix
Preface   xv
Acknowledgments   xix

Introduction   1

CHAPTER 1 | Global News Networks and State Power   21

CHAPTER 2 | Western Global News Networks and State Power 1   39
                Diplomacy

CHAPTER 3 | Western Global News Networks and State Power 2   81
                Intelligence

CHAPTER 4 | Non-Western Global News Networks   125
                Diplomacy and Intelligence Gathering

CHAPTER 5 | Conclusion   153

APPENDIX 1 | Interview with Terry Phillips   165

APPENDIX 2 | Methodology   173

References   179
About the Author   213
Index   215

LIST OF TABLES AND FIGURES

Table 1 Typology of global news networks   3

Table 2 Typology of GNN-state relationships   9

Table 3 GNN ideal types engaged in diplomacy   48

Table 4 Types of GNN intelligence gathering   84

Table 5 Intelligence-gathering ideal types   110

Figure 1 GNNs and intelligence flow   37

Figure 2 Semtex testing on the fuselage of an aircraft   119

Figure 3 Red Mercury formula   121

Figure 4 Chinese GNN organization structure   131

FOREWORD

Peter Laufer

Soon after the Soviet Union invaded Afghanistan, I was dispatched in my role as an NBC News correspondent to Peshawar. The frontier Pakistan city—still today packed with spies, soldiers, refugees, and journalists—is just down a jammed highway from the Khyber Pass, a strategic cross-roads along that fraught and porous border. I was there meeting with people the US government (and NBC) called freedom fighters, negoti-ating to join them on an attack foray back across the line into Afghanistan that would pit their Springfield rifles against Soviet tanks and helicopter gunships.

These CIA-financed ragtag soldiers were Al Qaeda forerunners, but in those confused days they were America's foot soldiers in the Hindu Kush. Or so the Reagan administration thought. Rumors were circulating at the Dean's Hotel (where the waiters asked us to keep our beer bottles hidden under the table) that the Soviets were seeding the trails through the mountains with mines camouflaged in vibrant colors and shame-lessly shaped like toys. Proving the stories true would be a propaganda coup for the anti-Soviet West. How cruel: they would risk blowing off the hands of intrigued innocent children only to further what already appeared to many of us observers on the scene as a doomed military mission.

One Somerset Maugham–soaked evening I found myself at the US consulate in Peshawar dining with the consul and a fellow reporter from one of the news wire services. As the US taxpayer–provided drinks flowed, the consul mused about the mine rumors and the dastardly dam-age they could do to limb and life. He knew we were planning a trip up to the pass and beyond.

"If you find any evidence of the mines," he said in what I remember years later as a soft, conspiratorial voice, "it would be of great value to your country were you to bring it back and give it to me." He warned us, of course, against picking up any unexploded ordnance. He envisioned fragments that could be identified by American experts as both resembling plastic toys and being of Soviet origin.

Back under the languid ceiling fans at the Dean's Hotel after the soiree, my colleague and I mulled over the consul's request. We're both red-blooded Americans, neither of us supported the Soviet invasion or its Afghan policy, and we certainly opposed minefields disguised as playgrounds. But we both considered ourselves independent journalists working for private independent newsgathering organizations. "We're not government agents," we told each other, and then agreed that were we to find Soviet mine detritus, we would report the news. In that case, we rationalized, it would be no compromise to give such evidence to the consul. On the contrary, it would just be a variation on our reporting work, with the consul the sole audience for the version of the story we would tell him, a version that could include the actual war matériel.

In *Spin Wars and Spy Games*, Markos Kounalakis acknowledges that my wire service colleague and I were not engaged as spies while we were clambering around Pakistan's North-West Frontier Province. Rather, Kounalakis labels us what he calls nonstate foreign correspondents, ready to aid our home country if it did not compromise our professional ethics, especially vis-à-vis policies we personally opposed. Our search efforts for mines would be at most a footnote in the ongoing power struggles playing out along the Afghan-Pakistan border. And it is hard to imagine that in the rush-rush of today's twenty-four-hour news cycle, along with Western newsgathering organizations' budget concerns, two roving American reporters could enjoy the luxury of lighting out in search of stories for days, even weeks, out of touch with headquarters.

Kounalakis argues that as the Western nonstate journalism role of independent investigator and critic diminishes, what he labels non-Western state-sponsored journalism grows at an alarming rate. He shows how these state-sponsored news outlets profit by employing Western-trained journalists who can no longer find work at home in a disrupted profession struggling with an antiquated business model. Hence, he writes, non-Western news organizations "build and deploy targeted, effective, and cost-effective, plausibly deniable intelligence-gathering institutions aligned perfectly with the state's strategic—as well as soft power—goals. The result is a formidable non-Western intelligence agency and world-wide diplomatic service with little pretense that it serves freedom of speech."

In an apartment on the Arbat in Moscow that I shared with Kounalakis and other Western reporters when we all were foreign correspondents, one of us attached a note under the telephone. In bold print it warned, "Speak only about the weather." We assumed all our calls were monitored because the government knew our job was to ferret out the news, not act as their docile stenographers.

The research and analysis in *Spin Wars and Spy Games* proves our phone warning is all but an artifact of a bygone era. Kounalakis shows that even when Western news outlets continue to field reporters overseas, "a combination of intimidation tactics, including non-accreditation, censorship, legal registration, physical threat, or arrest," often is used to blunt their effectiveness, while the state-sponsored journalists (should they be called spies or at least propagandists?) "work closely with state enterprises to propagate an ideological orientation as one more tool in a policy toolbox that gives them greater reach, increased access, and more points of engagement in the work of political, educational, commercial, and military diplomacy."

In addition to their engagement in espionage and as de facto diplomats, these state-sponsored reporters find themselves serving a valuable societal role that only adds to the credibility of their cover story. When news breaks in the wilds of the world, they're often the only operatives available to rush in a timely manner to the scene. Kounalakis documents examples of their exclusive reporting that should be embarrassing to the cash-strapped independent Western broadcasters and newspapers who were forced to credit their state-sponsored competitors for footage, photographs, and quotes.

No question that, even in this period of tight budgets and radically changing business models, brave Western reporters laboring for dedicated journalism companies risk their lives doing work of crucial importance. But the playing field is far from level.

Just after the Iron Curtain rose, Kounalakis—who has spent much of his career as a foreign correspondent—and I took an overland trip across Eastern Europe together. At the time he was considering a teaching position in Ohio. In those pre-GPS days, a paper road map was unfolded on his lap as we headed toward Bulgaria one day, with me driving and him riding shotgun navigating. "I better take that job in Ohio," he mused while checking our route. "I can get us to Sofia, but I don't know my way from Cleveland to Columbus." In the decades since, he's caught up on his Buckeye State geography, and all those years in the field from Kabul to Berlin and on to Havana, Beijing, and Cincinnati, and all sorts of flash points in between, provide the ideal background for this timely book.

"I pledge allegiance to the flag of the United States of America, and to the Republic for which it stands." Those words we learned as schoolkids can tumble out of Americans' mouths without thought. But what do they mean to us journalists and academics when so often our work assigns us a role adversarial to our own government? No question that, even in this period of tight budgets and radically changing business models, brave and dedicated Western reporters going out in the wilds for dedicated journalism companies risk their lives doing work of crucial importance. But the international playing field, as Kounalakis shows us, is far from level. Many—nay, most—of our state-sponsored professional competitors, especially those working for Chinese and Russian news agencies, do not spend a moment wrestling with their allegiances, let alone their consciences. They have a primary job to do, and scoring a news scoop for public consumption is of secondary concern at best.

ıııııııııııı

We live in an era when the president of the United States refers to America's longtime newspaper of record as "the failing *New York Times*" and calls his own nation's journalists "the enemy of the American people." The term *fake news* is used to tar news and information with which our polarized society disagrees. Meanwhile, as Kounalakis makes clear, America's adversaries labor quietly and tirelessly, taking advantage of a growing void of Western-style independent journalistic presence.

We ignore the timely findings of *Spin Wars and Spy Games* at our peril.

> *Peter Laufer, PhD*
> James Wallace Chair Professor in Journalism
> University of Oregon School of Journalism
>   and Communication
> *December 30, 2017*

PREFACE

There are more foreign correspondents in the world today than ever. They don't belong to the big media names of Western journalistic institutions, however. Nearly all of those Western institutions have dramatically cut back the number of correspondents who report on the world and closed down foreign bureaus. The precipitous drop in foreign corresponding—the type grounded in a Western tradition of fairness and accuracy and conducted by experienced senior journalists with adversarial relationships to power—raises the question of how societies and elites will be informed about the world in the future and how that information will shape perceptions and policies within and between sovereign states.

The world's largest global broadcast news network is no longer CNN or the BBC or any other Western name brand network; in fact, the previous dominance of these networks in global newsgathering and distribution is rapidly diminishing.

The world's largest global news network today is state-sponsored CGTN (formerly CCTV, China Central Television) when its resources are considered in combination with its state-run adjunct, the Xinhua news agency. RT (formerly Russia Today) is the world's most viewed news channel on YouTube, leveraging Russian state resources for production and non-Russian private sector infrastructure for its vast distribution. Western news networks had a near monopoly during the latter half of the twentieth century, a situation that helped catalyze the Cold War's end. In the early twenty-first century, however, Western nations no longer dominate the global informational realm. This new asymmetry has significant foreign policy implications. This book explores why.

All global news networks perform the counterintuitive functions of diplomacy and intelligence gathering. Though foreign correspondents are neither spies nor diplomats, they perform both intelligence-gathering and diplomatic functions, whether formally or informally. The larger institutional framework in which they function makes their work and work product materially relevant to the states they serve, whether they do so wittingly or unwittingly.

For those in the journalism profession at large, this performance runs counter to common perceptions, both in the public at large and within the profession, with the practice a secret known only among a limited number of foreign corresponding practitioners.

The material nature of the work done by global news networks goes beyond the dominant understanding in the academic literature that analyzes these networks and their work as performing a public diplomatic practice and supplying a source of power within a smart power framework that is limited mostly to the soft power side of the smart equation.

Further, as global news networks produce both soft and hard power, thanks to their integral role in intelligence flow, there is potentially a new aspect to the current geopolitical shift in material power.

As a result of Chinese state policies to grow the print, broadcast, Internet, and mobile networks of the state-controlled media, CGTN and Xinhua, China is fueling a dramatic increase in foreign corresponding bureaus, reporters, editors, broadcast stations, and information-gathering and dissemination infrastructure around the world. The investment is leading to exponential growth in presence and production. "While our media empires are melting away like the Himalayan glaciers, China's are expanding," said Orville Schell, director of the Center on U.S.-China Relations at the Asia Society.[1]

Former secretary of state Hillary Clinton went so far as to say that the United States is currently "engaged in an information war." She concluded that testimony to the Senate Foreign Relations Committee in 2011 by saying starkly that in the information fight against emerging international broadcasters, "we are losing that war."

IIIIIIIIIIIII

When I started this work in 2012, it was clear that Russia and China were expending enormous resources to build their global news networks with

---

1. Barboza 2010.

no expectation that there would be either commercial success or financial return for the state. The question that drove my research was why any state would invest such vast resources. What is the expected return, if not financial?

This book provides the answer. The return on their investment, at a minimum, has been a dramatic increase in their intelligence-gathering and diplomatic capacities. What I did not anticipate is that this evolving global news network infrastructure built by America's adversaries would provide the means to conduct effective and ongoing influence operations on vulnerable Western democratic states and their electorates, as the 2016 presidential election showed. That influence may yet prove the most rewarding return of all.

Markos Kounalakis
Hoover Tower
Stanford, California
January 2018

ACKNOWLEDGMENTS

First, I wish to acknowledge those who worked hardest and closest with me on this work, Central European University colleagues Matteo Fumagalli and Erin Jenne, as well as Oxford University's Philip N. Howard. This book also benefited enormously from the diligent work of my research assistants, Judit Szakacs and Kennedy Jawoko. Their help was invaluable. Any shortcomings are my own.

The Hoover Institution at Stanford University is my academic home and continues to support my work. I am privileged and honored to be here and appreciate Professor Dave Brady's fifteen years of clear and unvarnished guidance. This book was written, edited, and finalized in an office adjoining former president Herbert Hoover's on the eleventh floor of Hoover Tower.

The Hoover Press is the perfect house for this homegrown publication, and special thanks go to the dedicated production team led by Chris Dauer.

I am grateful to the many journalists, NGO workers, and academics who helped me with this book but must remain anonymous given their candor and our mutual agreement. You know who you are and I thank you deeply.

Finally, and most important, I thank my wife, Eleni, and my two boys, Neo and Eon, who gave me the time and space to do what needed to get done. They have my undying love and affection.

Markos Kounalakis
San Francisco, California
January 4, 2018

INTRODUCTION

It was a momentous time in the twentieth century when a new electronic technology allowed messages to be sent instantaneously across borders by short audible data bursts. The first political leader to exploit the technology put it bluntly: "The matter is *of immense importance* (a newspaper without paper and without wires . . . all Russia will be able to hear a newspaper read in Moscow)."[1] The technology was shortwave radio. The writer was V. I. Lenin. When the newspaper *Pravda* published this in 1926, nine years after the initial Bolshevik broadcasts in Morse code, Lenin clearly envisioned the potentially unlimited opportunities of being able to transmit messages far and wide via radio.

The goal of these early radio transmissions was to broadcast ideas and promote revolutionary ideals to a distant and often illiterate mass, moving quickly from the impersonal Morse code in 1917 to audible transmission of Lenin's passionate speeches. The next to go on air internationally, with the direct help of radio inventor Guglielmo Marconi, was Pope Pius XI, who established Vatican Radio shortly after the Vatican was granted full sovereignty in 1929.[2] Many states eventually followed and developed their own international broadcasting capacities, but these were the first two state broadcasters to believe they could proselytize the distantly unconverted and speak to their remote loyal flock.[3]

---

1. Lenin [1926] 1973, 473, emphasis in the original. The full citation follows: "The matter is of immense importance (a newspaper without paper and without wires, for with a loudspeaker and with the receiver which Bonch-Bruyevich has developed in such a way that it will be easy for us to produce hundreds of receivers, all Russia will be able to hear a newspaper read in Moscow)."

2. According to Bucci, Pelosi, and Selleri (2003), the pope was personally involved in setting up the first historic transmission from Castel Gandolfo.

3. Matelski 1995; Street and Matelski 1997. Street and Matelski's work is a comprehensive historical analysis of the use of radio for religious, as well as political, proselytizing and propaganda.

From the very first days of the technological advancement allowing for cross-border transmission and instantaneous mass communication, transnational global broadcasting has been used to varying degrees and in different ways as a tool of international statecraft.[4] While the goals may have remained the same, broadcasting has evolved tremendously during the last century; the reach of global networks has become vast. Now, as WikiLeaks shows, any individual owning a mobile phone has access to global news networks, enjoying "the communication power that was the monopoly of the nation state in the previous century."[5]

The contemporary descendants of the early state broadcasters are today's larger and more complex institutional news ecologies, global news networks[6] (GNNs) often controlled and underwritten by the state—organizations such as the Broadcasting Board of Governors' Voice of America and Radio Free Europe (BBG), Russia Today (RT), Al Jazeera (AJ), and China Global Television Network, formerly China Central Television and Xinhua (CGTN/X), as well as the individuals, either employed there or working with those GNNs, who are an increasingly integrated part of this broader news ecology. Equally important parts of the broader international media ecology are nonstate news institutions—and the individuals within them—and hybrid state/nonstate GNNs, most significantly CNN and the BBC, who work collaboratively, symbiotically, or in parallel with individuals and other national newsgathering broadcast, Internet, and print institutions in open and nonsovereign media environments to round out the institutional global newsgathering and distribution system.

This book recognizes the historical and contemporary soft power of the mass broadcasting and disseminating functions of GNNs. Further, it

---

4. Wasburn 1997. In this review of Gary D. Rawnsley's volume, Wasburn looks at the struggle between broadcasters and their state sponsors in the execution of their established and historically consistent roles in state information, disinformation, and in particular, diplomatic functions during war and peace. Most studies, however, focus on the propagandistic and ideational role within statecraft.

5. Cull 2011, 2.

6. The term, coined by the author here and used throughout this study, bears no relation to the Philippines-based cable television channel with the same name.

takes a deep dive into GNN functions that deliver news and information to narrower and sometimes targeted state audiences with the effect, if not always the desire, of delivering information and data as a hard material resource.

What follows in this introductory chapter is, first, a discussion of the concept of global news networks (GNNs), especially how that concept has evolved and how its functions relate to the state. The remainder of this chapter will proceed with a brief discussion on the work's relevance in today's geopolitical sphere. Predominantly reliant on elite interviewing, the study is informed by individuals who agreed to waive anonymity as well as those who demanded anonymity, given the sensitive nature of this research. The case study method is employed to look at the practices and performance of both Western GNNs and non-Western GNNs.

Global News Networks: Definition and Typology

Table 1 shows a limited representation of what constitutes a state, non-state, or hybrid GNN.

	CNN, *New York Times*, Associated Press, Bloomberg	BBC World, Internews Network, HRW	RT, Al Jazeera, CCTV, Xinhua, BBG, Deutsche Welle
Nonstate (Type)	X		
Hybrid (Type II)		X	
State (Type III)			X

Table 1. Typology of global news networks

A GNN in this study is defined as a network of nationally identified and aligned institutions and individuals that report, collect, curate, edit, broadcast, and distribute print and electronic productions,[7] relying on foreign offices or bureaus and expatriate or traveling researchers, reporters, and correspondents. Their publicized work product reaches or targets international audiences.

The main definitional characteristic of GNNs for this study is their formal relationship to the state, primarily defined by management, assignment, and editorial GNN structures but also by the informal state relationship and the level of direct or indirect state financial underwriting, grant funding, or request for proposal (RFP) fulfillment. Some GNNs are exclusively funded and managed by the state (state, type III), whereas others are exclusively funded via their commercial enterprise or nonprofit fund-raising (nonstate, type I), without state funds, relying on advertising and sponsorship revenue with no apparent structural direct state links or relationship. The third type (hybrid, type II) is a mixture of the first two types.[8]

For a broadcast or print news network to be included in the GNN typology, it must have programming or a distribution arm that targets an international audience and often includes multiple languages. In this study, GNNs always include a dominant English-language presence. A network that does not incorporate an English-language service in its news and information distribution is not considered a full GNN or a globally competitive institution for the purposes of this work. Other requirements include having global news collection and distribution

---

7. The reason for including print media in this definition is that though they are in decline, they both complement and remain heavily integrated with international broadcast media in multiple aspects of the newsgathering function and news value determination process. To varying degrees, multiple media organizations share or bundle resources, whether newsgathering or distributional presenting assets, and regularly mix and match their capacities. Together, the multiple manifestations and formal or informal combinations of national institutional media outlets form a significant portion of the complex and growing media ecologies of global news networks.

8. The categories in this typology are ideal types, not meant to correspond perfectly to reality. For instance, CGTN, formerly CCTV, carries advertisements in addition to its state funding, though the dominant advertising expenditures are indirect state subsidies, as either state-owned enterprises or state-negotiated advertisers are the main contributors to the $2.9 billion annual revenue stream (interview with CCTV-America, November 14, 2014).

channels (precluding some of the more regionally or diaspora-focused media networks), overseas broadcast centers, a minimal audience size, a minimal budget size, and the expansive capacity for multiple platform production and distribution (i.e., wire service, radio, satellite television, Twitter, Facebook, website, email alerting, etc.). A GNN, further, must employ not only nationals of the GNN home country but also nationals of other countries in either the news collection or management structure of the institution.[9]

Although global news networks traditionally comprise only formal news institutions and journalists, who made up the dominant news collection and dissemination process in the twentieth century, this work extends the understanding of what makes up this information and news ecology to include nontraditional newsgathering and dissemination institutions that currently feed into the larger media ecology, still dominated by formal journalistic institutions at the international level. The nonjournalistic institutions in this study include both international nongovernmental organizations (INGOs) and the academic research community (and to a limited degree, corporate institutions and executives), where research and publication are the staples of the profession and complement—or even, at times, supplement—the journalistic institutions that are the focus of most media analysis and the academic literature when trying to understand media effects on foreign affairs. These nonjournalistic institutions are unique in this sphere because they at times access privileged information.[10]

---

9. The GNN framework developed here is, naturally, not the only way to analyze and categorize existing transnational/international media networks. Chalaby (2002, 2005a, 2005b, 2006) proposed an alternative typology in which the focus is more on the intended audience than on the state-network nexus. A well-researched comparative analysis of Al Jazeera English and the Venezuelan Telesur channel by Painter (2008) categorizes international broadcasters by their relation to the dominant "Western" worldview as hegemonic or counterhegemonic and analyzes, among other things, whether they follow the "Western" journalistic value of impartiality or are openly ideological. There is also a wealth of literature studying media networks from the perspective of the/a European public sphere (see, for example, Brüggeman and Schulz-Forberg 2009). For the purposes of this book, however, the typology based on ownership, managerial, and editorial structure proposed here seems to be the most useful.

10. On the flip side, this information gathering also means INGOs are regularly accused of spying activities or of fomenting dissent and aiming to destabilize governments. In his study of NGO relationships to the state, DeMars (2001, 194) writes that "most relevant academic

The inclusion of nonprofit organizations in the GNN concept recognizes the expanding role many of these organizations play in news production, particularly in foreign news production and crisis coverage, as established by a growing body of literature.[11] The INGOs included, such as Internews Network, Human Rights Watch (HRW), Global Investigative Journalist Network (GIJN), IREX, or even Save the Children, are arguably very diverse. Yet from the perspective of this study, they can justifiably be grouped together. With respect to news production, they often exhibit similar behaviors, and they are often subject to similar pressures and face proscription by certain governments. While their inclusion as a type of GNN may lack nuance and definitional distinction, they are together an important part of the GNN landscape.

As for their relations to news production, these nonprofit groups often are the only organizations reporting on the countries in which they operate, the only "boots on the ground."[12] These news and nonnews NGOs have grown to fill a vacuum for news and data collection and distribution overseas and, in some cases, to supplant traditional news institutions as the only nonnative organizations around.[13] As a Washington, DC–based director of a humanitarian and rights-oriented NGO put it, "There aren't any American reporters out in the bush. They show up once in a while for the 'bang-bang'—whenever there's a terrorist attack or an American gets killed. Basically, if you're going to get any news from out there, it's going to be from us. That's it. Nobody else gives a shit."[14]

---

and policy literature fails to address the real issues in this hazardous relationship." For example, Russian president Vladimir Putin and leaders of both democratically and nondemocratically elected governments in Asia have taken a hard-line approach to INGOs, restricting their formal activities and freedom via punitive and controlling legislation (on Putin's attitude to non-Russian NGOs, see Carothers 2006; Evans, 2006). There is also an evolving trend in states like Hungary, Israel, Turkey, and China to develop new and restrictive laws proscribing INGO activities within their borders.

11. Powers (2015) provides a fairly recent overview of the existing literature.

12. Powers 2015.

13. Conrad (2013) looks at two nonprofit organizations, the Pulitzer Center on Crisis Reporting and the International Reporting Project (IRP), and notes the shift to and growing dependence upon nationally based NGOs as "they have considerable authority over the changing field of US foreign correspondence" (Conrad 2013, par. 1; see also Conrad 2015).

14. Personal communication, 2014.

Another reason to include NGOs in the GNN category is that they often perform journalistic functions, producing what are sometimes generically referred to as white papers. Aid agencies have been shown to hire professional journalists and photographers to create what Grayson termed "NGO reportage."[15] These papers are now becoming similar to documentaries, using various multimedia platforms in the pursuit of a mass audience. They also pursue multiple broad distribution channels in their pursuit of policy impact and journalistic credibility. The NGO final product or press release often finds a direct distribution channel for entering in an unedited manner directly into the wider media landscape.[16] That development has come as a direct result of distributed and digital production and publication tools and Internet-enabled distribution channels, which have intermixed and coalesced with more traditional journalistic institutions and mediations.[17]

The information revolution has played a crucial role in putting academia in the GNN ecology. Academic researchers living and working in foreign countries are now also understood to be part of the GNN world as defined in this study. While there has been a long history of academic research abroad carried out in a relationship with intelligence-gathering institutions,[18] it is primarily the intelligence-gathering and disseminating capacities that digital technologies have provided for academics that enable them to participate in GNN structures.

Further, this study's understanding of GNNs includes Internet giants such as Facebook, Twitter, and Google. Although they continue to deny

---

15. Grayson 2014. See also Cooper 2011.

16. Cooper (2009) notes that the line between NGOs and media outlets started blurring in the 1990s, when aid agencies started "providing cash-strapped foreign desks with free footage and words" (par. 24).

17. For a critical overview of NGOs' communication in the digital media age, see Cottle and Nolan 2007. Franks (2008) offers a critical look at what she sees as the media becoming too reliant on aid organizations for news production.

18. D. Price (2000) discusses how one of the most respected American anthropologists, Franz Boas, in 1919 exposed that four of his colleagues had spied for the United States during World War I. What is more, although Boas clearly saw this as a "betray[al] [of] their science"(par. 1), according to much later declassified FBI documents, one of the scientists, Harvard archaeologist Samuel Lothrop, continued to work for US intelligence agencies during World War II, using his scholarly work as cover.

it,[19] many strong arguments have been made to treat them as media companies rather than simply tech companies or platforms.[20] But even without coming down on either side of this debate, the huge amount of data these companies handle and the influence they have over public discourse warrant their inclusion in the GNN ecology.

INGOs, academic researchers, and Internet giants are professional practitioners who join traditional newsgatherers to make up today's GNNs. However, practitioners of "citizen journalism"—those institutionally unaffiliated journalists who make up "a range of web-based practices whereby 'ordinary' users engage in journalistic practices"[21]—are not included. The role of citizen journalists is complementary to the institutional media ecology but, unlike some NGO work or academic research, it is not considered in the current literature as a supplanting force in global reporting or institutional foreign work.[22]

Table 2 shows the ideal types of GNNs and their relationship to the state. GNNs can be one of three types of institutions: nonstate, state, or a hybrid owned, operated, or controlled by both state and nonstate organizations. Further, the matrix bifurcates the world into Western and non-Western states. Per the parameters of this research, the non-Western GNNs reviewed are Russian and Chinese. The Western GNNs are dominated by native English-language GNNs but incorporate others who make up parts of Western trade, security, economic, and political alliances. Not only news organizations but also Western academia and Western NGOs are categorized according to their relation to the state. The non-Western GNNs populate only one of the matrix cells, that of the state-controlled GNN, while the Western GNNs are dominated by nonstate institutions, though they also include state and hybrid institutions. While non-Western commercial media entertainment and sports

---

19. J. Roberts 2016.
20. Griffith 2017.
21. Goode 2009, 2.
22. Otto and Meyer (2012) write that there has been a great deal of excitement and anti-institutional utopian projection regarding the rise of citizen journalism and the tools that enable it worldwide. "It has been argued that the importance of foreign correspondents has been overstated and that news agencies, social networks and citizen-journalism can fill the gap" (205). Otto and Meyer show this to be a false, and dangerous, expectation.

	Nonstate	State	Hybrid
Western	CNN, *NY Times*, *Guardian*, FAZ, INGOs (Doctors Without Borders), academia	INGOs, academia, BBG (VOA, RFE/RL)	BBG, INGOs (Internews, IREX), academia
Non-Western		RT, CCTV, Xinhua, INGOs, academia	

Table 2. Typology of GNN-state relationships

enterprises are populating the domestic media landscape in China and Russia, state broadcasters either directly owned by or heavily dependent upon the state for their operations remain the dominant GNN institutions.

The goal of this book is to investigate the current global news network landscape and to identify current trends to understand what geopolitical significance those trends may have.

The Changing GNN Landscape

GNNs have evolved both in practice and performance. Western transnational and traditional news networks had a near monopoly during the latter half of the twentieth century and are credited with helping to catalyze the Cold War's end.[23]

In the early part of the twenty-first century, however, Western media no longer dominate this global institutional and informational realm. The world's largest global news network (GNN) is no longer CNN or the

---

23. M. Nelson 1997; Johnson and Parta 2010. For a historical overview of US foreign correspondence since the European revolutions of 1848 and the role it may have played in US foreign policy, see Dell'Orto 2013.

BBC or any other Western newspaper or magazine publisher or name brand broadcast network. As seen above, the previous global newsgathering and distribution dominance of these networks is rapidly diminishing while today's GNN is made up of a broader and more complex set of institutions and individuals beyond strictly newsgathering operations.

Further, Western news organizations are increasingly turning away from foreign affairs. The trend and direction of the shift is clear: the diminution of Western GNNs[24] and the global rise of non-Western GNNs. The disappearance of the American foreign correspondent and overseas bureau is now a hard fact, documented and narrated by the now also defunct *American Journalism Review (AJR)*.[25] In 2011, the *AJR* published "Retreating from the World," the last of a series documenting the demise of Western foreign reporting. "Eighteen newspapers and two chains have shuttered every one of their overseas bureaus in the dozen years since *AJR* first surveyed foreign coverage. . . . All but two of them eliminated their last bureau sometime after 2003, the year the United States invaded Iraq. . . . Many other papers and chains reduced their coterie of foreign correspondents. . . . What's more, an untold number of regional and local papers have dramatically decreased the amount of foreign news they publish. Television networks, meanwhile, slashed the time they devote to foreign news and narrowed their focus largely to war zones."[26] At the start of 2016, the McClatchy newspaper company, the third-largest newspaper organization in the United States, announced it had shut down all of its remaining foreign bureaus. As noted by the Poynter Institute, which does research on the media, "McClatchy is among the last of the regional newspaper companies to maintain foreign bureaus, and its de-emphasis of international coverage follows similar moves made by *The Baltimore Sun, The Boston Globe, Newsday* and others."[27]

---

24. Otto and Meyer 2012, 205.

25. The first report on the issue was put together by the Pulitzer Prize–winning war correspondent Peter Arnett in 1998. In the article titled "State of the American Newspaper: Goodbye World," Arnett writes, "I'll put it simply: International news coverage in most of America's mainstream papers has almost reached the vanishing point" (Arnett 1998, par. 12).

26. Enda 2011, par. 22. Interestingly, there have long been worries about the disappearance of foreign news on television. Utley (1997, 2) called "the network television foreign correspondent an endangered species" twenty years ago.

27. Mullin 2015, par. 6

In the meantime, in the non-Western world, the opposite trend is taking place. The dominant shift in the current GNN ecology is the recent nascence (2000) and dramatic growth of China's CCTV, now called CGTN, and Xinhua news agency. With the current rate of growth and level of investment, state-sponsored China Global Television Network together with its adjunct, the Xinhua news agency (CGTN/X), will soon be the world's largest global broadcast news network.[28] Russia is also expanding a state-sponsored GNN: RT, formerly Russia Today, is reportedly the world's most viewed news channel on YouTube, with more YouTube subscribers than the YouTube channels of CNN and BBC News together,[29] leveraging Russian state resources for production and non-Russian private sector infrastructure for its vast distribution. Other state-controlled GNNs, such as Al Jazeera, are also making a significant push to expand their network, programming, and distribution.[30] Yet the broadcaster that stands alone for sheer size, ambition, and growth is the combined behemoth of CGTN/X.[31] In fact, according to the *Columbia Journalism Review*, the Chinese government has already "built the world's largest news organization," with funding estimated at "19 times the annual budget of BBC."[32] In fact, the BBC warned in 2015 that it would soon be marginalized by non-Western GNNs unless its budget cuts are reversed. "China, Russia and Qatar are investing in their international channels in ways that we cannot match, but none has our values and our ability to investigate any story no matter how difficult," the BBC wrote in its report.[33]

---

28. Mustafi 2012. As Anne Nelson points out in a report to the Center for International Media Assistance (2013, 6), "China Central Television has come a long ways since its founding as a domestic party propaganda outlet in 1958 . . . boasting three major global offices in Beijing, Washington, and Nairobi, and more than 70 additional international bureaus."

29. Shuster 2015.

30. Bullogh 2013.

31. X. Zhang 2010.

32. Mustafi 2012, 19. Official budget figures for CGTN/X are difficult to find but not impossible to extrapolate from the known figures used for wages (approximately 20 percent above standard salaries in host countries), distribution (e.g., costs for satellite and cable distribution), and foreign bureau operations. More difficult to establish are domestic budgetary items and expenditures, though some official figures have been released.

33. Plunkett 2015, para 15. A British politician also said that it was frightening how the BBC World Service was getting "outgunned" by Russian and Chinese GNNs (par. 17).

Given the clear trends in resource allocations among GNNs and the rise of CGTN/X[34] in the GNN ecology—with China and Russia investing unprecedented amounts to develop their global news networks—the central research question that drives this work is: How consequential are GNNs for enhancing state soft and hard power?

In much of the academic literature to date, international state broadcasting is considered an aspect of public diplomacy and its role an extension of soft power.[35] However, as recognized by some leading scholars in media research and international broadcasting, the analysis to date has lacked either nuance or operational understanding.[36]

Add to this a dynamic and ever-changing media landscape, where digital tools and Internet-based distribution methods are challenging concepts of censorship and control, altering the realm of information sovereignty, as well as the very business models and organizational structures of institutional and individual news collection and distribution networks that have dominated the industry during the last part of the twentieth century.[37] Further, much of the research and analysis on media and policy[38] has been concerned primarily with domestic effects on national, regional, or local electoral behavior and policy formation, often ignoring nondomestic foreign policy, national security, or overall geopolitical effects.[39]

---

34. In 2013, CCTV presented some early figures of its personnel and bureau structure: CCTV's "Europe bureau chief, Jianing Shen, reeled off a host of statistics, citing CCTV's 70 overseas bureaux, with their 446 staff (roughly the same as the [BBC] World Service), 157 of them local employees. Just three years ago, it had only 49 staff posted abroad" (Tryhorn 2013, par. 5). These numbers have steadily increased, though exact figures are not public.

35. Nye (2011), who identified and theorized Soft Power, recognizes that international broadcasting is more than just a form of public diplomacy and relies greatly on the currency of credibility in the twenty-first century, but he does not elaborate much beyond the need for media credibility.

36. Robinson 2001.

37. Miel and Faris 2008.

38. B. Cohen's seminal work (1963) on the role of the media in the American foreign policy-making establishment, like most consequent works on media and foreign policy, focuses on the previous preponderance of Western foreign correspondents and GNNs.

39. Naveh (2002) is one of many academics recognizing the dearth of research in this field, writing that "past studies of foreign policy decision-making neglected to deal with [the] complex role of the media. They described the media (if at all) as one of the channels of informing leaders of international events, as input for the decision-making process" (1).

GNNs are generally understood and analyzed in the academic literature strictly as tools of public diplomacy intended as a means of manifesting "soft power." Further, they are analyzed as a "softer" aspect within a broader "smart power" framework.[40]

This book challenges such understandings. Extant published research has focused on the limited and ideational effects of both state- and nonstate-sponsored GNNs (the so-called "CNN effect")[41] rather than on their *functional* roles—how GNNs are developed and operated to serve the state as "hard" material power—and *systemic* roles: how GNNs interact with the state, informing and affecting foreign policy decision making. In contrast, an extended smart power framework of analysis allows for a look not only at how GNNs perform a soft power role but also at their potential and real performance as tools of hard power. In particular, among other overlooked functions, the literature is essentially bereft as to how GNNs strategically and dynamically operate and whether they perform, both formally and informally, the hard power function of diplomacy and of a state intelligence-gathering and analysis organization.

This book focuses predominantly on uncovering these diplomatic and intelligence-gathering functions in the context of a changing global media landscape, where state-sponsored CGTN/X is a recent, booming, and now dominant presence in the current global news media ecology, if not yet globally in popular viewership. China's relatively new entry into GNN news media accompanies that state's rapidly rising global economic and military power. Whether its GNN can be factored in as a material part of China's power—and to what extent—is an overlooked yet ominous factor in measuring the state's overall achievement of parity with other powers and what that implies in a geopolitical context. As a consequence, GNNs in general and CGTN/X specifically are the objects

---

40. Nye 1990a. Nye introduced the concept and coined the term *soft power* in this early work.

41. Gilboa (2005a, 2005b) "investigates the decade long effort to construct and validate a communications theory of international relations that asserts that global television networks, such as CNN and BBC World, have become a decisive actor in determining policies and outcomes of significant events" (Gilboa 2005a, 27). Gilboa found that most studies failed to present conclusive evidence on the existence of the "CNN effect" and often exaggerated any potential effect the media has on policy making.

of this intensive case study, which aims to answer the central research question of how consequential GNNs are in enhancing states' soft and hard power.

This raises a series of questions regarding dynamic and relative global power shifts. If, in fact, as this work and its empirical data indicate, GNNs perform the hard power functions of intelligence gathering and diplomacy and can be seen as a source of state material power, then the question of why China and Russia are investing unprecedented amounts of financial resources to develop their global news networks becomes relevant.

Answering this research question requires in-depth study of how GNNs function; in particular, does CGTN/X function as a global extension of Chinese state soft *and* hard power? Do RT and other Russian global news products do the same for Russia? Beyond the scope of this study's research and conclusions, however, are questions of a state's intention and effect: What might define a GNN's success and how might its impact be measured? And what might CGTN/X's rise mean for world order and the way evolutions therein are narrated and reported? While these questions were posed directly to representatives of CGTN/X, the answers will require further study with a deeper, longitudinal examination of the performance and penetration of China's nascent GNNs.

Although China is an interesting case in itself, by looking at GNNs, and specifically CGTN/X, insight may be gained as to what motivates any state news and information broadcaster or institution to expend billions of dollars overseas annually—with little to no foreign revenue return—to achieve a marginal global viewership[42] for programming that

---

42. Real audience figures for CGTN and RT are hard to come by. Both RT and CGTN have been accused of exaggerating their market share, deliberately confusing "the theoretical geographical scope of its audience" with real audience reach (Zavadski 2015, par. 7, regarding RT). An RT spokesperson claimed the channel reaches 700 million people worldwide, but this figure could not be verified by independent rating agencies (Zavadski 2015). An Ipsos poll in 2015 found that 70 million people globally watched RT weekly (compared, for example, to BBC's 372 million) (Rutenberg 2017). As the *New York Times* remarks, "If RT thought it would be ranked anywhere near" the popular American GNNs, it would pay to be included in the Nielsen ratings, the standard metrics for US television (Rutenberg 2017, par. 20). For CGTN, a similar charge was made by Flew (2017), writing that instead of the "hundreds of millions," CGTN's viewership is likely to be closer to 50 million.

is often considered to be flat-out propaganda.[43] Even though the data on CGTN/X and RT are thin and the organizational history short, it was possible to draw a longitudinal historical overview of two hard power dimensions, diplomacy and intelligence gathering, for similar Western GNN structures and their patterns. The role of GNNs as tools of international statecraft and the way they constitute state material power begin to be revealed in the process.

To begin an investigation into the geopolitical implications of the recent GNN shifts from the Western toward the non-Western sphere, we must examine how GNNs function. In the process, there were clear indications that GNNs could be understood as an integral part of states' material power. Whether that material power can be converted by the state from potential power[44] to deployable or perceptible power is beyond the scope of this study, but the translation of GNN functions into material resources is real and significant. This relationship of GNNs—via their generation of material resources in intelligence gathering and diplomacy—to the state could indicate whether there is already a contemporary geopolitical effect as CGTN/X's exponential global growth occurs concurrent with a dynamic of drastically reduced global resource allocation and limited presence of traditional and mostly Western GNNs, such as BBC World.

Global news networks are part of a complex media ecology with myriad institutions and individuals performing soft power functions that include elite influence and agenda setting. But, as will be shown in

---

43. The efficacy and value of programming perceived as propaganda has always been a question in funding battles. Appearing in *Foreign Policy* during the Reagan administration, Nichols's 1984 article reflects a dominant strain of criticism of GNNs at the time but is still a common criticism to date: "In 1984, Washington will spend more than three-quarters of a billion dollars on propaganda, much of it on overtly persuasive programming that, for the most part, will fall on deaf ears" (Nichols 1984, 129).

44. In "The Changing Nature of World Power" (Nye 1990b), the question of power conversion is key to understanding if material resources—whether they be economic or military, for example—can be effectively and efficiently converted. Nye writes, "Power conversion is a basic problem that arises when we think of power in terms of resources. Some countries are better than others at converting their resources into effective influence, just as some skilled card players win despite being dealt weak hands. Power conversion is the capacity to convert potential power, as measured by resources, to realized power, as measured by the changed behavior of others. Thus, one has to know about a country's skill at power conversion as well as its possession of power resources to predict outcomes correctly" (178). In the case of this study, the hard material resources garnered by GNNs are in diplomacy and intelligence-gathering capacities.

the following chapters, these news networks also perform hard power functions of diplomacy and intelligence gathering. Each has formal and informal manifestations. The conflation of the soft power aspects of diplomacy, in specific public diplomacy, with the workaday and decidedly much harder aspects of active diplomacy has evolved and given diplomatic actions a softer and less effective patina, sometimes obscuring the path from diplomatic inputs to desired foreign policy outcomes.

GNNs have performed a significant diplomatic and intelligence-gathering function in both the West and elsewhere, regardless of GNN type. While the GNN's relationship with the state varies, all GNN types have a direct impact on a state's foreign policy outcomes.

The danger in discussing the existing relationship between GNNs and the state is that it reinforces the assumption of nations and administrations hostile to any nonnative news and information institutions operating and identifying trends, practices, people, and processes in those nations. Those institutions and individuals are regularly arrested for spying or other activities aimed at demanding more transparency from purposely opaque systems. *Bloomberg News* and the *New York Times* found out that it was detrimental to the bottom line, to their employees, and to their previously less constrained activities when they reported on the Chinese Communist Party leadership's relatives and their amassed wealth, hidden properties, and enterprise ownerships—as editorialized in "Billionaire Princelings Ruin a Chinese Vision."[45] The result? "The Chinese government responded by blocking all new journalist-visa applications from the *Times* and *Bloomberg*. Existing staff members could have their visas renewed (it makes bad headlines to expel reporters), but no new hires would be allowed to reside in the country."[46]

Relevance

There are more foreign correspondents in the world today than ever. They do not belong to the big media names of Western journalistic institutions,

---

45. Pesek 2012.
46. Demick 2015, par. 3

however. Nearly all of them have dramatically cut back the number of correspondents[47] and closed down foreign bureaus. The precipitous drop in foreign corresponding[48]—the type grounded in Western traditions of fairness and accuracy and conducted by senior journalists with adversarial relationships to power—raises the question of how societies and elites will be informed about the world in the future and how that information will shape perceptions and policies within and between sovereign states.

Naturally, not everyone shares the pessimistic outlook.[49] In their often-cited analysis of changing practices in foreign correspondence, Hamilton and Jenner claim, "The alarm [about the end of quality foreign correspondence] . . . is based on an anachronistic and static model of what foreign correspondence is and who foreign correspondents are. Foreign news will be delivered as long as a demand exists."[50] Kumar (2011b) also elaborates on the concept of "backpack journalism overseas" as a new form of foreign correspondence. Others put high hopes on citizen journalism as a means of supplementing, if not replacing, foreign correspondents. Further, it might be argued that the Western values of fairness, accuracy, and impartiality are not absolute; news openly giving voice to one side or the other might, some argue, also have its place in the market (see Painter 2008). In today's media-rich environment, everyone can find their news.[51]

---

47. As Sambrook (2010, 11) writes, "Although the impact of reducing budgets on Western news organisations, and on international coverage in particular, are much discussed, there is no single quantitative study which analyses the reduction in bureaux and coverage over the past decades. However, the general narrative is not in dispute."

48. Every few years, Kumar and the *American Journalism Review* (*AJR*) conduct a survey of foreign coverage and correspondents. In 2010 in the United States alone, "twenty papers and companies have cut their foreign bureaus entirely since AJR conducted its first census of foreign correspondents in 1998" (Kumar 2011a, par. 3). She further reports on the nonstate broadcast status and finds that "NBC distinguished between full-fledged bureaus and editorial presence, listing 14 bureaus and an editorial presence in four other countries"(par. 5). CNN is healthier in terms of the number of foreign bureaus, with a total of twenty-six internationally.

49. Indeed, Archetti (2012) claims we are experiencing not a decline but rather a renaissance of foreign correspondence.

50. Hamilton and Jenner 2004, 302.

51. Iyengar and Hahn 2009; Arceneaux and Johnson 2013. The consequences of selective news exposure have been studied primarily in a domestic setting in the United States. Researchers confirmed the existence of the phenomena (e.g., Coe at al. 2008), and concluded that it leads to a polarization of the audience (for example, Iyengar and Hahn 2009).

However, this study contends that something is irrevocably lost when a GNN closes down a foreign bureau for good. As Wu and Hamilton put it, "Episodic coverage of foreign affairs will not alert Americans to the growing reality that foreign affairs are, in truth, local affairs."[52] In addition, to the issue of American or Western perception, perspective, or policy, this is a question of material capacities, the dynamic shifts in those capacities and the geopolitical effect as they move from a Western near monopoly on those capacities to capacities globally shared—and potentially far outstripped—by non-Western powers.

As GNNs produce and project both soft and hard power thanks to their integral role in intelligence flow, there is potentially a new aspect to the ongoing geopolitical shift in material power. The main contribution of this work is a discussion of the hard power aspects of GNNs, which have been hitherto neglected by scholarly literature. The findings of this research show that international media can indeed play tangible diplomatic and information-gathering roles. When Western GNNs close down their foreign bureaus, their home states, as the later chapters will elaborate, lose the benefits of those capacities.

As a result of Chinese and Russian state policies to grow the print, broadcast, Internet, and mobile networks of the state-controlled CGTN/X and RT, China, in particular, is fueling a dramatic increase in foreign corresponding bureaus, reporters, editors, broadcast stations, and information-gathering and dissemination infrastructure around the world.[53] This investment is leading to exponential growth in presence and production. "While our media empires are melting away like the Himalayan glaciers, China's are expanding," said Orville Schell, director of the Center on U.S.-China Relations at the Asia Society in New York and former dean at UC Berkeley's Graduate School of Journalism.[54] As it

---

52. Wu and Hamilton 2004, 529.

53. Mustafi 2012. "To some degree, whoever owns the commanding heights of cultural development, and soft power, will enjoy a competitive edge internationally," declared a communiqué that came out of the October 2011 plenary of the Communist Party's Central Committee. Toward that end, the Chinese government allocated $8.7 billion in 2009–10 alone to "external publicity work" (Mustafi 2012, par. 3).

54. Quoted in Barboza 2010, par. 7.

will be seen later, a similar expansion of state-sponsored Russian media, comparable in many ways to that of CGTN/X, is taking place globally.

Former secretary of state Hillary Clinton went so far as to say that the United States is currently engaged in "an information war." She concluded that testimony to the Senate Foreign Relations Committee in 2011 by starkly saying that in the information fight against emerging international broadcasters, "we are losing that war."[55]

The Structure of This Book

This introduction has focused on the issue of whether GNNs possess hard power characteristics, manifest in the presence of both diplomatic functions and intelligence-gathering performance. Prior to the discussion of these empirically identifiable traits, chapter 1 presents a theoretical framework for the interpretation of the data.

Chapter 2 looks at the varied institutional and individual diplomatic acts of Western GNNs, both in a formal and informal sense, drawing on both historic precedent and contemporary cases where GNNs are extended, usually privately, often secretly, into this realm, despite public perception of nonparticipation in such activity. The chapter contains original data and a previously unreported case of direct engagement by both a news network and individuals in GNN-mediated conflict prevention in Haiti in the early 1990s. (A full transcript of the interview on the case is presented in appendix 1.)

Chapter 3 continues the discussion of Western GNNs' institutional and individual engagement in intelligence gathering, both formal and informal. This chapter reveals multiple previously undocumented cases where individuals and institutions performed intelligence-gathering functions in conscious collaboration with states.

Chapter 4 reviews the relevance of the previous two chapters and contextualizes how GNNs' material power, which had been dominated by Western GNNs throughout the twentieth century, is now challenged and,

---

55. Quoted in Crovitz 2011, par. 3.

in some ways, exceeded by China and Russia. Non-Western GNNs' practice of diplomatic and intelligence-gathering functions is explored in depth in this chapter. Confidential information attained by this study establishes direct intelligence linkages between CGTN/X and both the Chinese ruling party and the governing structure of the People's Republic of China, with an established practice of intelligence reporting as the main conduit up the chain of command. This study concludes that not only are globally growing GNNs able to propagate their national perspective, culture, ideology, policy preferences, and system via their soft power resources, but they are also adding to their material resource base via successful leveraging of GNNs' diplomatic and intelligence-gathering capabilities.

Chapter 5 concludes with a summary of the manifestations of GNNs' heretofore unacknowledged or unidentified material power. GNNs' material power and the hard power they possess via diplomatic and intelligence-gathering functions are contextualized in a broader geopolitical framework as a challenge to Western powers. This work concludes that insofar as the practices of GNNs are limited to a realm of public diplomacy and soft power—dominantly the power of persuasion—non-Western GNN presence is minimal and limited in geopolitical effect. The true value of GNNs is in their material power.

In other words, GNNs are understood by non-Western states to be extensions of a state's material capacities. Non-Western states understand and confront other nations' GNNs as intelligence-gathering institutions—arresting reporters and charging them with espionage, for example—and deploy their own non-Western GNNs to perform the functions of an intelligence organization or accomplish whatever tasks are required by the state. Western states, as reflected both in the interviews conducted with members of the GNN professional class and in the academic literature, continue to perceive and approach GNNs, with few exceptions, as if their value is entirely rooted in their public diplomacy practice and performance. Any reckoning of relative power shifts needs to take into account not only the quantitative shift in material GNN resources expended by non-Western states (in particular China), but also the efficacy of those GNNs in performing intelligence-gathering and diplomatic functions for Western state sponsors and nonsponsors alike.

CHAPTER 1 | GLOBAL NEWS NETWORKS AND STATE POWER

The complex relationship among GNNs, power, and policy is diffi-cult to penetrate. Transnational media compose a significant part of GNNs, certainly the most public and prevalent media institutions on the world stage, but most empirical studies of the media fail to reveal the totality of how a GNN's constituent institutions and individuals function and the extended roles they perform both independently and in association with states. Further, studies of their geopolitical effects seem limited to soft power aspects or epiphenomenal effects not directly ascribed to GNNs or the totality of their effective performance in both soft and hard power roles.

This work leverages unique access and elite interviews to uncover and synthesize practices that are not typically acknowledged as GNN performance. The actively obscured, often surreptitious, and generally dismissed nature of this performance—and the professional stigma attached to some of it—is empirically established in this work. GNN institutions and individuals who work for GNNs reveal the means and methods of their systematic participation in two specific hard power aspects of GNN performance: (1) active participation in diplomacy, both informal and formal, and (2) both formal and informal intelligence-gathering activity. Establishing these acts as intrinsic GNN behavior is the primary contribution of this work. I hope that providing a structure of analysis advances research into global political and policy implications as the dominance of Western GNNs gives way to non-Western GNNs in the twenty-first century.

The past twenty-five years have witnessed a boom in scholarly lit-erature regarding the media's potential role in policy making. As Kalb wrote in 1991, "Academics are now coming to appreciate what successful politicians have known for decades—that the press is a key player in the process of governance."[1] A similar exponential rise in interest can be observed specifically for issues related to media and foreign affairs. As political scientist Bernard C. Cohen, author of one of the field's seminal texts (1963) put it in 1994, "The study of the media and foreign policy, a cottage industry thirty years ago, has become big business today."[2] Living in the information age or (new) media age had caught up with scholars outside media studies.

At the same time, international relations as a discipline remained partly unaffected by the rise of interest in communication. Many of the important works on media and foreign policy come from outside of the discipline; the best ones offer a truly multidisciplinary approach, called for, among others, by Gilboa (2008). Theories based in international relations seem to have difficulty assessing the operations of the media. Some of the limitations and structural boundaries where international relations and political science appear confined to conceptual understanding of GNNs include: (1) GNNs are primarily viewed through a lens of soft power, where a focus is placed on the passive aspects of media—often as a conveyer belt—and on media effects in a framing, indexing, or priming framework and where the media have limited geopolitical agency; (2) GNNs are studied to a high degree within a national framework, looking at media effect and domestic policy and politics. For example, recent studies on "the Fox effect"[3] show how exposure to the Fox network has an effect on citizen polarization[4] and voting patterns,[5] but both studies are conceptually incapable of assigning a media effect to foreign policy and international relations outcomes outside the margins of policy or in cases where policies are ambiguous and media are seen as an exogenous catalyst leveraged by a stronger elite framing actor to voice a perspective or policy preference to garner either elite sympathy or popular support for that preference; (3) when recognizing media as an

---

1. Quoted in Gilboa 2001, 3.
2. Cohen 1994, 8.
3. Morris 2005.
4. Levendusky 2013.
5. DellaVigna and Kaplan 2006.

agential actor, studies do not ascribe hard power or material value to any geopolitical media effect; and finally, (4) GNNs have not received broad academic scrutiny, other than for their roles in soft power and public diplomacy—their global strategic effects have been mostly neglected, in part likely due to the twentieth-century monopoly of Western GNNs and a preponderance of Western media and communication scholarship.

GNNs and Soft Power

As discussed in the introduction, the international relations theory that attributes the most importance to the media is Nye's soft power / smart power framework. "Fully defined, soft power is the ability to affect others through the co-optive means of framing the agenda, persuading, and eliciting positive attraction in order to obtain preferred outcomes."[6] Nye sees this as directly linked to Lukes's third face of power, and he names the media as one of the important resources for soft power or smart power:[7] "If the United States is involved in more communication networks, it has a greater opportunity to shape preferences[8] in terms of the third face of power."[9]

In the media and international relations literature, this "shaping of preferences" has been analyzed in many studies in terms of agenda setting

---

6. Nye 2011, 20–21. Elsewhere, Nye formulates soft power this way: "If I am persuaded to go along with your purposes without any explicit threat or exchange taking place—in short, if my behavior is determined by an observable but intangible attraction—soft power is at work. Soft power uses a different type of currency (not force, not money) to engender cooperation—an attraction to shared values and the justness and duty of contributing to the achievement of those values" (2009, 7). However, it must be noted that Nye has been criticized, among other things, for not theorizing attraction (Bially Mattern 2005).

7. Since soft power is a part of smart power, the descriptive statements about the media's importance as a soft power resource are valid for smart power as well.

8. However, Lukes (2005, 490–91) calls for a more nuanced understanding of the shaping of preferences and argues for a distinction to be made between the conditions under which, and the mechanism through which, the "influencing" takes place; he also finds the lack of differentiation between different kinds of "influencing" problematic.

9. Nye 2011, 18. Later on, Nye provides a more concrete example: "Smart strategies must have an information and communications component. States struggle over the power to define norms, and framing issues grows in importance. For instance, CNN and the BBC framed the issues of the First Gulf War in 1991, but by 2003, Al Jazeera was playing a large role in shaping the narrative of the Iraq War" (20).

and framing. Perhaps the most important argument used in the study of these effects in foreign news coverage is that "for many, the sole source of information about world events is the press."[10] Further, Entman contends that media effects can be particularly significant in issues where "there are no old attitudes to defend," where audiences "lack detailed, expert knowledge or strong opinion."[11] Others argue that precisely because the media (particularly US media) provide no background for news events (particularly foreign news events), "most citizens remain dependent on news and infotainment media and the cues they offer for making sense of war and other aspects of foreign policy."[12] Thus, the media are expected to have a particularly strong effect on the audience in foreign policy issues.

While agenda setting in communication studies means simply "the idea that there is a strong correlation between the emphasis that mass media place on certain issues . . . and the importance attributed to these issues by mass audiences,"[13] in political science, research has focused on agenda setting as intrinsically linked to power. It was Dahl (1956, 1961), and even more prominently Schattschneider (1960) and, following him, Bachrach and Baratz (1962), who first recognized the importance of the political agenda for understanding power. In an often-cited passage, Schattschneider put agenda setting at the center of his power concept: "The definition of alternatives is the supreme instrument of power. . . . He who determines what politics is about runs the country."[14] Bachrach and Baratz developed Schattschneider's work further. Their concept of nondecision making can be understood as control over the agenda.[15]

---

10. Wanta, Golan, and Lee 2004, 367. A similar claim was made by Baum and Groeling (2010). It can be argued that, with the emergence of Web 2.0, the mass media are losing some of their sway. Exploring the debates around this argument is, however, beyond the scope of this work. Nonetheless, it could be ventured here that very few scholars would deny that the mass media are still important to informing the public.

11. Entman 1989, 351.

12. Aday, Entman, and Livingston 2012, 327.

13. Scheufele and Tewksbury 2007, 11.

14. Schattschneider 1960, 68.

15. Agenda setting in the two disciplines developed separately and remained distinct until the mid-1980s. Interestingly, empirical studies in the two fields have led to different results. While "hundreds of studies worldwide" have proven the existence of agenda-setting effects in media studies (McCombs 2005, 543), the studies carried out by political scientists have produced contradictory findings.

The international relations theory that attributes the most importance to the media is Nye's soft power / smart power framework. While a
number of historical works have explored the development of soft power
from Wilsonian times,[16] Nye argues that in today's new media age soft
power / smart power is of primary importance. "Politics has become a
contest of competitive credibility. The world of traditional power politics
is typically about whose military or economy wins. Politics in an information age 'may ultimately be about whose story wins.'"[17] Further, although
soft power has been criticized as a fundamentally American concept,
scholars have studied its application in a variety of national contexts,[18]
including Japan,[19] Turkey,[20] India,[21] and most important, both in terms
of the size of the literature and for the purposes of this project, China[22]
as well as Russia.[23] Importantly for the present project, in addition to the
interest in China's soft power in the English-language academic world,
as Nye points out, "hundreds of essays and scholarly articles have been
published in the People's Republic of China on soft power."[24]

Despite the impressive number of studies, critics still argue that analysis to date has lacked distinction or operational understanding. "[Inter-
national relations]-based approaches have rarely had a strong empirical
handle on the actual role and influence of news media. More often than
not, the role and function of media have been assumed."[25] Nye himself has
seldom provided case studies; his conceptual development of soft power
has a dominant role for media, but he does not elaborate on the function

---

16. See, for instance, Axelrod 2009.

17. Nye 2008, 100.

18. Thussu (2014) argues that the soft power concept should be "de-Americanized."

19. Otmazgin 2008; Watanabe and McConnell 2008; Iwabuchi 2015; Hashimoto 2018; Ichihara 2018.

20. Oğuzlu, 2007, 2013; Altunişik 2008; Yörük and Vatikiotis 2013; Balci, 2014; Ipek 2015.

21. Thussu 2013; 2016; Mukherjee 2014.

22. Kurlantzick 2007; M. Price and Dayan 2008; Paradise 2009; Vlassis 2016; Shambaugh 2013; Sparks 2015; G. Zhang 2017; Gil 2017; Voci and Hui 2018.

23. Herpen 2016; Rutland and Kazantsev 2016; Mkhoyan 2017. Rawnsley (2015) compares Russian and Chinese public diplomacy strategies.

24. Nye 2011, 88. For a thorough analysis of how the concept has been used in China, see Shambaugh 2013. Another important analysis is J. Wilson (2015a, 2015b), regarding how the fundamentally Western concept of soft power is interpreted and adapted in China and Russia.

25. Robinson 2011, 5.

or efficacy of media, creating the skeletal framework for the future development of media models appropriate to his soft power conceptual structure.[26] The soft power framework of understanding transnational GNNs is used to measure popular and elite effects on foreign policy making, but it is useless in measuring GNNs' hard power diplomatic and intelligence-gathering aspects and effects, the central focus of this work.

Yet within international relations, the primary use of soft power theories in analyzing GNNs' media effects provides the background against which this research project was carried out. To extend Nye's theoretical framework, we need to establish the presence and performance of GNNs' nonsoft power. That nonsoft power manifests itself as the diplomatic and intelligence-gathering characteristics that are uncovered and presented in this book. The prevalence of understanding and analyzing of GNNs within a soft power context and through soft power theories is not disputed in this work, nor is the reason for this: within the international relations literature, international state broadcasting is the dominant traditional GNN manifestation; the role of such institutions is traditionally considered an aspect of public diplomacy and an extension of soft power.

Soft power can be wielded through a variety of means; one of them is public diplomacy, "a long-term foreign policy asset";[27] "an instrument that governments use to mobilize these [soft power] resources to communicate with and attract the publics of other countries, rather than merely their governments."[28] Many writings in international relations that account for the media on some level fall under the rubric of public diplomacy studies. These range from historical overviews[29] to insiders'

---

26. As Robinson (2011, 5) puts it, "When Joseph Nye wrote in 1996 that 'America's increasing ability to communicate with the public in foreign countries literally over the heads of their rulers via satellite, provides a great opportunity to foster democracy' (Nye and Owens 1996), he did so with little evidence of both how, and to what extent, this was actually occurring."

27. Adelman 1981, 927.

28. Nye 2008, 95. While this kind of definitions remains dominant in both the academic and the lay literature, Gilboa (2008) argues that they are too limiting. He embraces the definition put forward by Signitzer and Coombs, who see public diplomacy as "the way in which both government and private individuals and groups influence directly or indirectly those public attitudes and opinions which bear directly on another government's foreign policy decisions" (Signitzer and Coombs 1992, quoted in Gilboa 2008, 57). This definition allows for the inclusion of nonstate actors, effectively abolishing the difference between public diplomacy and PR.

29. Dizard 2004; Cull 2008.

memoirs and analysis[30] and to case studies.[31] Yet as soft power theories were criticized for lack of nuance, it has been argued that the literature focused on public diplomacy suffers from a lack of engagement with non-historical issues, an overly US-centric approach, and oversimplification.[32] To rectify this, in a series of papers, communications studies expert Gilboa developed a system of conceptual models on how the mass media are utilized in foreign policy in general,[33] and in public diplomacy in particular.[34] Viewing the media "as an instrument of foreign policy and international negotiations,"[35] Gilboa makes an analytical distinction between diplomatic efforts that impose limitations on the media (secret diplomacy, closed-door diplomacy, and open diplomacy) and those where officials make use of the media.[36] The latter category includes public diplomacy, media diplomacy, "officials' uses of the media to communicate with state and non-state actors, to build confidence and advance negotiations, and to mobilize public support for agreements," and media-broker diplomacy ("journalists turning mediators"),[37] this last notion being his own conceptual invention. Of the three, only public diplomacy has been subject to much international relations discussion; the concepts of media diplomacy[38] and media-broker diplomacy have, unfortunately, not taken

---

30. Tuch 1990.

31. For example, Nisbet et al. 2004; Burns and Eltham 2009; Khatib, Dutton, and Thelwall 2012; or, on RT and CCTV, Rawnsley 2015.

32. Gilboa 2008, 56. This last problem is also repeatedly brought up by Nye, who painstakingly tries to refute the conflation of public diplomacy with propaganda (for instance, Nye 2004, 83). In the context of China, and from a sociology of knowledge perspective, Chang and Lin (2014) explore how international research has looked at China "through the prism of either propaganda or public diplomacy" (450).

33. Gilboa 2001, 2002.

34. Gilboa 2000, 2008. More recently, Gilboa (like many other researchers) turned his attention to new communication technologies, introducing the concept of digital diplomacy (2016). Since digital diplomacy is not directly relevant to this work, it is not discussed here in detail.

35. Gilboa 2001, 4.

36. Gilboa 2000.

37. Gilboa 2001, 15.

38. The term *media diplomacy* has been used, but often to describe different notions (and often simply as synonymous with *public diplomacy*). In the only book-length treatise on the subject, which, interestingly, covers British rather than American diplomatic efforts, Y. Cohen (1986) defines it as part of public diplomacy yet somehow different from it: "Media diplomacy is thus to be distinguished from 'public diplomacy' in that the latter encompasses not only information work and cultural activities, where the media are involved, but all public aspects of foreign

hold with other scholars. The notion of media-broker diplomacy, where "international mediation [is] conducted and sometimes initiated by journalists,"[39] is of great importance to this research; the concept of informal diplomacy deployed in this work is closely related to Gilboa's concept. This connects back to the soft power / smart power framework: when journalists are employed to carry out these nonjournalistic missions, they can be interpreted as resources bringing about hard power. This is a highly underresearched yet highly interesting phenomenon, and one which the present work aims to explore.

Institutional journalists, as well as some INGO employees and academics, often engage in diplomatic discourse, intermediation, and negotiation, as well as serving, in their least direct involvement, as couriers of fact and position. GNNs and their constituent members often act as private actors rather than performing their strict public role as observers and reporters of fact. The following chapter will review this long-standing performative role in greater depth and later chapters will reveal that this role is endemic to both Western and non-Western GNNs, though the relationship to the state will be seen differently, as Western GNNs are predominantly nonstate or hybrid institutions. These hard power diplomatic functions have not garnered as much attention in scholarly literature as the soft power aspect of GNNs.

In his work on hard and soft power, Nye put great emphasis on soft power being a capability, since many of his critics mistake it for a type of behavior or, more commonly, a resource. He also tries to avoid an overly simplistic identification of tangible resources with hard power and intangibles with soft power (although he does claim that it is often the case) by bringing up a number of counterexamples, such as patriotism, an intangible sentiment affecting military (hard power) outcomes. Typically, hard power resources can also produce soft power; he says, with Osama bin Laden, that "people are attracted to a strong horse rather than a weak horse."[40]

---

policy. . . . Media diplomacy includes all those aspects of public diplomacy where the media are involved as well as others not associated with public diplomacy including the sending of signals by governments through the media, and the use of the media as a source of information" (7).

39. Le 2006, 2.

40. Nye 2011, 86.

Another example of a hard power resource—wealth producing soft power—is that of CNN and the First Iraq War: "When Iraq invaded Kuwait in 1990, the fact that CNN was an American company helped to frame the issue, worldwide, as aggression. Had an Arab company been the world's dominant TV channel, perhaps the issue would have been framed as a justified attempt to reverse colonial humiliation."[41] In his later work, Nye completes the picture by pointing to the difference between the first and the second Gulf War: "CNN and the BBC framed the issues of the First Gulf War in 1991, but by 2003 Al Jazeera was playing a larger role in shaping the narrative in the Iraq War."[42]

When discussing soft power media effects in the contemporary world, the fundamental changes in the media landscape must be taken into consideration. Bringing about a dramatic reduction of communication costs and thus "exponentially increasing the number of channels of communication in world politics," the information revolution has had a major effect on "the patterns of complex interdependence"[43] between states. At the same time, Keohane and Nye are careful to emphasize that the information revolution did not occur in a vacuum but rather in an existing political system that has shaped it (and is being shaped by it).[44]

A further effect of the information revolution explored by Nye is the "paradox of plenty."[45] In today's world of information overload, attention rather than information has become the scarce resource. Gatekeepers who can separate relevant information from noise are in high demand; thus credibility is a "crucial resource and an important source of soft power."[46] Credibility is an undefined and untheorized but nonetheless central concept in Nye's argument. Not only is it a decisive soft power resource for

---

41. Keohane and Nye 1998, 90.

42. Nye 2011, 20.

43. Keohane and Nye 1998, 85.

44. An element of this they claim not to have foreseen is the dramatic increase in importance of "loosely structured network organizations," which are now, thanks to a significant drop in the cost of communication, in a position to better "penetrat[e] states without regard to border." While globalization is not a new phenomenon, as they point out, "earlier transnational flows were heavily controlled by large bureaucracies like multinational corporations or the Catholic Church" (Keohane and Nye 1998, 83).

45. Nye 2008, 99.

46. Nye 2008, 100.

the media, but it has become crucially important for governments, too, who are also implicated in a "contest of competitive credibility."[47]

GNNs perform this gatekeeper role at a high level. They are, if nothing else, built as reporting and analysis mechanisms with extraordinary access to political actors and other social leaders. The GNNs' professional, institutional role is to use omission and commission of fact to draw comprehensible and, at times, actionable narratives for both mass audiences and narrower state actors. The credibility and track record of these GNN institutions gives them greater credence in policy-oriented, epistemic communities as well as in analytical institutions that turn to reliable open-source data and information for policy formation and prescription. These functions allow GNNs to perform the hard power tasks of providing the data used in policy formation, but also to fulfill soft power aspects by helping to set agendas from a limited and perspective-driven reportorial and analysis stance. A Western GNN will note different points of interest and delve deeper into policies that reflect their own institutional biases compared to a non-Western GNN.

The development of the information society has certainly piqued the interest of communication studies scholars. As McCombs notes, many scholars predicted that the spread of new media would diminish media's effects on the public, and maybe also on policy.[48] The spread of new communication technologies continued to favor a diversification of news sources; some have argued that with the rise of customized, idiosyncratic news, mass audiences will cease to exist. Fragmentation of the audience, the argument goes, will lead to fragmentation of the public agenda. However, there are now studies showing that the changes are more limited than scholars had expected. McCombs compares the situation to cable television: you have access to a hundred channels, but you only watch a few of them.[49] He cites evidence to the effect that "attention on the web is even more concentrated than in the print world."[50]

---

47. Nye 2008, 100.

48. McCombs 2005, 544–45.

49. McCombs 2005, 545.

50. McCombs 2005, 545; see also Takeshita 2006. For a more recent review of the literature, see Weimann and Brosius 2016.

Beyond access and exposure, a further issue is whether new media are independent from traditional mass media. It has been noted that some of the more popular new online sites are connected to traditional media by their ownership structure.[51] For example, *CNN.com* is an extension of CNN, and *New York Times* online is a different manifestation of the *New York Times*.[52] Further, the so-called intermedia agenda-setting effect—that is, elite media influencing the agenda of smaller, nonelite news outlets—has already been demonstrated.[53] On the other hand, there is now solid evidence that online media often drive the agenda of mainstream traditional newspapers and television,[54] or at least that there is a reciprocal relationship between them.[55]

With respect to GNNs and the new media age—and with the extraordinarily notable exception of President Donald J. Trump's unprecedented information diet—this work has found noninstitutional journalists to be ineffective. Those who are not part of the larger GNN institutional system and do not feed into a valuable or valued policy-making system cannot substitute for the larger GNN institutional structures and their journalists, researchers, and academics.. Noninstitutional players are hampered by two problems that prevent them from matching GNNs' hard power performance. The first is the lack of access afforded to these smaller, independent players. A reporter or researcher with institutional relationships is granted higher-level access to elites and the policy-making community, as I was told in interviews with multiple impressive bloggers and news websites. I asked many noninstitutional players if they could conceivably get interviews with foreign heads of state or cabinet-level

---

51. For example, by McCombs 2005; Takeshita 2006.

52. Although it needs to be noted, Althaus and Tewksbury (2002) found in an experimental, microlevel study that the print and the online version of the *New York Times* led to different issue agendas among their respective audiences.

53. For example, Reese and Danielian 1989; Danielian and Reese 1989; Roberts and McCombs 1994; Golan 2006.

54. For example, Vargo and Guo 2017.

55. For example, Conway-Silva et al. 2017; Boynton and Richardson 2015. Much scholarly attention has been devoted recently to online media in general, and social media in particular, mostly to Twitter. Current US president Donald Trump's reliance on Twitter as the main presidential communication channel has led some researchers to call this "the Age of Twitter" (Ott 2017).

ministers. The answer, with the one exception of a journalist who had a personal long-term relationship with a leader (this journalist had been an institutional GNN reporter), was that it was "near impossible" for non-GNN personnel to get "anywhere near the presidential palace."[56]

The second problem is a lack of attention to strategic issues and a greater emphasis on the ephemeral and sensational. While some of the West's leading institutional GNNs have cut back on resources, new information organizations and individuals are driven more by ephemera in their "hunt for clicks and impressions."[57] The long-form analytical piece is disappearing in direct correlation to the disappearance of resources from the profession, and the "news hole" is being filled with sensationalism. "Henry Kissinger is not my audience," said one website manager who also relies on cats and short funny videos to populate part of the rolling front page of his product. Foreign affairs is not on his radar.

The third problem is noninstitutional GNNs' lack of reach to a policy-making or party institution that values and knows how to properly credit and weigh editorial choices and story placement (for instance, whether a particular story appears on the front page or buried in the business section). This may reflect an ongoing demographic transition, but one member of Congress said that she does not "look at the internet." When asked how information could be conveyed, she said to this author, "This may sound funny, but can you fax me?"[58] This same lawmaker relies on files of newspaper and magazine clips, as well as other in-house briefing materials, for her committee meetings. While GNNs and their output are well represented in this stack of published materials, there is no room in her information diet for raw or unprocessed fodder of unfamiliar provenance.

The second media effect that has come to dominate media studies since the mid-1990s[59] is framing, or "the process of selecting and

---

56. Personal communication, 2015.

57. Personal communication with Internet news editor, 2014.

58. Personal communication, 2014.

59. Weaver (2007, 144) includes a fascinating chart of the number of studies on agenda setting, framing, and priming published in communication studies journals between 1971 and 2005. It shows that agenda setting was the dominant of the three up until 1995, when it was overtaken by studies on framing. In the period 2001–5, almost three times as many papers were published on framing as on agenda setting and priming together.

highlighting some aspects of a perceived reality, and enhancing the salience of an interpretation and evaluation of that reality."[60] Some studies try to connect media framing and public opinion[61] or media framing and policy.[62] As for issue framing in GNNs, an in-depth study on Chinese agenda-setting narratives of intervention in the conflicts in Libya and Syria[63] draws a direct relationship between the media framing of a type III (state) non-Western GNN (total alignment with a Chinese state policy privileging sovereignty) and a type I (nonstate) Western GNN (close alignment but with dissent and contradiction regarding the expressed state policy of the United States, promoting the primacy of R2P—responsibility to protect).[64]

Studies on framing and public opinion, like those on framing and policy, have brought the discussion back to the question tackled in this chapter: How do media, particularly GNNs, influence policy? It can be argued that the media influence (foreign) policy by influencing foreign policy makers. Policy makers, it is argued, are members of the audience; thus they are subject to media effects on the audience. While this is undoubtedly true to an extent, Walgrave and Van Aelst warn against

---

60. Entman 2004, 26.

61. Brewer 2006.

62. Auerbach and Bloch-Elkon 2005.

63. M. Kounalakis 2015a, 44.

64. An earlier study (M. Kounalakis 2015a) shows that while the United States and Russia staked out opposing positions on Syria on the basis of either material concerns or national security, the Chinese interest in the dispute outcome was—and remains—less obvious. In a previous UN-sanctioned action enabling intervention in Libya to oust Muammar Gaddafi, China did not veto the Security Council action—despite its significant material interests in that country. A short time later, at the outset of the Syrian stirrings and talk of UN action, China made clear through both official state channels and aligned media that it would not enable a Security Council approach that could lead to intervention, either unilaterally by a third country or via a military coalition of state actors. This study uses a critical discourse analysis (CDA) approach to understand the official Chinese position in the case of Syria—a position that stands in contrast to its recent and prior intervention-tolerant foreign policy position on Libya at the end of the Gaddafi era. One conclusion of this study is that China is still formulating its dynamic and seemingly disjointed foreign policy position in the Middle East at present. China's promotes policy narratives of national "sovereignty" over the international community's "responsibility to protect" (R2P) and right to intervene in a nation's internal affairs if there is an overriding humanitarian purpose. China has moved away from R2P, and its state media privileges Chinese state policy. The study found a dominant anti-interventionist foreign policy posture propagated and promoted by China's dominant GNN transnational media channels.

simply extending audience effects on politicians by stating that "political agenda setting is a macroprocess and not a microprocess."[65] Peksen, Peterson, and Drury argue that what is at play here is rather that media attention "mobiliz[es] the public to pressure leaders to take action."[66]

Further, policy makers often see the media agenda as a proxy for the public agenda and media content as their best insight into public opinion.[67] From this perspective, it does not even matter whether the media reflect public opinion or influence public opinion; what matters is that policy makers believe they do.[68]

From the perspective of the GNN-state power relation, with regards to framing, it is highly important that research has repeatedly found that "as a practical matter, news organizations routinely leave policy framing and issue emphasis to political elites (generally, government officials)."[69]

One influential theory of media influence that appreciates the role of the elites is Entman's cascading activation model.[70] The model's starting point is the observation that different parts of the elite "peddle their messages to the press"[71] (or to use scientific jargon, engage in frame contestation), and in some cases the administration's framing of the event dominates, while in others "counterframes" prevail. The model, which suggests that "the media's political influence arises from how they respond—from the ability to frame the news in ways that favor one side over another"[72]—aims to account for both cases and thus to explain why "the media have varied from lapdog to watchdog."[73] In the expanded version, Entman (2008) hopes to define the necessary circumstances

---

65. Walgrave and Van Aelst 2006, 99. More recently, Walgrave and his colleagues set out to study this microprocess by surveying individual politicians (e.g., Midtbø et al. 2014; Sevenans, Walgrave, and Vos 2015).

66. Peksen, Peterson, and Drury 2014, 855.

67. Pritchard 1992.

68. Schudson (1996), quoted in Walgrave and Van Aelst 2006, 100

69. Bennett and Manheim quoted in Livingston 1997, 5. On the flip side, Peksen, Peterson, and Drury (2014) find that media framing effects on foreign policy are "conditioned by US strategic ties to potential targets . . . leaders balance the public's demand for action with the security imperative to maintain good relations with allies" (855).

70. Entman 2004, 2008.

71. Entman 2004, 4.

72. Entman 2004, 4.

73. Baum and Potter 2008, 54.

under which pro-American counterframes can be successfully deployed in the anti-American media environment of a target country. His model takes into account the different power positions of the actors[74]—it is a hierarchical framework with the dominant frames "cascading" down from the top—and can include differences in the influence of various media outlets as well as the display positions of particular news pieces. It also contains several feedback loops and interactions. The model shows that the success of counterframes is a function of cultural congruence,[75] and have an inverse relationship with media freedom: "Those countries where the mainstream political culture favors the United States and elites exert tight control over media provide the most hospitable environments for pro-American frames to penetrate."[76]

The elite function of foreign policy making is further reinforced by the elite role played by institutional GNNs. "We go to the same parties," said one journalist living and working in Europe. "I see the embassy people all the time."[77] Individuals working within elite structures, in particular GNNs, are granted unique access and privilege—and reciprocate that access and privilege to political and social elites.[78] In the international sphere, this elite structure is even smaller than it is in a nation's capital. In many instances, diplomatic missions overseas look to their nationals in GNNs as extensions of their diplomatic corps, relying on them for fresh reporting data, analysis, networks, contacts, and even policy suggestions. While this is done for the most part on an informal basis by Western GNNs, there is often a formal structure in non-Western GNNs, replete with direct reporting functions and hierarchical state-run systems of

---

74. As Aday, Entman, and Livingston (2012, 328) put it, "Cascading activation allows for other actors and institutions ranging from Congress to media to the public, and perhaps global advocacy networks, to shape issue definitions and other aspects of policy discourse. But . . . these secondary players are themselves often responding to the initial frame promoted by the White House."

75. Entman 2008, 94. This was recently empirically verified by, for example, Sheafer et al. (2014), who analyzed the framing of the war in Gaza in the winter of 2008–9 in the English-language media in twenty-six countries and found that "the closer the relative proximity between Israel and a foreign country, the greater the acceptance of Israel's views" (149).

76. Entman 2008, 96. Empirical works that utilize Entman's cascading activation theory include Canel 2012; Chaban and Holland 2015; Rowling, Sheets, and Jones 2015.

77. Personal communication, 2014.

78. Lichter, Rothman, and Lichter 1990; Nesbitt-Larking and Wingfield 2007.

reward and punishment. Chinese GNNs have formalized the reporting process from the field up the chain of command to the highest levels of the government and the party, depending on the value of the information and whether it is timely and actionable. While this system is not friction-free, it is structurally able to deliver adequate information and data to formulate a state policy or promote a state plan.

GNNs and Hard Power

As this overview of the literature indicates, substantial work has been done on GNNs' soft power effects, with some of the most significant causal relations established in the agenda-setting realm. With limited exceptions, GNNs, in their broadest sense and encompassing media and other global and transnational newsgathering and disseminating institutions and individuals, have not been systematically subjected to study of their hard power aspects.[79] Yet as Gilboa points out, journalists are sometimes used to carry out decidedly nonjournalistic missions, such as mediating between opposing parties. Sometimes they are directly implicated in intelligence gathering. This is a less familiar aspect of the media, in which it is used by the state as a hard power asset. Apart from Dover and Goodman's (2009) excellent work, international relations literature on this topic is almost nonexistent. While a few scholars, such as Gilboa and Robinson, either allude or directly venture into this field, they pose questions for future research and promote potential research agendas that otherwise go unattended, if not entirely unnoticed. The study of GNNs' hard power performance is inaccessible for the most part and unattainable without guarantees of anonymity, background assurances, and off-the-record interviews with guarded individuals protective of their individual roles as well as professional journalistic and NGO standards

---

79. However, digital media as such (and not GNNs) have been explored as hard power assets (although not necessarily using this terminology). Howard (2015), for example, lists a number of countries, such as China, Russia, Bulgaria, Romania and Ukraine, that have hackers on government payroll. Howard also describes incidents of "cyberwars" (295) in which states use viruses, a paid army of proregime contributors such as China's "fifty-cent army" (186), and bots on social networks to achieve particular goals.

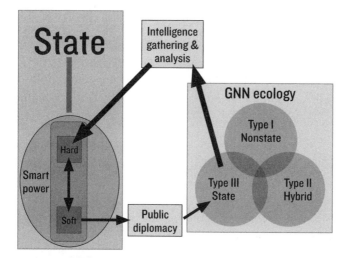

Figure 1. GNNs and intelligence flow

and ethics. The media literature review finds many entry points for the formal and informal performance of both diplomacy and intelligence-gathering roles, at institutional and individual levels, and leaves open the hard power roles performed by GNNs, which are misperceived by the public, overlooked in the literature, and publicly denied, but privately revealed.

The theoretical contribution of this work is to posit that GNNs — a conceptually new, broader newsgathering and data analysis structure with political intermediating potential and practice — possess, inherently and through active promotion and development, hard material power capacities deployable by states. These capacities are exploited via the formal and informal relationships between the state and GNNs, serving to enhance a state's potential hard and soft power.

Figure 1 depicts the intelligence flow between states and GNNs. As depicted, the state deploys strategies of smart power (via interacting soft and hard power). State soft power is expressed institutionally via its public diplomacy institutions and functions, including development of state media news networks. These state media news networks are a part of a larger GNN ecology that includes nonstate networks (such as CNN or the *New York Times*) and hybrid state/nonstate networks (such as

BBC), but also partially state-supported NGOs. This GNN ecology is a semiclosed system that interacts with itself, sharing sources, framing and priming for each other, and setting conventions for collection, presentation, production, and distribution of a final product manifesting itself most visibly as a mass media product. That product is then one of the consumables used by the state's intelligence-gathering and analysis functions to develop and produce their products. This formal relationship develops familiar products such as media briefs and reviews, as well as news synopses. This is only one aspect of the intelligence-gathering and analysis relationship. The other one is between the GNN ecology and state systems of intelligence gathering and analysis and involves exclusive interactions, relationships, and information.

To date, GNNs have mostly been seen as state-sponsored news organizations (such as the Western Voice of America, and the non-Western RT or CGTN in the non-West), rather than the increasingly complex and varied institutional structures that currently perform various GNN functions. The literature consequently reviews these narrower international broadcasters nearly exclusively as institutions extending a state's soft power. Hard material power assigned to these structures and institutions is neither generally perceived by the public nor broadly validated by academics. Despite this lack of theoretical understanding, states recognize — mostly stealthily — that GNNs possess and generate hard material power outputs. In November 2017, the United States made explicit its previously unexpressed view that Russia's RT and Sputnik networks were not considered independent news organizations and needed instead to report their activities to the Justice Department by registering and reporting under the Foreign Agents Registration Act (FARA). How states interact with GNN institutions depends on the type of GNN structure, whether a type I (nonstate-sponsored) structure, type II (hybrid) GNN, or type III (state-sponsored) institution. GNN type does not determine whether the constituent institutions of a GNN develops material hard power nor their efficacy; it does determine structures and defines the formal or informal relationship to the state, party, and policy-making elites.

CHAPTER 2 | WESTERN GLOBAL NEWS NETWORKS AND STATE POWER 1
Diplomacy

This chapter examines the role of global media institutions and foreign correspondents in diplomacy and reviews historical diplomatic functions of GNNs. At times an integral part of their professional role and at others a by-product of their status and structure, institutional journalists and media organizations that dominate GNN structures engage in activities outside the publicly received and widely perceived functions of reporting, writing, and broadcasting. In the course of their professional performance, they interact directly and as agential actors with states and their representatives and often participate—actively or passively, formally and informally—in the iterative and communicative diplomatic processes between states and policy makers. State foreign policy outcomes are often a direct result of GNN intervention and interaction, with significant and historically recognized outcomes that would not likely have been achieved without this class of mediating professionals acting outside their dominant roles[1] as observers, reporters, researchers, and public analysts.

One of the first and more comprehensive studies to incorporate the diplomatic functions of a GNN, in this instance Al Jazeera, is Shawn Powers's doctoral dissertation.[2] Powers creates a matrix of seven geopolitical effects of international media. He states that of these seven,

---

1. For an ethical discussion of the professional role of journalism, see Arant and Meyer (1998), which focuses on conscious activities that go beyond the traditional roles of news capture and dissemination and examines the self-perception and responsibility felt by journalism professionals who engage in nontraditional roles. A host of work covers journalists' roles and responsibilities before and after the digital age. Two often-cited books are McQuail's *Journalism and Society* (2013), and Kovach and Rosenstiel's *The Elements of Journalism* (2014).

2. S. Powers 2009.

most of which fall into the realm of agenda setting and elite influence, two are directly related to the diplomatic function: diplomacy and media-brokered diplomacy. He found that the seven identified functions "are commonplace consequences of international media that can be observed as influencing international politics."[3]

Global news networks are part of a complex media ecology in which myriad institutions and individuals perform soft power functions that include elite influence and agenda setting, as well as the hard power functions of diplomacy and intelligence gathering, both formal and informal. Conflating public diplomacy—the rubric under which most scholars and professionals place the work of GNNs, in particular type III (state-sponsored) GNNs—with other strategic aspects of diplomacy, such as negotiations and two-track diplomatic participation, has given GNNs a weaker, more passive role in the literature on the practice of diplomacy. Diplomacy is sometimes understood, in general and popularly, as a soft power practice.[4]

Diplomacy, however, has always had a harder edge than current perceptions and discussions allow.[5] Démarches have been a standard diplomatic practice, and the tough negotiations that precede an outbreak of military hostility between nations are often the result of heated diplomatic dialogue, threat, or walkout.[6] To be sure, a credible diplomatic

---

3. S. Powers 2009, 13.

4. This approach is reinforced in the academy as well as statecraft, as during former secretary of state Hillary Clinton's presentation of a three-legged stool of power (the "3 Ds"), where hard power refers to defense, soft power to diplomacy and development, and all together make up "smart power" (Nye 2009).

5. Clausewitz and Scherff 1883. Diplomacy, in Clausewitz, is a definitive and identifiable expression of power, one of a spectral set of tools available to states. Political practitioners have interpreted Clausewitz's oft-cited aphorism "War is an expression of politics by other means" to express the spectrum of diplomatic state options. In the prenuclear age, Lenin was a keen follower of Clausewitz's work. Kissinger used the aphorism to reinforce forward-leaning diplomacy and invalidate total war in the nuclear age in his book *Nuclear Weapons and Foreign Policy* (1957). The conundrum in Kissinger's analysis is that diplomacy, too, becomes a weaker tool in the face of nuclear proliferation and where sovereign states no longer need to align or balance when they possess nuclear weaponry, as with contemporary North Korea.

6. The range of diplomatic practice was apparent to me during my work as a foreign correspondent, as a diplomatic spouse, and in interactions with former secretary of state George Shultz, former undersecretary of state for political affairs Nicholas Burns, and many others over the last thirty years. While the classic 1917 book *Diplomatic Practice* by Sir Ernest Mason Satow

action needs to have material resources to back it up, but even in cases where a nation's material resources are limited, diplomacy can use tactics like naming and shaming or effective marshaling of allies, a regional body, or a world community to support a diplomatic cause backed by military might. All this to suggest that diplomacy comes in both soft[7] and hard manifestations, and sometimes the hard and soft characteristics find seemingly dissonant combinatorial expressions.[8] The diplomatic spectrum of tools ranges from the attractive (soft) to the coercive (hard).[9] The perceived firmness of diplomacy is contextually contingent.

Larson identifies the media as participating in foreign policy in at least three ways: "They provide the view of reality most frequently and heavily relied upon by diplomats in making policy. They also receive and widely disseminate official accounts. The third role involves journalists directly in the diplomatic dialogue, as exemplified by ABC's 'Nightline,' on which Ted Koppel frequently interviews heads of state or senior diplomats."[10] Expanding on Larson, this chapter reviews three forms of diplomacy in

---

(2009), recently updated, is still used as a popular reference, it focuses on the legal aspects of diplomacy, with less attention to the personal and unconventional practices diplomats leverage. I have been in the presence of Richard Holbrooke as he berated a harsh German critique of America's racial inequality and moral authority; personally experienced the skill of Nicholas Burns as he appealed to a broader Greek public over the heads of his official Athens interlocutors; and saw how George Shultz brought economic and business interests to bear on the policy preferences of the diplomatic corps. The range of available tools and tactics is broad and often reflects personality traits and proclivities, but in all cases they give the diplomat a wide attractive and coercive diplomatic range. While the classic description of the range of measures at diplomats' disposal is Satow's *Diplomatic Practice* (2009), a more contemporary look at diplomatic practice and its multiple manifestations can be found in *Madam Ambassador* (E. Kounalakis 2015).

7. Leonard 2002. The title of Leonard's essay, "Diplomacy by Other Means," is a play on the Clausewitzian-derived aphorism. Leonard bridges some of the dissonance and distance between the hard and soft power tools, recognizing that soft power is not always perceived or performed as soft and referring to the contradictions as sometimes "a velvet fist inside an iron glove" (56).

8. For a comprehensive sweep of the empirical manifestations of diplomacy's many forms as practiced by a former US secretary of state, see Henry Kissinger's *Diplomacy* ([1994] 2012). Kissinger's volume is a solid primer on the topic. His book refers regularly to historic and contemporary diplomatic actions where "tough" diplomacy, ultimatums, and walkouts are practiced. While these practices are the most visible exertion of diplomacy's hard power, it would be a mistake to understand apparently milder diplomatic acts as lacking either enforcement or a coercive edge, as the tip of a sword is sometimes delivered by a silver tongue.

9. This was discussed in more detail in M. Kounalakis and Simonyi (2010), a more complete treatise on diplomatic tools and the diplomatic power spectrum.

10. Larson 2004, 35.

which GNNs are engaged: formal diplomacy, informal diplomacy, and an all-encompassing manifestation where GNNs intersect or parallel diplomatic practice.

Formal Diplomacy

GNNs and their practitioners have long performed formal diplomatic functions, either despite or because of their roles and journalistic capacities. This formal diplomacy has been conducted both by individuals working for GNNs and by GNN institutions themselves.

Correspondents and other individuals working in pre-GNN institutional journalism have been documented as performing formal diplomatic functions. As early as the nineteenth century, people such as Britain's Valentine Chirol performed diplomatic functions while also working as a journalist. As described in Fritzinger's *Diplomat without Portfolio*, this peripatetic journalist for Britain's *Times* was regularly used as a back-channel diplomat between the English and Germans. "Thanks to his almost unique position—part diplomatist, part information conduit, part expert on the East, Near and Far, and on Europe—Chirol had played a major part in the working out of the Anglo-Japanese Alliance, had gone to Berlin to discuss Anglo-German relations. . . . All these quasi-official assignments took place under Lansdowne [the British foreign secretary]."[11] Chirol's split loyalties and successful dual role as a diplomat and journalist were only possible due to the prestige and prominence of the *Times*, which gave him high-level access, resources, editorial support, and cover, while the Foreign Ministry was able to leverage and profit from his activities, while maintaining plausible deniability in diplomatic engagement or proposed solutions. Chirol, however, always saw himself as a journalist first, and his expertise grew out of his journalistic activity and professional experience. These were identified by Britain's foreign minister and put to direct use without Chirol needing to sacrifice his professional standing or position.[12]

---

11. Fritzinger 2006, 277.

12. After two decades as a foreign reporter and war correspondent, Chirol retired from the *Times* in 1911. One year later he was knighted for his advisory role to the Foreign Ministry and

Another example is Stephen Bonsal, who worked directly for the American foreign policy apparatus while he was a foreign correspondent for the *New York Herald*, his reporting going directly to policymakers in the US and British governments. Interestingly, in an 1892 newspaper column in the literary magazine *Athenaeum* where Bonsal's reporting was questioned, British diplomat Sir Charles Euan-Smith defended the quality of his work: "Mr. Bonsal nevertheless affirms that he sent nothing which was not official. He not only acted at Sir Charles's request, but his dispatches were read to several members of the embassy staff, and the contents made known to the minister himself."[13] Bonsal's official diplomatic work was not deemed his primary activity; to his prominent pre-GNN journalistic institution and in his own mind, his reporting responsibilities came first—reporting for his publication and the citizenry it served.[14]

As discussed in chapter 4, the Chinese practice a more direct form of diplomatic representation via their state-sponsored institutions, using their news agency Xinhua, for example, to serve as a de facto embassy. As a nation, they are, however, not alone in using people outside the diplomatic corps to perform full diplomatic functions, particularly in countries they do not officially recognize or where diplomatic relations have been severed.

While the concept that a GNN—whether a journalistic organization or an INGO—performs de facto or de jure diplomatic services is exceptional in states with type I (nonstate) GNNs, the practice is not unheard-of in states with predominantly type III (state) GNNs. A corollary to this practice of statecraft by an entity other than the state is found in the realm of international diplomacy, where foreign states are imbued with the power to perform diplomatic functions for other states in their stead. Often this role is played by a "protecting power,"[15] a third country

---

shortly thereafter joined the British diplomatic corps. "At the tenth annual meeting of the Royal Institute of International Affairs, Major General Sir Neill Malcolm called him 'The friend of viceroys, the intimate of ambassadors, one might almost say the counsellor of ministers, he was [also] one of the noblest characters that ever adorned British journalism'" (Fritzinger 2006, 481).

13. Charles Euan-Smith in the *Athenaeum* (1892), 735.

14. Bonsal covered the major global events of the late nineteenth and early twentieth centuries for the *New York Herald* (1895–1907) before becoming President Woodrow Wilson's private translator and adviser at the 1919 Paris Peace Conference (Bonsal 1944). In 1945, he received a Pulitzer Prize in History for his book, *Unfinished Business*.

15. Levie 1961.

that represents the interests of the protected country. Greece, Turkey, and the United Kingdom have acted as protecting powers for the island republic of Cyprus since decolonization in the 1960s. Hungary briefly performed this role for many countries—including the United States—in Libya during the kinetic activity leading to the overthrow of Colonel Gaddafi. This is sometimes done unofficially through third-party representation (as the United States did with the Swiss embassy in Iran), or via the downgrading of diplomatic missions (such as the US Interest Section that operated in Havana during the years leading up to the normalization process started under former president Barack Obama).[16] However, except for the Chinese, nations do not use news agencies or news organizations as official representation to other countries.[17] China and the news agency Xinhua are unique in such bald use of a news operation in diplomatic and official functions, though Russia, too, openly admits a direct relationship between its GNNs and the state's diplomatic corps.

Russian and Chinese GNNs can be viewed as diplomatic missions in their own right or, at the very least, as diplomatic outposts. This is sui generis for news organizations worldwide, with nonstate and hybrid GNNs often distancing themselves from the state and maintaining a publicly adversarial relationship.[18]

However, there are many cases in which individuals in GNN institutions and GNNs themselves are systemically leveraged in ad hoc fashion, surreptitiously or with plausible deniability for their formal state-induced or state-imposed diplomatic roles. During my time as a diplomatic spouse in Hungary, the use of my journalistic network, credibility, and authority

---

16. These cases are interjected in this book to illustrate the practice of proxy diplomacy that sometimes empowers GNNs to represent or negotiate on behalf of a state. Reasons for the state's absence can be multiple. In Iran, for example, the United States did not have a diplomatic presence following the taking of US hostages in 1979. This proxy power is sometimes informally relegated to Western GNNs.

17. K. Hamilton and Langhorne 2011.

18. Hallin 1989. The public perception of objectivity and an adversarial relationship was early on recognized as an incomplete picture of journalism's relationship to the state: "Simultaneous with the rise of the ethic of objectivity and the growing autonomy of the journalist within the news organization was another fundamental change in the nature of American journalism: a tightening of the bonds between journalism and the state" (Hallin 1989, 69).

was leveraged at official diplomatic functions—in particular, as a bridge to the embattled national journalism community subjected to the new Hungarian government's restrictive media laws—not in the course of my professional journalistic duties (restricted by the US State Department) but rather as a result of my spousal relationship with the US ambassador to Hungary.[19]

A particularly interesting case of a pre-GNN Western journalist being used for official diplomatic functions concerns Ray Stannard Baker. At the end of World War I, President Woodrow Wilson enlisted this well-regarded muckraking journalist, who worked for the *New Republic* and the *New York World*, to report directly to the White House and the State Department.[20] His book, *A Journalist's Diplomatic Mission*, details the postwar Paris Peace Conference, where he not only observed but actively participated in promoting America's interests in diplomatic negotiations, while helping to formulate or proscribe dictated terms to align with President Wilson's interests and desired outcomes. Baker later wrote a biography of President Wilson. Baker, like Chiron and Bonsal before him, was an active journalist but performed diplomatic functions at the highest level, whether as an analyst or a go-between in negotiations. This practice foreshadowed a GNN practice that continues to this day. Informal as well as formal nonprofessional diplomatic GNN functions were performed primarily by journalists during the nineteenth and twentieth centuries, when the West had a nearmonopoly of journalistic institutions reporting

---

19. E. Kounalakis 2015. While some of my professional activities are elaborated upon in this volume, my perspective and unofficial diplomatic performance are not presented in any detail. As I was considered a specialist in media law, having chaired the first multinational conference that drafted Iraq's media laws in the postinvasion period in 2003, my expertise was drawn upon broadly by the US embassy community, as were the credibility and connections from a long career in journalism. None of these acts were public or publicized. There were regular meetings with editorial staff of the country's leading media organizations, from *Népszabadság* to Magyar Rádió to online news sources. Many editors and reporters regularly conveyed private concerns and observations regarding a multitude of issues to me, in part due to my diplomatic relationship, but just as often on a collegial and professional basis. Some of my journalistic findings during the course of my wife's diplomatic mission to Hungary were also actively relayed to the embassy, though the actionable nature of the information—if any—is not a part of the public record.

20. Baker et al. 2012. Baker later became President Wilson's press secretary and participated in diplomatic negotiations at the Paris Peace Conference.

overseas. In the twenty-first-century, GNNs have their own players—journalists and others—performing similar roles, only with a broader base of institutions and a greater number of non-Western actors.

In a contemporary Western GNN context, former president Barack Obama's ambassador to the United Nations, Samantha Power, performed diplomatic actions prior to her appointment as a government official, while she was working as a journalist and author, though the formality of the relationship is unclear. Certainly, she was regularly consulted on her human rights work and the conditions she observed and solutions she conceived.[21] All this happened while she was working within institutional GNN structures, significantly the *Economist*, the *Boston Globe*, *U.S. News and World Report*, and the *New Republic*. These important and respected journalistic organizations gave her the credibility and access to be able to stretch her work from strict reporting to advocacy and, informally, state representation.

Despite her engagement with Western states on an informal diplomatic level, it was only at the end of her institutional journalistic role that she began to publicly perform her official diplomatic duties. Power's Pulitzer Prize for her book *A Problem from Hell* (2003), which discussed genocide as well as her foreign policy insights and human rights activities, garnered great attention. As a result, her diplomatic advice was sought by both policy makers and politicians. As Zengerle writes, "Not long after Obama was elected to the Senate in 2004, he invited Power, whom he'd never met, to lunch so he could pick her brain about foreign policy."[22] She is one of a number of international journalists and GNN personnel who turned long diplomatic relationships into formal diplomatic careers.[23] In the contemporary context, Steve Bannon, executive chairman of Breitbart News, played

---

21. Zengerle 2013.

22. Zengerle 2013, par. 5.

23. I also worked closely and remain collegially close with former *Time* Moscow correspondent Jay Carney, who eventually took a policy adviser role with Vice President Joe Biden before becoming presidential spokesman for President Barack Obama. As was true for most other Western institutional GNN reporters, Carney's time in Moscow included regular meetings and interactions with political and economic counselors at the US embassy, as well as the ambassador. Samantha Power may be one of the higher-profile GNN individuals who later worked in government, but her participation in diplomatic functions is not unique.

a significant role both before and after the election of Donald Trump, using his personal and media resources to mediate and advise globally.

The list of journalists turned diplomats is long and includes 2016 US presidential candidate Rand Paul's adviser Richard R. Burt, once a *New York Times* correspondent who covered deeply and engaged actively in arms control issues and later became the chief negotiator for the Strategic Arms Reduction Treaty (START I). Another high-profile diplomat, former US special envoy to Afghanistan and Pakistan Richard Holbrooke, went in and out of diplomatic service, working at one point as an editor at *Foreign Policy* magazine and contributing editor to *Newsweek International*. He later married journalist and author Kati Marton, who also formally engaged in diplomacy during his lifetime. Marton discusses this issue in an op-ed piece for the *New York Times* titled "The Weapons of Diplomacy, and the Human Factor." Here she notes, "Since Richard believed in using all available tools in diplomacy . . . he seated me between Milosevic and Bosnian President Alija Izetbegovic and instructed me to make the two deadly foes talk to each other."[24] The newspaper where Marton recounted this story, the *New York Times*, given its reputational status and industry-respected role as "the newspaper of record,"[25] is the quintessential Western type I (nonstate) institution, exemplifying an access, status, and impact nearly unmatched in the West. Though Marton,[26] a second-generation journalist, was not in the employ of the *New York Times*, she and others recognize the importance and visibility of a *Times* op-ed. Richard Holbrooke often used his journalism background and network to make sure that his policy perspectives and diplomatic overtures were given additional weight, most often by placing the work in the *Times*.[27]

---

24. Marton 2011, par. 4.

25. Okrent 2004.

26. Including Kati Marton in this book brings up a difficult chapter in the history of journalists who worked for Western GNNs—in particular, Marton's parents, who were Hungarian journalists working for the American United Press (later UPI) and Associated Press (AP). Both parents maintained a close working relationship with the US embassy in Budapest and the US ambassador. Their activities behind the Iron Curtain earned them the official title of "enemies of the people," leading to jail and worse, as documented in Marton's book (2009).

27. Personal communication with Holbrooke family member, April 20, 2015.

Diplomacy Ideal Types (WEST)	Informal	Formal
Individual	Phillips, Marton	Scali, Burt, Holbrooke, Baker, Power
Institutional	CBS, *New York Times*, *Washington Post*	State-sponsored GNNs: BBG (VOA, RFE/RL), BBC World Service

Table 3. GNN ideal types engaged in diplomacy

An ideal breakdown of functions and diplomatic performances can be seen in Table 3. The detailed features and functions of informal and formal diplomacy, as well as institutional and individual performance within these roles, is the subject of this section. As with most ideal types, the hard-drawn lines of activities are subject to crossover, and individuals and institutions might arguably be placed in either different or multiple cells.

Table 3 categorizes the formal and informal roles played by GNNs, at both an individual level and an organizational level. This chart is a framework of GNN ideal types engaged in diplomacy, with specific individuals and institutions placed in the appropriate category. The individuals and institutions are examples; they are the ones discussed in this book, but one can think of many more instances of each category. The matrix does not recognize the overlap of those engaged both in formal and informal categories.

The first cell recognizes individuals engaged in informal diplomatic work and includes Kati Marton, Terry Phillips, and myself. The second cell includes individuals previously identified as performing a formal diplomatic role.

The third cell shows the institutions identified in this chapter as having performed a diplomatic role on an informal basis on behalf of their host nation. The fourth cell identifies state-sponsored GNNs that perform de facto (and in the case of Xinhua, de jure) diplomatic functions. The BBG is the United States' Broadcasting Board of Governors and the official government agency that oversees and directs individual broadcast news networks, including the Voice of America (VOA), Radio Free Europe/Radio Liberty (RFE/RL), Radio Free Asia (RFA), Radio Marti and TV Marti, and the Middle East Broadcasting Network (MBN).

Informal Diplomacy

As a logical extension of a GNN employee or related entity engaging in direct formal diplomacy, the diplomatic function is often performed by established GNN institutions — often news bureaus — and individuals in an informal fashion. Kati Marton crosses over between her formal role (as at the dinner party) and the informal role she played during her career, performing multiple GNN diplomatic functions. The informal GNN diplomatic role sometimes crosses over into the formal. Further, there is a twofold informality to this type of diplomacy: how individuals related to GNNs are perceived and how those same individuals and institutions perceive themselves.

External Perception
How GNNs are perceived is key to their primary performance and the legal frameworks in which they are allowed to function. Much of the external perception of GNNs is determined by how structures are funded (whether state, nonstate, or hybrid) and which nation hosts the organization (where it is headquartered and which citizenship is held by a GNN-employed individual). Geniets finds that even when GNNs are state owned, their funding models vary, as does their financial (and in part, their legal and political) dependence on their benefactors: "These international broadcasters are either state-funded or commercial, or (as in the case of the BBC and Al Jazeera), a hybrid of both funding models. That said, only one of these broadcasters, namely CNN International, is primarily focused on revenue generation."[28] Of the international

---

28. Geniets 2013, 60.

broadcasters, only CNN International is not state owned or operated, either wholly or in part. This funding structure creates for these GNNs— otherwise self-proclaimed independence-oriented organizations[29]—the accurate perception of having a direct link to the policy preferences and goals of their financial funders: the state. In a series of studies, Samuel-Azran found that accusations that Al Jazeera was a tool of Qatari interests rather than an independent news organization were, in the case of Al Jazeera Arabic, mostly true.[30] Gary Thomas's "Mission Impossible"[31] provides an analysis of the inherent perception conflict within Western state-sponsored GNNs and their mission to promote state policy preferences, where nonadministrative rank-and-file employees perceive their roles as that of independent journalists within a government agency. Thomas is a twenty-seven-year-old Voice of America veteran who argues that the self-perception and performance challenge hinges on disparate interpretations of the mission: "Policymakers have long viewed US international broadcasting as part of the public-diplomacy effort.... [T]he journalistic coherence that Central News brings to VOA has been rendered impotent."[32] Thomas recognizes that contemporary political pressure and legislative interest are creating state-sponsored GNNs that are even more focused on "advocacy, not journalism"[33] in the context of increasingly adversarial global relations and war.

It is not only state-sponsored GNNs that face a perception problem as a result of having direct relations with the state or having their content or viewpoints dictated by the state. Despite organizations' structural and financial independence, the accusation is viewed as credible.[34] CNN and

---

29. The BBC, for example, has purposes spelled out in the Royal Charter and Agreement that allow for its operation and are the constitutional basis for the organization. The BBC states as its primary value that "trust is the foundation of the BBC: we are independent, impartial and honest." The claim of independence has always been in question; for example, "the IRD [British Information Research Department] maintained a strong relationship with the BBC" (Dorril 2002, 78).

30. Samuel-Azran and Pecht, 2014; Samuel-Azran et al. 2016; Samuel-Azran 2013. Specifically, these studies found that Al Jazeera Arabic showed a strong alignment with Qatari interests, while Al Jazeera English tended to adhere to the journalistic norms of independence and objectivity to a much greater extent.

31. Thomas 2013.

32. Thomas 2013, par. 5.

33. Thomas 2013, par. 20.

34. Shotwell 1991.

Fox News are regularly singled out as organizations that seem to reflect US policy preferences and, further, promote outcomes desired by the state.[35] President Donald Trump has distanced himself and his administration from CNN, asserting that the network is pursuing an anti-Trump agenda and is a leading purveyor of "fake news." The charges are grave and the perception popularly considered unfair, but the implication is that CNN does not represent the domestic policy preferences of the Trump administration, though its international performance and role may continue to be perceived as wholly American.

This perception holds true globally. Foreign sovereigns usually regard any agent or flag bearer,[36] whether an industry or a news organization, as representing the interests of the nation in which it is incorporated or where it has its headquarters, regardless of whether a formal or financial relationship exists. GNNs are no exception. A most extreme example of this is the Russian Duma-enacted law, which primarily applied to the activities of foreign NGOs within Russia, officially equating registered foreign NGOs as foreign agents.[37] This perception was legally formalized in Russia and Turkey, where NGOs and journalists for foreign state news organizations were required to register as foreign agents. The US Foreign Agents Registration Act (FARA) of 1938 works similarly. Until recently,

---

35. Jaramillo (2009, 138) writes that in stark contrast to the adversarial posture toward American government and institutions in their domestic reporting, CNN and Fox News present a more unified nationalist narrative regarding American foreign policy, while also defining non-American GNNs as lackeys for their own nations' policies: "The overwhelming description of Arab television on CNN and Fox News Channel, then, was that it was a vehicle for pro-Hussein propaganda." Several other studies also found that different though they may be on domestic issues, when reporting on foreign issues, CNN and Fox News often offer similar perspectives, reflecting dominant US ideology (e.g., Guzman 2016.)

36. Just as ships and other materiel can be requisitioned by a state, so journalists can be enlisted in the pursuit of national interests or during wartime. Materiel can be legally acquired via the United States Merchant Marine Act, commonly referred to as the Jones Act. According to the Merchant Marine website, "The Merchant Marine is the fleet of ships which carries imports and exports during peacetime and becomes a naval auxiliary during wartime to deliver troops and war materiel. According to the Merchant Marine Act of 1936: 'It is necessary for the national defense . . . that the United States shall have a merchant marine of the best equipped and most suitable types of vessels sufficient to carry the greater portion of its commerce and serve as a naval or military auxiliary in time of war or national emergency . . .' During World War II the fleet was in effect nationalized."

37. See "Russian Political Parties Banned from Making Deals with Foreigners or 'Agents,'" *RT*, November 11, 2014, http://rt.com/politics/204399-russian-foreign-agent-political.

the US act was mostly limited to requiring foreign agents and lobbyists to register, although starting in the 1940s, the Soviet news agency TASS and other Soviet news outlets were included, and currently Chinese media outlets such as *China Daily* or Japan's NHK Cosmomedia are also registered.[38] Of great importance for this book, in November 2017, RT's American operator[39] and Sputnik's radio broadcaster in the United States registered under FARA.[40]

The most popular case of flag-bearing industries representing a nation or national interests concerns national airlines[41] or shipping lines,[42] which by law can be impressed into national service as a result of a real or perceived national emergency. In cases where the GNN is a state enterprise, the same logic and legal structure applies, as state-owned enterprises in other countries could not function without direct state support.[43] Even when a GNN and its representatives insist (or insist too much) on their independence, the perception is that GNNs represent the interests of the states where they are headquartered.

Self-Perception

This logic extends to state GNNs, where news organizations are both perceived and deployed as foreign agents.[44] According to an article in the *Diplomat*, both China and Russia extend the practice of characterizing foreign NGOs as foreign agents to include news agencies, de facto if not

---

38. Report of the Attorney General to the Congress of the United States on the Administration of the Foreign Agents Registration Act of 1938, as amended, for the six months ending June 30, 2017, accessed December 27, 2017, https://www.fara.gov/reports/FARA_JUN_2017.pdf.

39. Stubbs and Gibson 2017.

40. Eckel 2017.

41. Yglesias 2013. As Matt Yglesias points out, there exists in the United States a cabotage act, although it is seldom used: "In practice, despite fighting two wars simultaneously for a decade, CRAF [the Civil Air Reserve Fleet] seems to have been activated just once at the very beginning of the Iraq War when the Pentagon activated 47 passenger aircraft and 31 wide-body cargo planes" (par. 10).

42. Whitehurst 1965.

43. Geniets 2013.

44. Famularo 2015. As Painter (2008) writes in his *Counter-Hegemonic News*, "There seems little doubt that many of the state-funded channels are a means of augmenting national prestige in the way that a national airline might" (5).

entirely de jure. In that article, Famularo quotes former White House national security advisor Stephen Hadley, who "expressed his fear that Vladimir Putin is privately arguing to Xi Jinping that the United States and its Western allies are 'seeking to destabilize and change both governments; that it is this effort that is responsible for the instability and demonstrations in both Ukraine and Hong Kong; that the agents of this Western effort are civil society groups, NGOs, free media, and dissidents; that these "agents of foreign influence" must be stamped out in both Russia and China; and that the United States and its allies need to be confronted at nearly every turn.'"[45]

For nonstate-run GNNs where individuals and institutions lack a formal relationship to the state, there is an informal relationship, in part developed as a function of assured access and sovereign protection. A reporter for CNN or the *New York Times* in a particular area, for example, can have unique access to American policy makers or analysts, and as a host of studies prove, they often do, directly or indirectly.[46] It is often assumed, furthermore, that journalists can pass information from their area of expertise or the foreign country from which they are reporting to those who represent their home country's national interests. My findings have shown regular, if fettered, contact with policy makers. One interviewee recalled his process: "Check in with an embassy when arrive in a country . . . usually get some sort of briefing. Then circle back and debrief before getting out of town."[47] Sometimes a background briefing is arranged before departure for another country, with foreign ministries obliging, even encouraging and initiating, such briefings with high-profile journalists and columnists. "You get a full overview and they give you an idea of what they are most concerned about" is how another American journalist characterized an official predeparture briefing: "They want you

---

45. Famularo 2015, par. 18.

46. See, for example, A. Davis 2009; Carpenter 2007. My operating premise here, supported by my findings and reinforced by studies such as Carpenter (2007), is that elite news organizations and GNN institutional structures have greater access to elite sources, while nonelite or "citizen journalist" organizations have limited access. The Carpenter study (2007) was exceptional in that it showed nondifferentiation when it came to access of military sources. Otherwise, elite source assumptions were reinforced across government and regarding industry access.

47. Personal interview with *Diplomats* American newspaper journalist, October 2013.

to also test a few things when you meet with certain people when you get there."[48]

The practice of information exchange and diplomatic direction is done on a regular basis, even though it is seldom discussed in public. Organizations such as the Overseas Press Club recognize the practice and try to help professionals weigh the ethical pros and cons of this generally recognized informal diplomatic relationship in the context of a nonstate-owned GNN. On November 11, 2014, the Overseas Press Club in New York City arranged a panel discussion titled "Useful Sources: What Should Be the Relationships of Reporters to Diplomats, Especially in Times of Crisis?" The program guide offered a summary of the common foreign correspondence issues up for discussion: "The program is designed to provide newly assigned foreign correspondents tips on how to handle day-to-day basic working relationships with diplomats, both American and foreign. Topics to be discussed include embassy briefings, confidentiality, how to deal with CIA staff and military attachés."[49]

GNN personnel rarely write about these relationships or discuss them publicly in their broadcasts. But at the panel meeting organized by the Overseas Press Club of America in 2014, State Department historian Lindsay Krasnoff talked about the traditionally close relationship between diplomats and foreign correspondents: "There was certain trust on the part of U.S. diplomats that the information that they gave the journalists who visited them, and on the other side there was certain restraint and self-censorship on the side of journalists to maintain the diplomat's trust in terms of not publishing all that they witnessed," until a later time when the information was not as time-sensitive or actionable.[50]

On occasion, when a public reckoning of nonstate-operated GNN relationships with a state are revealed or otherwise become transparent,

48. Personal interview with American network broadcast producer in Washington, DC, November 2014.

49. Overseas Press Club of America, "Useful Sources: What Should Be the Relationships of Reporters to Diplomats, Especially in Times of Crisis?," *YouTube*, 2014, https://www.youtube .com/watch?v=M_7OS4M7HrE&feature=youtu.be.

50. Overseas Press Club of America, "Expert Panelists Discuss Reporter-Embassy Relations," November 11, 2014, https://www.opcofamerica.org/Eventposts/expert-panelists-discuss -reporter-embassy-relations, par. 14.

journalists often apologize or explain that they participate in diplomatic intervention or humanitarian activity only in extreme emergencies.

When about fifty thousand Yazidis, members of a religious community in the Middle East, were trapped on a mountaintop in 2014, a CNN reporter helped some of the refugees onto the rescue helicopter.[51] This was seen as an exceptional (and commendable) act because the reporter was working with aid workers and as a result directly engaging in a humanitarian effort seen as outside the core role for someone who is expected to be strictly an observer. The moral aspects of media workers interfering or refraining from interfering in what they observe have been intensely debated. For example, in an article for the *American Journalism Review*, Smolkin reviewed the ethical responsibility of engaging in humanitarian aid efforts during crises and concluded with a cautionary note: "Remember, though, that your primary—and unique—role as a journalist is to bear witness. If you decide to act, do so quickly, then get out of the way. Leave the rescue work to first responders and relief workers whenever possible."[52]

On the other hand, journalism as a profession is frequently criticized for reporters not participating in such activities. Occasionally, however, journalists' engagement goes beyond the Good Samaritan scenario that requires journalists to act in extreme cases. The informal yet effective diplomatic role played by a journalist in defusing nuclear tension and confrontation during the Cuban missile crisis is one high-profile case. Similarly, GNNs' engagement in humanitarian relief, while not directly a diplomatic function, can augment state power under the rubric of "humanitarian diplomacy."[53] What follows are instances of GNNs directly engaged in traditional diplomatic functions.

There are various ways GNNs may engage in diplomacy. On the institutional diplomacy level, GNNs may perform diplomatic functions formally and informally, in a passive or active manner. Passive informal diplomacy involves the administrative and editorial layers of GNN institutions, as they inform and mediate for government representatives and

---

51. Taibi 2014
52. Smolkin 2006, par. 69.
53. Lund 2001, 17

policy makers on an ad hoc level. This is the most public relationship between GNNs and the state. It is depicted in cinema and experienced in most state capitals around the world. Exchanges in such contexts are informal and exploratory, though the venues and the participants can be targeted for exploration prior to an event.

A formal passive relationship between institutional diplomacy and GNNs is also possible, where GNN institutions receive diplomatically relevant or critical information or instructions and are used as passive intermediaries. This is often the case when institutions receive letters or email traffic "over the transom" (unsolicited), with the GNN thrust into a role rather than seeking it out. It is often the case for a GNN overseas that unique information or dissident calls arrive unexpectedly and uninvited.

In an informal active relationship, the GNN takes an intermediary role in its normal course of operation and along the lines of its mission. The placement of opinion pieces,[54] advocacy of a position or policy, and the leveraging of unique "over the transom"[55] received exclusive information to perform a diplomatic function are typical examples of this behavior.

The active formal relationship, which has been discussed in some detail, involves the engagement of a GNN institution to perform direct, active, and outcome-oriented diplomatic functions. The unique aspect of GNN institutions is usually the access available and cover allowable for plausible deniability of the act and to perform the function outside the usual formal channels. GNNs are used by state leaders and foreign offices both purposefully and as a matter of course, leveraging GNNs' strengths, access, insights, and analytical skills on behalf of the state in pursuit of enhancing state power.

---

54. For case studies on "op-ed diplomacy" (Gilboa 2005c), see Golan 2013, exploring the op-eds on the 2011 Egyptian revolution published in European editions of two American newspapers; and Golan and Lukito, 2015, on framing China as a global power in editorials and op-eds in the *New York Times* and in the *Wall Street Journal*.

55. A ProPublica investigation into Chinese espionage shows the questionable but useful nature of "over the transom" information: "Paul Moore, a former top FBI Chinese counterintelligence analyst, said cultural differences between the West and East pose challenges for investigators trying to determine if Chinese are involved in intelligence operations. 'Was this a Chinese intelligence operation, or just something that came in over the transom?' he said. 'It sounds like Chinese people acting like Chinese people. It looks foreign to us—and suspect'" (Gabrielson 2014, par. 94).

Informal Diplomacy: Individuals

Perhaps the greatest impact in a diplomatic performative function came from the role played by John Scali, the ABC News reporter who carried messages between Soviet and American officials during the 1962 Cuban missile crisis. L. Gelder detailed Scali's role in an obituary in the *New York Times* in 1995: "Mr. Scali acted as courier, Government spokesman and negotiator for the Kennedy Administration before the crisis was peacefully resolved" (par. 11). When Scali was asked if he would do it again, "'the answer is yes,' he said. 'At times like that, a reporter has no choice. Because whatever he can do to save humanity from destruction, even just an ounce worth, he must do—and that's not just patriotic flag waving.'"[56]

He was essentially a negotiator, even establishing policy positions in the process. Scali played an active diplomatic role.[57] Scali's official GNN role at CBS gave him the unique access required for him to perform this act. It also provided the perfect cover for his actions, so that external questions regarding his interactions with the Soviets could be attributed to his professional role as a journalist.

Another profound and well-documented example is the hand that *CBS Evening News* anchor Walter Cronkite had in setting up negotiations between Israeli prime minister Menachem Begin and Egyptian president Anwar Sadat. As recounted by Cronkite and affirmed by others, the Begin-Sadat on-air discussion eventually led to the Camp David accord ending hostilities between those two states.[58] As Cronkite told NPR, "The terms of a settlement seem simple and clear. It was the human factors that complicated things—pride, politics and power. What was needed was for someone to drop a handkerchief, a moment of opportunity that would permit the parties both movement and cover. In 1977, I found myself playing that role in what would become the first direct exchange between Egypt and Israel."[59]

---

56. Gelder 1995, par. 13.
57. Garthoff 1989. Before Garthoff's recounting of the Cuban missile crisis negotiations between the United States and the Soviet Union and the central mediating role played by John Scali, Scali himself published a full narrative of the events in "I Was the Secret Go-Between in the Cuban Crisis" in *Family Weekly* (1964).
58. Cronkite 2007.
59. Cronkite 2007, par. 4–5.

Cronkite's role was extraordinary and his public admission of his intermediation a rarity. Cronkite was self-deprecating and downplayed the important role he played: "As for Cronkite diplomacy, I'm sure that it initiated nothing the two principals were not already prepared to undertake. If I dropped the strategic handkerchief, they chose the time and manner of picking it up. But the openness of television offered a powerful incentive that secret diplomacy did not. The political consequences of a public failure improved the ultimate chances of diplomatic success, and statesmen willing to fail publicly are a courageous lot."[60] Walter Cronkite points out how a GNN, in this case a Western type I (nonstate) broadcasting organization and its employee, brought a unique contribution to the enhancement of state power. While Cronkite speaks to his particular experience, and the case of television, he provides a clear template for how Western GNNs use their public role, popularity, and stature to perform unique diplomatic functions otherwise reserved for the state. Further, the unique access and power, hallmarks of institutional GNN structures, are reinforced in the Cronkite example, where his argument extends to the relative insignificance of noninstitutional journalistic players, such as bloggers or citizen journalists, who lack the stature or the structure to affect large-scale diplomatic events and outcomes.

Journalists and GNN personnel sometimes engage in diplomacy even without urgent humanitarian or global existential crises. One case involves myself and Terry Phillips, who was in 1994 acting bureau chief for CBS News ("the Tiffany network")[61] in Port-au-Prince, Haiti. This is a previously unpublished case of journalists actively engaging in direct diplomatic action. Like myriad other diplomatic actions by GNN professionals, this one has been kept secret for over twenty years, in part because of the professional concerns of the participants while we remained active in our careers. Ethical questions regarding professional conduct and journalistic roles entered into the decision-making process

---

60. Cronkite 2007, par. 41–42.

61. CBS was referred to as "the Tiffany network" because of the perceived high quality of its news organization and popularly respected newsmen during the tenure of CBS founder William S. Paley.

prior to the intervention and remained a concern after the fact, keeping this instance out of the public eye to avoid collegial judgment.

In the summer of 1994, military conflict on the island nation of Haiti was avoided partly through the participation of Phillips and myself. Phillips, who was in Haiti at the time of the crisis, and I became involved in a series of actions that made us intermediaries between the governments of Haiti and the United States and ultimately aided in achieving a peaceful resolution.[62]

Though Phillips shares some of the ethical concerns discussed by Smolkin (2006), he firmly believes that journalists should engage in non-journalistic functions if they "can do good": "We are often in a position to know things that other people don't know, to have connections with people that other people don't have, and I think we oftentimes either ignore or deliberately avoid serving in other capacities, and I think it's unfortunate. We can clearly do some good when these opportunities arise. . . . I wish we would do this more deliberately and more often" (appendix 1).

Other cases, both American and non-American, where journalists interviewed for this study have intervened in the diplomatic process directly, if informally, have been kept confidential as per an understanding between myself and the interview subjects. The instances include a case in Chechnya (1992), one in Georgia (1992), one in Armenia, two in Afghanistan (1991 and 2004), one in Yugoslavia and, later, Croatia (1991), and one in Poland (1989).

Legal Obligations to Engage in Informal Diplomacy

Of course, in wartime, journalists, like other citizens, often have a legal responsibility to protect—and at times support—the efforts of their government. For journalists, regardless of their nationality, this usually takes the negative form of restrictions on reporting and dissemination of information, primarily on activities that would be construed or judicially

---

62. The full circumstances are recounted in appendix 1. In the interview, Phillips describes two further diplomatic interventions.

interpreted as aiding or abetting an enemy.[63] These restrictions include adhering to rules of engagement, not reporting troop movements, and following other strictures as determined by law and custom. In the United States, the principles were laid down in the oft-cited Minnesota Supreme Court decision *Near v. Minnesota*, 683 U.S. 697 (1931), regarding prior restraint. The court ruled that certain restrictions can be imposed on the press.[64] These practices apply to journalists and their employers, who have obligations to publish or not publish. Such was clearly the case during World War II, when military censorship was in full force. American journalists covering combat wore uniforms, held nominal ranks, and were subject to direct commands by superior officers. *Washington Post* journalist Sam Stavisky heard in 1942 that the US Marine Corps was forming a special unit for journalists called the Combat Correspondent Corps. The Marine Corps was planning on transforming a few civilian reporters into Marines and assigning them to the Pacific.[65]

The relationship between media and the military has always been complex. For the great historian Thucydides, field reporting and analysis was born of action he witnessed and participated in as an army general. Since those ancient days, the relationship between reporters and the military has always been intense.

However, in recent years, the relationship has become more complicated as reporters and defense departments have implemented a formal embedding structure with, for example, US forces. As noted in "A Comparison of Embedded and Nonembedded Print Coverage of the US Invasion and Occupation of Iraq," the voluntary embedding of reporters during times of war—where access to one side's military personnel is restricted—resulted in greater association with the military. In particular,

---

63. Loane 1965; Sarbin, Carney, and Eoyang 1994. Most nations have a form of treason law. Its application and interpretation varies widely.

64. "**Legal Question:** Is censorship by prior restraint of a newspaper allowed under the First Amendment? **Decision: No,** except in crisis situations such as reports of troop movements, or incitement to violence or overthrow of government, or publication of obscene material" (JEM First Amendment Project, "Near v. Minnesota, 683 U.S. 697 [1931]," *University of Tennessee Knoxville*, accessed February 18, 2018, https://firstamendment.cci.utk.edu/content/near-v-minnesota-683-us-697-1931).

65. Stavisky 1999.

this study found a different "overall tone toward the military, trust in military personnel, framing, and authoritativeness between embedded and nonembedded articles."[66]

Legal principles of reporting during wartime remain the same today as they were during World War II, but the nature and immediacy of reporting—as well as the immediacy of news distribution in the Internet era—create dynamics hitherto unknown.[67] The relationship between RT and the Russian military is strong, and has gained greater attention following the recent Russian military engagement in Ukraine.[68]

People employed by GNNs can engage in informal and formal diplomacy in either a passive or active manner. Further, the practices and patterns uncovered in the interview process revealed witting and unwitting performance of those practices. For individuals engaged in passive informal diplomatic activity, innocent sharing beyond open-source distributional methods involves person-to-person engagements where notebooks are opened and data shared that is unavailable to a broader public or sponsoring institution. The activity is a friendly, passive, informal act that yields insight and access to people and circumstances that shape diplomatic actions, according to policy makers interviewed.

The passive formal relationship between GNN individuals and state agencies or individuals is best represented by directed diplomatic action or information gathering that is understood by the GNN individual as being outside the professional and ethical realm of strict reporting or analysis but, according to GNN individuals interviewed, mostly acceptable. This could involve a state official requesting that the GNN individual

---

66. Haigh et al. 2006, 139. More recent studies also found that embedding reporters influences their reporting (e.g., Maguire 2017.)

67. D. Bennett 2013.

68. M. Kounalakis 2014b. As pointed out in this newspaper article, "Tune in to Russia Today and you can watch conventional programs like 'Larry King Now' or 'Venture Capital.' On some recent programming, however, RT's party line bias was so heavy-handed that it prompted one anchor to resign on-air in protest over the Kremlin's Ukraine policy. D.C.-based Liz Wahl went off script on the RT-America program, saying, 'I cannot be part of a network funded by the Russian government that whitewashes the actions of Putin. I'm proud to be an American and believe in disseminating the truth, and that is why, after this newscast, I'm resigning.' Another RT host, Abby Martin, strayed from the party line, going rogue on-air by saying, 'Russian intervention in the Crimea is wrong'" (par. 23).

mediate with transferal of specific information or data to achieve a diplomatic outcome otherwise unavailable to the state agent and outside the realm of competence or available information for the GNN actor. "Pass this on to your government" is how one interview subject described this action. The subject then described a time when, in the course of interviewing a high-level government official where his nation had no national diplomatic representation, the source asked him to deliver a diplomatic negotiating point to his country of citizenship.[69] It is remarkable that GNN institutional players have unique opportunities when representing themselves as such rather than acting as independent, unaffiliated, noninstitutional journalists. Without institutional support and structure to give them access and credibility via internationally branded news organizations (which often appear in foreign editions overseas and in international newsstands and at airports), it is unlikely that they would be asked to perform even a minor diplomatic courier role. *Newsweek* and *Time* correspondents during the 1980s and 1990s, for example, were highly visible in their overseas bureaus and were regularly approached by state representatives to discuss, sometimes on background and sometimes off-the-record, issues of state strategy and diplomatic sensitivity.

The third form of individual GNN diplomacy is active and informal, the result of individuals seeking or attending briefings where sensitive but unclassified information is imparted and exchanged. Such engagements raise specific questions or are intended to garner pointed interactions between GNN individuals and otherwise inaccessible foreign individuals and institutions. The GNN individuals actively seek the interaction with their native governments and present their governments' position and perspective to interview and research subjects. Specific negotiating points are indicated and specific diplomatic data sought by the state agency via the GNN individual, who is actively aware of the process and wittingly performing it while maintaining an informal relationship to the state. In some instances—for example, following informal interactions with the American embassy—a *Newsweek* correspondent was prompted to ask specific questions regarding a foreign nation's policies concerning

---

69. Personal interview with a GNN individual, Berkeley, California, 2015.

a third nation. The questions were pointed and consequential, including issues regarding nuclear weaponry and the state's position on the third nation's approach and policy. The questions were intrinsically interesting to the journalist, but he likely would not have asked them because he lacked the background and policy context prior to his interactions with the American state representative.[70]

Finally, an active formal diplomatic engagement is also possible. This is transactional and involves the GNN individual, regardless of the institution to which he is assigned or employed, taking a forward and witting action of direct diplomacy, as in the case of John Scali. The GNN individual need not be a direct employee of the state, but may act on behalf of the state while maintaining a primary professional identity with a GNN institution or unaffiliated GNN distributional institution. While a non-GNN individual could theoretically perform this role, research for this study showed a near-exclusive reliance on individuals working in institutional GNNs. The reasons given included a published track record and time spent together during GNN coverage of state activities (often as "State Department beat" reporters or because "I knew her when she covered the Pentagon"). The attitude of state representatives was that bloggers (with the exception of a few individuals who moved to blogging from institutional GNNs) and citizen journalists were "cowboys," too independent or "untethered" to be reliable partners in this activity.[71] As with nearly all traditional practices in type I American GNN structures, this paradigm may no longer prove as dominant during the Trump administration, where organizations previously considered fringe now have greater access to the White House and institutional players find their access and influence more constrained.

Formal and Informal Intersectional Diplomatic Functions

In the realm of individual passive informal diplomacy, GNN employees naturally perform certain functions, generally categorized as cocktail

---

70. Personal interview with an American journalist, 2015.
71. Personal communications with state representatives, 2014, 2015.

party conversations. These casual chats typically occur at foreign embassy receptions or over coffee between an industry executive or NGO administrator and a government official.[72] In such encounters, individuals exchange rather than proffer information. Journalists often test the margins, perhaps to get a second source on a story without the source being aware of confirming facts, even though she or he may suspect that this is the case. In the course of informal fishing for information, the journalist gives up some information he or she has collected as a show of goodwill, an enticement, or at times a bluff, as reported by a majority of this study's interviewed subjects. In the case highlighted in chapter 3, when information on potential terrorist activities was flagged by a correspondent for the US embassy's military attaché in Prague, the information exchange was preceded with information that was less valuable to test the limits of sharing. The *Newsweek* reporter noted an exchange with a former Communist Party arms dealer who shared information regarding members of the new, interim non-Communist government of Václav Havel and their involvement in questionable arms sales to the Middle East. "I had to give up a piece of information he likely already had, or should have had. It was a test. I wanted to see if he would give me something in return. And it was probably a test for him, too. How reliable am I? Am I just BS-ing him? Trying to get something for nothing?"[73] The exchange produced detailed and important information regarding Soviet activities in the early days of post-Communist Czechoslovakia.

With regard to this mutually beneficial information exchange—an important act of informal diplomacy—most reporters interviewed for this study discussed the fact that journalistic reports typically use 5 to 10 percent of what is in their notebooks.[74] That is especially true in broadcast

---

72. The *South China Morning Post* reports that recognizing the high value of journalist-generated information, in 2014 the PRC made it illegal for journalists to share unpublished work. "According to the directive, the rules cover information, material and news that journalists may deal with during their work, 'including state secrets, commercial secrets and information that has not been publicly disclosed. Reporters, editors and anchormen should not disseminate state secrets in any form via any media and they should not mention such information in their private exchanges or letters,' the new rules stipulate" (Li and Chen 2014, par. 6–7).

73. Personal interview with an American journalist, 2015.

74. Some newspapers, like the *New York Times*, have infrequent columns titled "Reporter's Notebook," where some of the valuable and interesting information that does not make it into a

news, where content is constrained and time limits and medium emphasis on imagery and sounds dictate the level of detail and complexity of analysis.[75] This means that journalists have a lot of names, numbers, and peripheral data that might not even bolster the thesis of the story—but might be even more valuable as currency for collateral use.

Articles, analyses, broadcast productions, and reports intended for US audiences, for example, routinely require an American perspective. It is not unusual for reporters to gather a large quantity of material, more than required for the final report, that is of interest to a domestic audience. That leaves a surplus available for unpublished, informal exchange. As one of the journalists interviewed for this study put it, "This is perfect for doing a 'notebook dump' with someone over lunch."[76] According to a diplomat based in Europe, this data can lead to diplomatic openings, and "the exchanges themselves are a part of the [diplomatic] process."[77] There is also an intelligence-gathering aspect to this practice. The crossover between formal or informal diplomatic activity and formal or informal intelligence gathering is not uncommon.

Thus, as a foreign correspondent who has worked in multiple countries of Africa, Europe, Asia, and the former USSR explained, something in the reporter's informal chatter might strike a particular chord during conversation with a diplomat. The source might offhandedly verify a fact. The subsequent quid pro quo might be to add, "I'd be curious to know what that person would say if you were to ask. . . ."[78] In such a case, journalists share an analytical perspective and approach rather than secrets.

Consequently, a journalist might have a follow-up debrief with the same person because of a curiosity to know what was uncovered. In my experience and in the majority of interviews conducted with GNN professionals for this study, reporters are regularly debriefed in such cases

---

reporter's stories is able to see the light of day in a mass publication and with alternative contextualizations. Most reporter notebooks remain unmined for their ancillary value, deep data, source contacts, and side notes—often making them invaluable to those who are able to cull specific data and information that is regularly exclusive.

75. Lang 2000.

76. Personal interview with an American journalist, June 2, 2013, Germany.

77. Personal interview with a diplomat, December 2012, Prague.

78. Personal interview with an American journalist, June 2013, Budapest.

to allow for the triangulation of answers and information because of undisclosed but available open-source or discovered information. The elements listed above help journalists shape an approach in dealing with a subject. This is truly a symbiotic relationship.[79]

Further, there is a level of judgment and perception that occurs based on the comportment, dress, and seeming intelligence of journalists. It affects how they are perceived by the subjects of their work. This is as true in the political world as it is in financial circles[80] and diplomatic milieus.[81] How big is a journalist's team? What does his/her infrastructure look like? Does he/she have the latest in equipment, or is he/she a lone wolf recording with an iPhone? All these things project the relative power of GNN institutions in the host country where a foreign correspondent or bureau is located. Impressive office addresses, the latest studio technologies, multiple bureau employees, globally respected brands, and familiar reporting talent combine to project the importance, professionalism, and power of institutional GNNs while also putting into relief the inadequacy and weakness of noninstitutional players. The same is true for the academic and the INGO. Brand-name institutions matter to the consumer if not to the capacity or quality of scholarship. But a Harvard or Stanford academic has an easier time opening doors than the guy from Fresno State (unless the work is in Armenia, where Fresno has a uniquely important institutional standing due to the number of Armenian-Americans at the university). INGOs rely on the size of their institution and its brand identity to gain access and have impact. The Red Cross and Red Crescent have outsize reputations and budgets that allow them to enter transitional regions or countries that are under extreme stress or in need of humanitarian help. Similarly, Doctors without Borders, the Nobel Prize–winning organization that often finds itself in the midst of turmoil in areas that face

---

79. While I was based in Moscow during the early 1990s, working for two different American GNNs, I and Mark Bauman also wrote for a Russian newspaper, *Nezavisimaya Gazeta* ("Independent Newspaper"). The columns were in effect informal (or semiformal) approaches to issues of the day and—infused with our global analytical and field understanding—often included policy recommendations and insight.

80. Baron and Markman 2000.

81. Kraut and Poe 1980. Kraut and Poe's psychological study found that "comportment mediated the effects of demographic characteristics and had direct effects on decisions" (784).

political as well as medical difficulties. Perhaps there is a transition underway where some web-based humanitarian organizations are now able to build the size and impact of their organizations quickly and effectively, but those organizations have not yet become institutional players in the GNN firmament, according to a few Western embassy representatives outside the United States with familiarity in humanitarian undertakings. GNNs still rule in this regard.

At the same time, states have recognized the value of journalism as a diplomatic extension, particularly given how inexpensive and nimble it is relative to other forms of diplomatic and intelligence-gathering institutions. When states lack GNN ownership, they give up direct control over the process of leveraging or directly using journalists as diplomatic interlocutors and analysts, though this arrangement provides greater diplomatic plausible deniability.

Two senior State Department officials affirmed the lack of control over Western type I (nonstate) GNNs and, notably, lamented the loss of the open-source intelligence (OSINT) and analysis that fed their own policy shops and country desks. "We get a lot of our information from foreign correspondents," said one, who then insisted that these journalists are important sources of information who "help us take the temperature of a country." Another senior American official said that the importance of GNNs and their personnel in the field had increased as security concerns "keep our people behind the wire," meaning that Western embassies increasingly resemble fortresses, where official embassy personnel who would otherwise circulate around the country were now required to stay within the safe confines of cordoned-off areas or places deemed secure. In this environment, "journalists are a lifeline" to the outside world, according to this official. Many of the officials I interviewed asked how this diminishing GNN resource could survive and return with a strong presence in the future.

Those government officials I interviewed were all dismissive of the current foreign affairs bloggers, with a few exceptions (one is University of Michigan history professor Juan Cole, whose *Informed Comment* blog on the Middle East was mentioned more than once). One criticism was that these blogging sites lack an editorial layer to check facts and impose a balanced analysis, instead taking on an advocacy role in their approach to a country or region. In contrast to their dismissal of the usefulness or reliability of citizen journalists, the officials had a positive attitude regarding institutional journalists. All of these senior officials admitted to having prominent journalists from leading institutions as friends with whom they regularly communicated.

A former US congressman with relations to the intelligence and diplomatic community said that given the diminution of Western resources due to the collapse of the business model of type I (nonstate) GNNs, there was even greater reliance on those resources that are still active and healthy. He mentioned a particular Western magazine with deep worldwide access and a program that allows them to have a direct dialogue without infringing on journalistic integrity.[82]

This loss of control (and policy deniability) extends further over the developing forms of web-enabled citizen journalism, where anyone with a mobile phone can perform parts of a journalistic function—in particular where simple coverage of breaking news can create a compelling and competitive news product.[83] The rise of citizen journalism and the contemporaneous, if not consequent, loss of Western nonstate institutional GNN resources constitute a relatively new phenomenon, but some changes are immediately identifiable, such as noninstitutional GNNs' loss of access and questionable levels of credibility.[84] It is too early to measure the effects of the move to a more citizen- and popular-based network of information-gathering individuals and collectives, but noninstitutional access to elites and foreign affairs decision makers is clearly more limited, and hence opportunities for formal or informal diplomatic engagement are markedly proscribed when compared to the dominant Western and

---

82. Personal communications with former US congressman, 2013.

83. Reich 2008. The whole question of noninstitutional journalism and noninstitutionally related individuals performing journalistic functions is a broad field of study in contemporary media and communications whose importance to this work involves credibility and access. Without mass or elite credibility or access, noninstitutional actors are not considered part of the otherwise tightly knit GNN network, though their performance may prove catalytic over time (as suggested by some scholars ascribing causal outcomes during the "Arab Spring"). But Reich (2008) speaks to the more common current analysis of "citizen journalism," finding that "ordinary citizens can serve as a vital complement to mainstream journalism" (739).

84. Reich 2008, 739.

non-Western GNNs. The new organizations in foreign correspondence have thus far focused on the sensational and violent, as with Vice News, and eschewed the official and analytical reporting by institutional GNNs that serve states' diplomatic and intelligence needs.

In the case of NGO workers within the GNN framework, individuals' informal diplomatic activity often takes on a more "on-the-ground, grass-roots and local-level flavor," according to a former employee of Save the Children.[85] This engagement, according to another NGO interviewee, gives states and policymakers an otherwise unavailable localized and systemic autonomous decision-making process conducted at the local and regional level by individuals who are not formally engaged in seeking diplomatic outcomes.[86] The resulting effective outsourcing of diplomatic activity to an autonomous field worker allows for "a more nimble action" that bypasses organizational chart peculiarities, said another NGO worker, or ministerial relationships and state nepotistic realities.[87] One NGO executive who was working on archaeological access in Colonel Gaddafi's Libya described in great detail a unique deal to turn parts of the Libyan coastline into a protected natural habitat and archaeologically protected sanctuary.[88] His direct dealings with Gaddafi's son, Saif al Islam al-Gaddafi, involved direct diplomacy at a time when diplomatic representation of the Western NGO's home country was unavailable or ineffective.

Much like an official embassy's personnel rank and national status and power, GNN institutions and individuals parallel state agencies and representatives regarding the efficacy of their institutions' and individuals' abilities to perform diplomatic functions. GNNs rely on access and credibility to effectively perform informal or formal diplomatic functions. Just as it is more difficult for a chargé d'affaires from a small nation to get an appointment with the prime minister of a host nation than it would be for the ambassador (or secretary of state) of a much larger nation, it is much

---

85. Personal interview with former Save the Children worker, September 22, 2014, Palo Alto, CA.

86. Personal interview with an NGO worker, December 3, 2014, Los Angeles, CA.

87. Personal interview with NGO worker, December 3, 2014, Los Angeles, CA.

88. Personal interview with NGO executive, November 4, 2014, Washington, DC.

harder for a blogger than a staff correspondent for a major national daily newspaper (or the anchor of a major network nightly newscast). Sacrificing the earlier dominance of Western GNN news bureaus gives up power and presence as well as access.[89] This is a nontrivial point when assessing the geopolitics of GNNs, where access, credibility, elite influence, agenda setting, diplomatic functions, and intelligence gathering have been the hallmarks of Western GNNs in the twentieth century.

Access

Access is limited not only for unaffiliated non-GNN players but also for preferred GNNs, as in Africa, where only CGTN is granted access to African leadership.[90] Since this power is relative, a potential formula is clear and a question arises: When a non-Western GNN, such as Xinhua in Africa, is the predominant international operation and a Western GNN, such as the *New York Times*, is absent, does China's material power and influence rise and America's drop? And even when Western GNNs are present to perform soft and hard power functions, given their informal relations to the state, are they as capable of performing the diplomatic functions they performed successfully in the twentieth century where Western GNN resources are limited, access diminished, credibility diluted, competition expanded, power diffused, and voices cacophonous? Wekesa and Yanqiu found that in Africa, "commentators saw the entry of CCTV as replacing the then downsizing, retrenching and shrinking

---

89. Tumber and Webster 2006. In their critical analysis of the work of war correspondents, Tumber and Webster summarize the importance of sources by stating, "Access to sources is paramount for all journalists" (80).

90. Wekesa and Yanqiu 2014, 20. One of the more dramatic developments as Western GNNs decline while non-Western GNNs, primarily CGTN, strengthen, is that access opportunities shift dynamically. "Most journalistic and academic analysts take cognizance of the fact that Western broadcasters (and to some extent Al Jazeera) are often too adversarial to the extent that they are seen as foes by the leaderships of many African countries. Of course, Western journalism celebrates this as watchdog journalism; seeking to ensure that authorities are held accountable to the people. Taking advantage of the fact that Western broadcasters have boxed themselves in by placing themselves in opposition to government, CCTV has become probably the only international broadcaster on which one can find exclusive presidential interviews" (Wekesa and Yanqiu 2014, 22).

Western media such as BBC, France 24 and that, increasingly, Kenyans were consuming 'global perambulations' of Chinese media."[91]

During my research in Africa, which included a ten-day research visit by my Ugandan assistant, Kennedy Jawoko, who engaged in wide-ranging interviews and on-site visits with CCTV personnel, government officials, and varied media audiences, my results correlated closely with the findings of Wekesa and Yanqiu.[92]

National Alignment and Attitudes

Presence of GNN personnel is part of the equation that makes GNNs' diplomatic functions effective, but Western news organizations also have stylistic aspects, traditional approaches, and a confrontational style that run contrary to successful diplomacy. This is in no small part because of Western traditions of historical independence in and, perhaps more important, a traditionally adversarial relationship to governmental power among Western GNNs, especially in the United States.[93] Interviews conducted for this study indicated overwhelmingly that the adversarial stance was heightened toward non-Western foreign governments. At the same time, greater sympathy toward one's home country was also a theme in interviews conducted with all but one European war correspondent, who had a harsher, more aggressively dismissive understanding of his home government. This generally sympathetic psychological aspect of national support aligns with previous studies,[94] though some research

---

91. Wekesa and Yanqui, 2014, 11.

92. In all cases of data collected from CCTV, the interviews were done under an agreement of confidentiality (both in the United States and in Africa) because all CGTN/CCTV employees are required to sign a nondisclosure agreement with their employer. Just as importantly, CCTV employees felt a real threat of job loss or reprisal if their identities were revealed and criticism was conveyed. Tightly restricted information disclosure characterized these interviews, with palpable fear expressed by all CCTV parties except consultant Jim Laurie, who had express permission to represent and externally discuss CCTV. A more detailed review of the work that Chinese GNNs are undertaking in Africa is found in chapter 4.

93. Louw (2010, 52) cites Professor Larry Sabato's historical understanding of the shift in American journalism: "American journalists abandoned lapdog journalism in favour of an adversarial watchdog approach as a result of the Chappaquiddick accident and Watergate."

94. Garon 2012. While the issues of diaspora, exile, refugee, expatriates, and foreign workers are complex and have a large literature, the concept of national affinities is undergoing a

also shows that over an extended period while on permanent assignment or with full expatriate reporting, co-option and alignment with the new, nonnative host country is also a potential psychological effect.[95] Patriotic empathy (if not outright patriotism) is easier for GNN personnel when abroad than at home, as the majority of interviewees reflected. That sentiment varies between wartime and peacetime, as revealed by interviewees for this work and elsewhere in the literature.[96]

Furthermore, the perspective of journalists who parachute into a country to cover a particular event can be contrasted to the perspective of those who live there and operate in a bureau. Although being (semi)permanently stationed in a foreign country also has its dangers,[97] not having staff on the ground can be problematic both for newsgathering[98] and for any ancillary diplomatic performance. More than one interviewee noted the absence of Western GNNs from the deteriorating security environment in Syria, though there were GNN representatives from China and Russia.

The Chinese presence in Africa and the CGTN/CCTV broadcasting base in Kenya gave that network unique presence and access to some of the more dramatic stories of the last few years, including the Westgate shopping mall attack and the Garissa University attack. In both instances, footage shown on Western GNN news networks was often sourced from CCTV.[99]

---

redefinition with technological evolution. According to Garon (2012, 1), "In all political, economic and social spheres, the role of social media and non-mediated communication has systematically reduced the role of the state and empowered a new network dynamic that will define the coming decades of the Twenty-First Century."

95. Kirkhorn 1999.

96. Kovach 2002.

97. Living in a country for a longer period can lead to what, in diplomatic circles, is referred to as "going native"—a pejorative term to be sure. That is a key reason for cycling embassy staff out of a country. As for journalists, in a collection of studies of professional ethics, Fakazis (2003) analyzes the equivalent of the "Stockholm Syndrome." As she puts it, "Like the early pioneers of participant-observation, journalists often worry that empathy can lead a journalist to 'go native'" (49).

98. As BBC World Service's *Focus on Africa* editor S. Mayoux told Marsh in a personal interview, "If the only thing you do is parachute in, generally yes, white males in full body armor into a conflict for a week and then take them out, you're failing. You need to do that bit, but you also need to cover the bit before and the bit afterwards" (Marsh 2016, 67). Then he went on to explain that he could not afford to have a reporter in every country.

99. Though it should be noted that the *New York Times* had a still photographer, Tyler Hicks, in situ at the time of the attack. He subsequently was awarded a Pulitzer Prize for his work. Globally distributed video footage of this story, however, was dominated by CCTV.

Ultimately, who collects facts and builds local relationships is crucial to building and maintaining the access and credibility necessary to perform the journalistic function and any diplomatic bridging or movement in bilateral or multilateral ways. All the interviewees asked in this study reinforced the importance of GNN institutional presence.

Where institutional presence is lacking, Western GNNs often rely on local "stringers" or "satellite bureaus" where native employees are engaged.[100] Depending on overseas local talent, working in the blogosphere to perform the journalistic diplomatic functions discussed above for a Western domestic audience risks an important disconnect. Often, from a diplomatic as well as a journalistic perspective, essential questions are not asked or not contrasted with the foreign policies of other nations, but instead focus on the immediate, sometimes parochial, and are often much more general in approach.[101] This may be due to unconscious sympathy for the host government, or be designed to avoid undesirable consequences—where a local employee or a stringer's family lives, where his livelihood depends on good relations with the powers that be in the home country. A cautionary approach can also be motivated by desire as well as fear. One CGTN employee in Washington, DC, confided that a particular Chinese national colleague wanted to permanently extend her stay in the United States, perhaps through a green card marriage. The colleague was actively maintaining good relations with the home office but soft-pedaling some stories so as not to be offensive, as she saw it, to the host nation where she wanted to permanently reside.[102] This may be a case where a state's interest and the GNN are not aligned due to a personal desire to change patriotic allegiances. Whether this is characteristic of those working for non-Western GNNs would be conjecture only,

---

100. Sundaram 2014a. Sundaram wrote a thorough account of the life of a stringer overseas. In addition, he also wrote a summary of his experiences for the *New York Times*, concluding, "Life as a stringer, even for those eager to report from abroad, is daunting. It's dangerous, the pay is low and there is little support" (2014b, par. 21).

101. Sundaram 2014b. The lament for the loss of media presence is expressed in this *New York Times* column by Sundaram: "The Western news media are in crisis and are turning their back on the world. We hardly ever notice. Where correspondents were once assigned to a place for years or months, reporters now handle 20 countries each. Bureaus are in hub cities, far from many of the countries they cover" (2014b, par. 1).

102. Personal interview with a CGTN employee, October 16, 2013, Palo Alto, CA.

but it must be noted that this discrepancy between a GNN's potential intelligence and diplomatic capacity and the interest of the state is due to a separate personal agenda.

Occasionally, the opposite may occur: local journalists might have a dissident orientation, where a local newsgatherer has an agenda or an adversarial approach toward the society and politics of the nation in which he permanently resides. Regardless of the standing or orientation of the GNN stringer or local hire, a perspective that directly reflects a particular GNN's national interest will be missing.[103] This is one reason stringers or freelance journalists are seldom used as the main source of information for a US audience in countries with notoriously oppressive regimes.[104] According to two North American editors who confided diplomatic engagements and foreign ministry relations with their own countries, at the very least the analysis needs to be filtered so that the final product is distilled through a Western point of view that is relevant both to policy makers and to the public.[105]

GNN Functions Paralleling Diplomatic Practice and Forums

In addition to the diplomatic functions discussed above, GNNs and individual journalists can also publicly perform a diplomatic function (not to be confused with public diplomacy). In these cases, GNN personnel perform a diplomatic function publicly, at times on live television or radio, by interviewing policy makers, juxtaposing politicians, or pressing for express policy formation, response, or preference via their medium. A prominent example is former CNN talk show host Larry

---

103. On the flip side, some welcome this change for exactly this reason. Bunce (2015), for example, shows that the rise of the local journalist in Africa as opposed to the outsider Western reporter was greeted with the hope that more diverse voices might replace the homogenized "Europe-made" image of Africa. Bunce's research shows that this hope has been realized only to a limited extent due to the constraints imposed on the local stringers by the GNNs they work for. According to Bunce, the work of the local journalists is shaped by these GNNs' need to make a profit targeting their Western audiences and their Western journalistic values of objectivity and noninvolvement. For a recent review of how Western journalists actually portray Africa, see Nothias 2016.

104. Larsen 2010.

105. Personal interviews in 2013.

King's long-standing tradition of interviewing heads of state on the air.[106] King's questions (and his guests' answers) had wide-ranging diplomatic effects on state policy.[107] The discussions raised negotiating points for subsequent engagement.[108]

Another example of a journalist publicly carrying out diplomatic work is the former host of ABC's *Nightline*, Ted Koppel.[109] The program was launched shortly after the 1979 kidnapping of fifty-two American citizens at the US embassy in Tehran. *Nightline* could be called the "People's State Department." Koppel often had Middle East representatives, such as Palestinian Hanan Ashrawi and Israeli Benjamin Netanyahu, debate their respective positions.[110]

From time to time, weekend talk shows have foreign leaders as guests. One notable case was the April 2009 interview ABC's George Stephanopoulos (himself a former aide to President Bill Clinton) conducted with then–Iranian president Mahmoud Ahmadinejad. The questions were so sharply crafted that one could mistake them for a diplomatic exchange. Stephanopoulos was so experienced, well trained, and attuned to the perspectives of the State Department and the White House that he did not need either formal or informal preparation (let alone debriefing). His Iran policy inquiries on nuclear talks a few years back, for example,

---

106. Indeed, you can call this very public diplomacy.

107. In his memoir, former congressman John P. Murtha (2010) details media pressure on his approach to Somalia policy and his initial opposition to troop deployment, especially how it was formulated, articulated, and debated on *Larry King Live* in 1992.

108. *Larry King Now* is a relatively new program, currently produced and distributed by Russia's RT.

109. Despite the popular and official understanding that Ted Koppel engaged in a form of diplomacy and that his program, *Nightline*, was the venue for performing diplomatic public negotiations and staking out positions, Koppel abhors this characterization. He said in an interview on WNYC's *On the Media*, "I hate the term '*television diplomacy*' because it's an oxymoron. It doesn't exist" (October 6, 2001). Koppel vehemently rejected the notion that his journalistic institution was vulnerable to serving the state, in whatever capacity, and maintained that journalists are independent and that television programs such as his did not have a policy agenda.

110. Phil Donahue and Vladimir Posner performed a similar function in their occasional space bridge programs, allowing ordinary American and Soviet audiences to interact with one another. Neither man was part of a news network, though they worked with news broadcasting organizations. This is an example of broadcasting on the margins of journalism and, but for their celebrity, visibility, and success, a slight departure from the sort of journalistic diplomacy function I discuss here.

were highly relevant and directly put, focusing on the issue of preconditions and establishing certain diplomatically negotiable parameters for future formal diplomatic negotiations, whether direct or in a two-track framework.

Though the policy talk show format was developed by Western broadcasters and epitomized by shows like *This Week, Meet the Press,* and *Face the Nation,* as well as various programs on BBC, CNN, Deutsche Welle, France 24, and others, the format has been replicated by various non-Western news organizations—in particular Al Jazeera, RT, and CGTN. The unique aspect of these policy talk shows is that they attract senior policy makers, giving the network access to those policy makers but in a format that can at times force policy pronouncements or allow what could be called television diplomacy. On CGTN, for example, host Nathan King brings high-level government officials to a professional-looking studio and tries to influence policy by posing challenging questions. A program with former secretary of state Hillary Clinton's adviser P. J. Crowley actively reinforced the contention of the host and the Chinese government that the world has a vote in American foreign policy, in particular on the Iran nuclear deal, where China was engaged and ultimately a signatory party in the final agreement.[111] The assertive diplomatic stance was directly reflected in the publicly televised production.

New York Times columnist Thomas Friedman (who regularly met with former president Barack Obama) has great access around the world. He is one of the few with some authority to exchange messages at every level.[112] In fact, in February 2002, Friedman published a Middle East peace proposal in his column following a dinner party and direct talks with Saudi crown prince Abdullah—an "intriguing" idea that was followed up by President George W. Bush in a phone call with the Saudi crown prince.[113] Friedman enjoys high-level access not only in Washington, DC, but in

---

111. King 2015.

112. Even an otherwise very critical article makes the point that Friedman is "perhaps the single most influential newspaper columnist on the planet, reaches an audience of a few million people in a nation of 300 million" (Pareene 2013, par. 2).

113. Bebow (2002, par. 7) cited growing criticism of Friedman's diplomatic intercession: "Friedman came under fire for acting as much like a diplomat as a columnist. A *Boston Globe* editorial said it 'wasn't a textbook way to conduct international relations.'"

capitals around the world. His columns frequently suggest policy solutions, regardless of how workable the idea. He has as many detractors as he has fans, but all of his readers recognize the unique access to world leaders he and his network enjoy, and he is in great demand as a guest speaker at global conferences.[114] But for US reporters, the farther one gets from the news centers of Washington, DC, and New York City, the fewer news resources are deployed in this manner.

Some non-Western networks follow the example of the American talk show. Most notably, Al Jazeera America brought newsworthy American policy makers (and dissident voices) to its US studios along with well-known broadcasters and journalists in the studio and in the field. Al Jazeera America hired name brand talent like Chris Bury, David Shuster, Joie Chen, John Siegenthaler, Soledad O'Brien, and Ali Veshi—who had previously been with American networks like CNN, Fox, CBS, ABC, and NBC. RT does much the same. Al Jazeera America, however, had a slight disadvantage, with limited national distribution and an on-screen logo proclaiming its Arabic ownership, often making guests wary and deterring potential viewers.

By contrast, RT initially resembles any other American channel, and Larry King's presence reinforces the mainstream nature of their productions. RT has approached and at times surpassed Al Jazeera's spectacular production values. *CrossTalk with Peter Lavelle*, which uses an evolved *Nightline* format—with advanced production features, music, graphics, clips, bumpers, breaks, and energetic performance—is a hard-charging program that brings in mid- to high-level officials, think-tank analysts, journalists, academics, and policy makers of varied stripes, led by the host, to discuss and formulate positions and responses.[115]

---

114. *Rolling Stone* magazine took aim at the Friedman speechifying juggernaut, referring to his speech at "OligarchCon 2015 (i.e. the Davos World Economic Forum in Switzerland)" and offering a t-shirt to the best interpreter of Friedman's speech in the "Thomas Friedman said something awesome at Davos" contest (Taibbi 2015).

115. This self-referential programming asks questions about its own existence and role in policy: "Media wars have entered new territory: Secretary of State John Kerry, EU officials and the NATO military alliance all have singled out this television station, RT, as some kind of security threat. Since when is holding and broadcasting a different opinion or narrative a threat to global media freedom?" (introduction to the program on March 27, 2015).

Diplomacy and Intelligence Gathering

The formal diplomatic functions of international journalism include (a) a news bureau serving as a de facto embassy, (b) a correspondent serving as a de facto ambassador, and (c) reporters used to perform an intermediary role as an envoy. The success of GNN personnel in performing diplomatic functions often hinges on credibility and access. In some cases, journalists engaged in acts of intelligence gathering and outright espionage. Some of those individuals operated under official diplomatic cover. The following chapter will delve farther into the formal and informal performance of GNNs' intelligence gathering.

On the informal diplomatic side, GNN personnel and journalists perform an uninitiated diplomatic function as intermediaries and envoys. They are asked, for example, to serve as private messengers for information that will not enter the public realm. They sometimes take the initiative to suggest policy approaches during interviews or off-the-record conversations. Raising points or issues that have never been considered is a diplomatic function; it is not a feature of newsgathering or reporting. It is leading the witness and can help to shape an outcome. This collection of informal diplomatic GNN processes can further serve to inject new perspectives, shape an agenda, or influence elites within a policy-making framework.

This chapter has outlined historical and previously unexamined or unpublicized formal and informal cases of an established GNN institutional and individual practice and the wider, most inclusive professional media ecology.

As explained in the introduction, in stark contrast to the rapid, steady growth of non-Western GNN resources, there has been an equally steady and rapid decimation of the Western journalistic presence on the world stage. The decline of that cadre, while designed to improve the corporate bottom line, has unintended consequences for American and European power. In short, with the diminution of Western GNNs, the West may essentially be losing a tool of diplomacy.

While this chapter has concentrated on the formal and informal institutional and individual diplomatic functions performed by GNNs, these diplomatic engagements and debriefings often align with and at times become nearly indistinguishable from intelligence-gathering interviews or interrogations, whether conducted formally or informally as a part of an intelligence-gathering network. This parallel GNN function of intelligence gathering is the subject of the following chapter.

CHAPTER 3 | WESTERN GLOBAL NEWS NETWORKS AND STATE POWER 2
Intelligence Gathering

A normative or performative study of intelligence and security is beyond the scope of this work but has a rich literature that engages and elaborates on the value of intelligence gathering for states. In any overview of intelligence, the authoritative work and ur-text is *The Art of War* by Sun Tzu,[1] which explains the rationale for and value of intelligence gathering and outlines the methods and structure for intelligence-gathering networks.[2] Sun Tzu's work is included in *Craft of Intelligence* by Allen Dulles ([1963] 2006), the first and longest-serving civilian director of the CIA, who pays homage to Sun Tzu in his historical overview. Later, Dulles extends the early work into analysis of the contemporary justification and structural enhancements to the craft of intelligence within a post-Westphalian global nation-state system.

Contemporary literature locates intelligence gathering within security studies,[3] presenting it as both a method and an expression of

---

1. Sun Tzu 2002.

2. Any work in political science would seem remiss without reference to Thucydides and Ancient Greece, and so it is appropriate that intelligence gathering was a key aspect of classical societies' military and political statecraft strategy (Russell 1999). Russell's study recognizes at the outset Thucydides's understanding of a state's reliance on intelligence gathering as a strategic tool and survival tactic, quoting the ancient: "Without fail, a man harms his foes thus: those things that they most dread he discovers, carefully investigates, then inflicts on them" (Thucydides 6.91.6, quoted in Russell 1999, front matter).

3. L. Johnson 2007. Intelligence, despite the tendency to silo it academically within military and security field of intelligence studies, is recognized as a broad practice that is intrinsically interdisciplinary. The handbook edited by Loch K. Johnson (2007) is a collection of essays, predominantly from academics and practitioners in security studies who recognize the intersection of intelligence with other fields. Most relevant for this work and the importance of GNNs' informal intelligence gathering is the recognition of the unique value of "open source intelligence" (OSINT) (Steele 2007).

material power within the structures of defense and diplomatic functions.[4]

This chapter focuses on the roles GNNs have played in intelligence gathering writ large, with a focus on their formal and informal functions. The reach, credibility, and power of Western GNNs were largely unrivaled throughout the twentieth century.[5]

Given this Western dominance, much of the structural analysis of GNNs in this chapter is based on intelligence gathering performed by Western organizations and individuals. The following chapter on non-Western type III GNNs relies on a behavioral extension of this Western model and incorporates the new GNN institutions of the twenty-first century, while identifying unique non-Western characteristics. Newer non-Western GNNs have been subject to less scrutiny and little structural or behavioral transparency, with the exception of a few cases that will be elaborated in the following chapter.

The research for this chapter focuses on the role of global media institutions, foreign correspondents, international nongovernmental organizations (INGOs), and other GNN institutions in intelligence gathering while reviewing pre-GNNs' and GNNs' historical intelligence functions. The institutions and individuals in those institutions that I examine are primarily within the traditional news generation field and mostly comprise journalistic and media organizations.

Just as diplomacy is an integral part of Western GNNs' formal and informal roles, intelligence gathering is also central to their function. As posited in this work, the functions of diplomacy and intelligence gathering stray from the realm of soft power or public diplomatic expressions of power into the realm of hard power functions that supplement or

---

4. See, for example, Clinton 2010. Hillary Rodham Clinton embraced the concept of smart power during her tenure as US secretary of state and promoted, as she did in this piece, the three-legged stool of smart power as including strong defense, diplomacy, and development. In approaching the material nature of intelligence gathering, the role of development is generally not explored in the academic literature other than as an epiphenomenal attribute associated with INGOs that receive state underwriting or military backing.

5. Nelson 1997. Nelson shows that the Western radio broadcasts during the Cold War were globally unrivaled and that, despite the presence of countering non-Western media, they were predominant in terms of audience, credibility, and ultimately, impact. The relevance of this domination was, quite simply, that the West had more boots on the ground, more presence, and greater intelligence-gathering capacities overall by overwhelmingly preponderant margins.

complement the multiple hard power tools found in a toolbox dominated by military and other material capacities.

GNNs participate in intelligence gathering, at times on a directly contractual basis or based on a structural exigency. My research indicates that, for Western news institutions, the role is most often performed as a by-product of their status, structure, and access as journalists and media organizations, which allow them to engage in activities that are outside of their generally accepted functions of reporting, writing, and broadcasting.

In the course of their professional performance, GNNs interact directly with the state and, in certain circumstances, operate as active, independent agents. Further, this performance is at times an institutional extension of state structures, state power, and state representatives. GNNs often participate — actively or passively, formally and informally — in the iterative, analytical, and communicative intelligence-gathering processes in states and for policy makers and intelligence analysts. State foreign policy outcomes are often a direct result of media organization and journalistic discovery and analysis, with significant historically recognized outcomes that would not likely have been achieved had media professionals not acted outside their dominant roles as observers and public analysts, as exemplified by the Cuban missile crisis negotiations or the Haiti case detailed in appendix 1.

While the popular perception of intelligence gathering involves operatives working undercover for a sovereign nation's defense or for state analytical forces, far more intelligence gathering is done in a more subtle, less formal, disengaged, and publicly justifiable manner, in which type I GNNs without a direct relationship to the state (unlike either type II [hybrid] or type III [state-run] GNNs, which populate the non-Western GNN media ecology) service the state's intelligence needs, often without suspecting that they do so. The work products, publications, and broadcasts of this work—popularly referred to as "the news," "reports," "studies," "white papers," and so on—are known in intelligence circles as open-source intelligence (OSINT).

These two types of GNN intelligence gathering were earlier characterized as either witting or unwitting, as Wilford puts it in his important

	Informal	Formal
Witting	Operational reporting (e.g., military field reports)	Task-oriented, directed, or contracted reporting (IMV)
Unwitting	Institutional briefs, analytical, intelligence organization uses of open-source intelligence (PDB, INR, CIA, FBI, DIA)	Ostensible task-oriented, directed, or contracted reporting; use of ancillary data or information

Table 4. Types of GNN intelligence gathering

book, *The Mighty Wurlitzer: How the CIA Played America* (2009). Wilford details how the Central Intelligence Agency's political warfare chief was able to manipulate journalists (and others) in the course of his work by playing any propaganda tune he desired during the Cold War. Put differently, the spymaster played people and got them to do his bidding.

I differentiate further, not only parsing the concepts of witting and unwitting but also extending the earlier framework to incorporate formal and informal intelligence gathering. Further, intelligence gathering can be done informally yet wittingly, as well as formally and unwittingly. Table 4 depicts the various combinations and cases represented in my data collection.

In the first cell of Table 4, informal intelligence gathering is done in the normal course of reporting, but the reporter is cognizant (witting) that the work has intelligence value—as, for example, when a field report designates the coordinates of a hostile missile strike, data that can be used for ballistic forensics or targeting and calibrating. In the second cell, formal reporting is done wittingly—as in the Defense Department's underwritten International Media Ventures (IMV) organization—to gather and report detailed operational intelligence on individuals, roles, locations, and targeting data. The third cell represents informal collection of data whose open-source reporting is then used by individuals and organizations in the course of their institutional practice, though the analytical work product is invisible to the originator, who often maintains either a willing ignorance or active lack of concern about the use of the open-source data used in the presidential daily brief (PDB) or by intelligence and law enforcement agencies. Finally, a contracted reporter may believe that his work is targeted, but the ancillary data delivered makes the individual ignorant of the true purpose of the reporting (often the case when reporters are dispatched to militarily significant zones to take photographs and report with nonmilitary objectives).

I refer to both formal and informal intelligence gathering as an extension of Wilford's early characterization of intelligence-gathering participants as either witting or unwitting. In the course of the research, there was an early tendency for research participants to conflate informal intelligence gathering with unwitting and formal with witting. I distinguish between the two, as GNN institutions—and individuals working within those institutions—can be formally engaged in intelligence gathering yet unwitting as to the intelligence goals or value of the intelligence gathered. Equally, one can be informally engaged in intelligence gathering and be witting as to its value.

The GNN intelligence-gathering matrix sets informal and formal relationships to the state against the witting and unwitting understanding of the producer of intelligence—whether or not the work product is intended or contracted for exclusive or open-source consumption. In the first cell, where informal relations exploit wittingly employed institutions and individuals, the work is often the product of war correspondents and other field reporters and researchers who are delivering real-time or near real-time data (as in a CNN report on Scud missile interceptions). These reports are not intended for intelligence use and were once either ignorantly or innocently broadcast for their sensational appeal and general human interest in matters of war and peace, but they are currently understood ultimately to have ballistic data embedded in them and, in real time, allow for targeting calibration and psychological operations response. Some states either block or channel this data and, it is suspected, can sometimes manipulate or counter it, but the central point is that state noncontracted GNN institutions and individuals are performing an informal intelligence function—and are conscious of the consequences of such performance.

Cell 2 juxtaposes a formal state relationship with a witting understanding of the use of reports. This is a more straightforward and often transactional relationship that has, but for its opaqueness, the capacity for metrics and milestones to measure the quality and quantity of outputs, performance, deliverables, and outcomes. It is the hardest cell to populate with examples because of the clandestine nature of the activity. International Media Ventures (IMV) is a group that worked in the Iraqi and Afghan battlefields to deliver operationally actionable information directly to the Department of Defense via an unaffiliated nongovernmental intermediary. As will be apparent in another matrix graph, the witting aspects of the operations were limited to IMV's administration, while its frontline reporters and correspondents were unaware of the military value of their on-the-ground reporting. Their unwitting status was supported, maintained, and reinforced by IMV's ability to place the work product into mass media products, giving both the data collection and the collector the necessary cover to claim an open-source character for the work product.[6]

The third cell of Table 4, unwitting informal activities, includes the most widely used and popularly perceived understanding of open-source intelligence gathering by GNNs. These are news reports and broadcasts, NGO briefing papers, think-tank white papers, as well as academic research and publications, which, on a daily basis, depending on the topics, region, and focus of policy makers, make up the bulk or, at the very least, part of the collected and distributed data that is processed, weighed, and acted upon as an integral part of the analytical process and operational decision making. This product is the most familiar to the general populace: the reporting delivered in newspapers, on television and radio, or on major online news sites. It is also work that was often found, at least until the Trump administration, in the daily presidential daily brief (PDB), clipped and used by intelligence, security, military, and

---

6. Horton 2010; also Filkins and Mazzetti 2010.

policing forces, and relied upon by the diplomatic corps as well as policy-making agencies. While the purveyors of this work product may be aware that there are specialty uses for their data (*Wall Street Journal* reporters recognize the value of their market intelligence and political risk analysis to hedge fund managers, for example), foreign correspondents believe that presenting their findings in reports to a wide, unrestricted audience dilutes the strategic value of the open-source data. "We feed the public; we've got a mass audience. What spooks do is feed a very small, very secretive, very exclusive group of people—that's not us," said one former American foreign correspondent who reported on the end of the Cold War from Moscow and was regularly accused of spying by both officials and suspicious members of society, who noted he was "always asking too many tough questions. But, basically, I was just reporting. It didn't help that I regularly ate lunch at the [U.S.] embassy."[7] Like other GNN reporters, this correspondent said he "knew" his work was being "sifted" by American officials, but he always knew his work was not state directed, that it was unwitting.

That understanding of his work as unwitting—whether truly felt or willfully believed—was prevalent among GNN personnel, whether reporters, INGO workers, or the few academics who were interviewed for this work. Even when asked how reports were used, this foreign correspondent described his work in the field as being free of intelligence value. He reported on the early stages of the war in Yugoslavia in 1991, and he required GNN institutional resources to cover the war well and to get unique access to President Franjo Tudjman. His reports were followed up with a call from a political officer at the American embassy, and he easily shared exclusive insights and contacts with the official. When confronted with this argument, he responded, "We're just committing journalism, that's all."[8]

In our last case, the unwitting nature of a formal relationship involves subterfuge, opacity, and misleading management of the data-collecting resource, so that the work product contracted by the state is not the main

---

7. Personal communication, 2014.
8. Personal communication, January 2014, Palo Alto, CA.

data in which the contracting party is interested but rather ancillary data collected as a by-product or accident of the initial assignment. Photographers often fill this role by being assigned specific geographic, militarily strategic, urban, or unexplored rural areas in which to take pictures, where the background, street scene, commerce, movement, or gender makeup is of more strategic value than the ostensible subject of the images. Photographs of the seventieth anniversary of the Pyongyang regime yielded many images of military parades and precision drills, but those photographs are still being reviewed for useful data concerning military hardware, leadership personnel and their proximity to Kim Jong-un, and popular reactions to and performance of ideological presentations, all described in a *Stratfor* article titled "China Flaunts Its Missile Arsenal."[9] While most of the useful intelligence-oriented North Korean imagery was provided by Pyongyang's state media, this example illustrates how visual and descriptive information can have dual use for the public and state intelligence agencies. All GNNs use their resources to obtain imagery of otherwise unobservable locales, whether difficult-to-reach areas or conflict zones. Safe passage and security at such locales have traditionally been more assured to GNN personnel, as attested by Terry Phillips: "My cameraman and I would never have gone to cover the war in Mogadishu if CBS didn't send me."[10] In certain conflict zones, such as the Iraq War, in which embedded GNN personnel were provided safety and security during the conflict, the formality of the relationship was clear between an unwitting participant and the state, represented by the military in this case, as bonds built between units and reporters. While photographers are the most obvious unwitting players involved in a formal relationship, the same holds true for others engaged in reportage, where observations of ancillary information and data collection are the focus rather than the ostensible reason for the reporting trip.

---

9. Intelligence analysts wrote, "Military watchers around the world eagerly anticipated China's Sept. 3 military parade to commemorate the 70th anniversary of the surrender of Japan and the end of World War II . . . keeping an especially attentive eye out for the potential display of new weaponry and equipment. China showed off a large number of cruise and ballistic missiles during the parade, highlighting the scale of its expanded missile arsenal" (Stratfor 2015, par. 1).

10. Personal communication, 2015.

In addition to looking at the role of GNNs as such in intelligence gathering, the GNNs themselves can be broken down into hierarchies. GNN type I–III institutions can be divided into a class of owners and administrators ("Administrative & Managerial"); as opposed to the individuals working in GNN type I–III institutions but not part of management ("Reportorial"). Both administrative and reportorial staff can perform at an informal or formal level.

As explained in the case of IMV, there are various levels of understanding regarding the uses of data collection and reporting: a reporter or operative may be unaware of the administrative or management layer's strategic use and value of a work product, or that use and value may be opaque to the producer, whether for operational security reasons or as a matter of protocol. In this case, it can be said that the employees at the reportorial level are unwitting informal participants in intelligence gathering, while those at the managerial level are wittingly and formally engaged in it.

Journalists interviewed for this work admitted that they rarely speak privately about their role in intelligence gathering and never publicly— and most certainly not while actively engaged in such activities. That is, in part, because performing this function has legal ramifications, requires secrecy and operational security, and could have political, diplomatic, military, judicial, and other severe consequences not only for individuals but also for institutions and states. GNN personnel engaged in this function suffer from a societal and professional stigma that is attached to it,[11] with ethical debates and scathing critique heaped upon those who actively profess or are discovered to engage in espionage using a journalistic cover or in intelligence gathering that is consciously sympathetic to any side in a narrative battle or in wartime.

In rare instances—usually after years of surreptitious work, sometimes revealed only in posthumously released documents—a journalist

---

11. Shafer 2010. Shafer touches on the parallels between spying and reporting, as well as the ethical dilemmas involved in the work (par. 12). "Both journalists and spies recruit sources, collect and annotate information, verify it, interpret it, write it up in reports, and disseminate it. There the similarity ends. Journalists are supposed to stay on this side of the law, this side of libel and invasion of privacy, and this side of turpitude."

tells his or her story and, in the course of the confessional, may name names. On the formal side, there are numerous documented cases, some brought forth as a result of congressional inquiry in the United States,[12] others as a matter of judicial inquiry or arrest, or by defectors and double agents who count on publicity for personal security.[13]

On the informal side, the best known of these cases is a contemporary German journalist who wrote the book *Gekaufte Journalisten*.[14] The book names Western individuals and GNN institutions actively engaged with the state and its multilevel functions, including—but not limited to—its intelligence-gathering apparatus across secretariats and departments.

Intelligence: A Material Capacity

States need intelligence. History shows the long tradition of intelligence and its use of surreptitious and undercover work,[15] including frequent exploitation of those operating or reporting under the guise of a false or hidden secondary activity,[16] the equivalent of modern day nonofficial

---

12. See, for example, Bernstein 1977. Much of the previously confidential information gathered by this well-known Watergate correspondent came as a follow-up report after testimony and documentation presented to the so-called Church Committee in the US Senate, chaired by Sen. Frank Church (D-ID) in 1975. This 25,000-word cover story for *Rolling Stone* remains one of the greatest exposés of the relationship between American journalistic institutions, reporters, editors, and the CIA, as detailed in the sections of this chapter devoted to formal intelligence gathering.

13. Edward Snowden's case (see Greenwald, MacAskill, and Poitras 2013) has been broadly publicized. Snowden continues to conduct high-visibility interviews (for example, on BBC) and participate in free-speech conferences via Skype, and a documentary about him, *Citizen Four*, has won an Oscar. The case of Edward Snowden is complex and, while revealing GNN complicity in espionage, falls slightly outside the realm of journalist spy. The strategy Snowden employs, however, for maintaining personal security and survival is keeping himself in the public eye, a standard approach for vilified individuals and potential state security threats. "Yes, I could be rendered by the CIA. I could have people come after me. Or any of the third-party partners. They work closely with a number of other nations. Or they could pay off the Triads. Any of their agents or assets," he said (*Guardian*, June 11, 2013, par. 21).

14. Ulfkotte 2014. Udo Ulfkotte, who worked at the *Frankfurter Allgemeine Zeitung* for seventeen years, describes in great detail the methods, approaches, and relationships that evolved during that time and created an alignment between journalists and Western state institutions and goals.

15. Sun Tzu 2002.

16. Shulsky and Schmitt 2002.

cover agents (NOCs).[17] In the invasion of ancient Greece by the Persians, the Persian king Xerxes regularly used spies to discover his adversaries' strengths and weaknesses, often forcing turncoat natives to save themselves and their families by performing this function.[18]

During the Cold War, both East and West actively engaged in this work, as detailed in Allen Dulles's definitive work (2006) on practice and tradecraft.

Foreign intelligence gathering—unlike domestic spying on citizens or subjects—while open to normative analysis and judgment, is a global practice, a means as much of preventing war as of measuring adversaries' intentions and capacities to ward off assault and occupation. In fact, it is a time-honored, if highly misunderstood and criticized, profession with a deep historical record to confirm both its successful[19] and unsuccessful[20] performance in war and peace.[21] It enables action as much as inaction; where credible foreign intelligence exists, not all of this intelligence is actionable.[22]

If there is a code of honor, respect, and reward in the intelligence community for its assets and systems, this is not the case for spying and formal intelligence gathering by those outside of the spy profession and, in particular, those who gather intelligence for a wider public rather than a smaller subset of state analysts and policy makers. In fact, it is considered one of the most pernicious and reckless acts for a journalist, undermining the credibility, access, and reliability of the profession,[23] and further,

---

17. V. Wilson 2012. Valerie Plame Wilson is one of the highest-profile nonofficial cover (NOC) agents to be revealed publicly. Her account of her outing by officials in the George W. Bush administration describes in detail her path to becoming a NOC. During conversation with the author on February 5, 2015, Ms. Plame was cautious about answering sensitive questions that could reveal or intimate confidential information but confirmed details previously revealed publicly.

18. Hale 2009.

19. Elhassani 2011.

20. Taylor 2013.

21. Hinsley and Simkins 1990.

22. This was dramatized in the film *The Imitation Game* (2014), based on the story of Alan Turing. The plot involves breaking an enemy's code, gaining knowledge of troop movements and battle plans, but choosing not to take lifesaving preventive actions to avoid revealing knowledge of the enemy's capacities.

23. Klein 2014.

putting those performing their public function in grave danger of being accused of spying.[24] In 2015, the *Washington Post* Tehran correspondent Jason Rezaian was convicted of espionage and sentenced to a prison term in Iran but released in January 2016. Unsurprisingly, Rezaian's newspaper emphatically denounced such allegations, calling the charges "absurd and despicable."[25]

While the case against Jason Rezaian is exaggerated and instructive, there is a tradition of personnel from state and hybrid GNNs being in the direct employ of the intelligence agencies of foreign sovereigns.[26] The United States has publicly stated that it no longer engages in this type of direct journalistic engagement after years of directly funding specific GNNs, most notably Radio Free Europe/Radio Liberty.[27] The CIA has said it no longer uses journalists as operatives, and this assertion is reinforced by security and intelligence scholar Robert Jervis from Columbia University.[28] Within the United States, the FBI occasionally used journalists as a front for investigations, though the practice has been officially restricted since 1992.[29]

Unclassified documents from the CIA years of RFE/RL yield a trove of operational data on the hand-in-glove relationship between

---

24. This was explored in more detail in M. Kounalakis (2014a).

25. Baron 2015, par. 3.

26. Dover and Goodman's *Spinning Intelligence* (2009) is perhaps the most comprehensive overview of the formal and informal relationships between journalism and intelligence agencies. This anthology touches on the historical relationships between the two enterprises and the contemporary need for news reports to complement and complete intelligence analyses, with the front matter of the book describing "the CIA's reliance on open sources for intelligence purposes."

27. In this self-reported history, Radio Free Europe and Radio Liberty candidly acknowledge their previously clandestine relations: "Initially, both RFE and RL were funded principally by the U.S. Congress through the Central Intelligence Agency (CIA)" ("History," *RadioFreeEurope/RadioLiberty Pressroom*, accessed February 18, 2018, https://pressroom.rferl.org/p/6092.html).

28. Ioffe 2015. Jervis is quoted in this magazine article as arguing that journalists are not actively engaged by the CIA, saying, "For us, especially after the reforms in the wake of Watergate that reined in the C.I.A., there was a lot of pushback from journalists that this was putting them in danger, so we backed off" (par. 10).

29. Upano 2003. The restrictions are stringent, but they allow exceptions, as highlighted in this article from Reporters Committee for Freedom of the Press: "The 1997 Intelligence Authorization Act was signed into law by President Bill Clinton, allowing the ban on the use of journalists to be waived with notification to Congress and presidential approval" (par. 19).

this Western type III state-sponsored, intelligence-gathering, pre-GNN broadcast organization and the American intelligence community. The US Office of Policy Coordination worked through the American Committee for Liberation (AMCOMLIB) during these years to develop a plan for propagating information to the Soviet Union and the captive states of Eastern Europe, and to participate in intelligence gathering and analysis. AMCOMLIB was established because, as Frank Wisner, the former southeastern European head of the Office of Strategic Services (OSS) and, later, the head of the Directorate of Plans at the CIA in the 1950s, wrote in a now-declassified CIA memorandum from August 21, 1951, there was a need for the "establishment of a cover committee."[30] Later, State Department documents reveal an analysis by those within AMCOMLIB on the issue of restraints on pre-GNN RFE/RL when West Germany regained its sovereignty.[31] Declassified documents from this era allow for an understanding of the broad-based underwriting, management, mission, and legacy of the current Western type III (state-sponsored) GNN institutions and their alignment with state policy and goals as well as their service in enhancing state power via their organized and underwritten policies and practice.

Cloak and Gown

It is not just journalistic institutions and individuals who make up GNNs, but also the larger NGO world,[32] which continues to increase its engagement, both formal and informal, in reporting, writing, editing, and

---

30. "Office of Policy Coordination History of American Committee for Liberation," August 21, 1951, History and Public Policy Program Digital Archive, Obtained and contributed to CWIHP by A. Ross Johnson. Cited Ch1 n60 in his book *Radio Free Europe and Radio Liberty*, CIA mandatory declassification review document number C01441005, accessed May 5, 2016, http://digitalarchive.wilsoncenter.org/document/114354, par. 3.

31. "State Department Views of Radio Liberty Broadcasting," February 11, 1953, History and Public Policy Program Digital Archive, Obtained and contributed to CWIHP by A. Ross Johnson. Cited in his book *Radio Free Europe and Radio Liberty*. CIA mandatory declassification review document number C01441016, accessed May 5, 2016, http://digitalarchive.wilsoncenter.org/document/114472.

32. Wright 2015.

other information-gathering and dissemination processes, in particular as the capacity of traditional Western news organizations diminishes.[33] In a Nieman Lab study at Harvard University, "NGOs as Newsmakers," the authors note that "civil society actors such as NGOs and advocacy networks are becoming increasingly significant players as the traditional news media model is threatened by shrinking audiences, the availability of free content online, and the declining fortunes of mainstream media."[34]

As a result of the increased capacity for news, data, and information gathering and dissemination in the academic world, researchers in foreign countries increasingly participate in the broader GNN constellation of newsgathering and dissemination. Their work has often engaged historically—if not dominantly, then distinctly and identifiably—in "cloak and gown" activity,[35] where archaeological, sociological, anthropological, economic, political, and nonhumanitarian overseas work has regularly been done with direct funding from or a reporting relationship to foreign intelligence-gathering institutions.[36]

A wide variety of defense and intelligence organizations continue to engage directly with scholars,[37] including the US Department of Defense's Minerva Initiative.[38] The importance of academics to Western GNNs is

---

33. DeMars 2001; Spyksma 2017. Spyksma shows that NGOs can "fill a global news gap" by reporting from areas that are not covered. The relationship between intelligence agencies and NGOs is intensely debated and controversial, but whatever the intensity or proximity, according to DeMars, "most relevant academic and policy literature fails to address the real issues in this hazardous relationship" (193). My experience with various NGOs operating overseas have informed this work and their inclusion within a comprehensive GNN framework.

34. M. Price, Morgan, and Klinkforth 2009, par. 2.

35. The phrase *cloak and gown* is a play on the popular spying phrase *cloak and dagger*, in this case specific to the use of GNN institutional academics and researchers in the practice of intelligence. The phrase was popularized by the book *Cloak and Gown: Scholars in the Secret War 1939–1961* (Winks 1996). A *New York Times* review of the book noted the conflict between the formal and informal relationships of intelligence gathering and analysis by scholars and the inherent problems therein: "The line between asking anthropologists about the cultures of the Pacific theater and using them as covers might be blurred, but it was a dangerous one that many American (and some other) universities crossed" (Hodgson 1987, par. 9).

36. D. Price 2000; LeVine 2012.

37. Moos, Fardon, and Gusterson 2005.

38. This program for scholars describes its mission as follows: "The Minerva Research Initiative is a Department of Defense (DoD)–sponsored, university-based social science research initiative launched by the Secretary of Defense in 2008 focusing on areas of strategic importance

increasing as traditional newsgathering resources diminish. While Western GNN type I journalism institutions have been usually understood to maintain some distance from state structures and capacities, NGOs and academics with direct funding ties to the state are open to greater scrutiny for their relationship to the state and their potential for enhancing its power. The Social Science Research Council recognizes the Minerva Project's potentially controversial funding from the US military: "The initiative indicates a renewal of interest in social science findings after a prolonged period of neglect, but it also prompts concerns about the appropriate relationship between university-based research programs and the state, especially when research might become a tool of not only governance but also military violence."[39]

Further, the legal protection embodied in the reporter's privilege now recognizes institutional academics for their GNN role as newsgatherers, with legal precedent for their work and protections for their activities.[40] As noted throughout this work, all GNNs, both Western and non-Western, now make up a more complex institutional news, information, and analysis ecology that includes and harnesses the work of other institutional researchers and analysts. Academics are naturally a part of this and have at times become important in feeding both the informal and formal GNN intelligence system. As noted in "The Reconstruction of American Journalism," the GNN ecology is opening itself more to nontraditional newsgathering institutions: "The Internet has greatly increased access to large quantities of 'public information' and news produced by government and

---

to U.S. national security policy" ("Mission and Vision," *Minerva Research Initiative*, accessed February 18, 2018, http://minerva.defense.gov/Minerva).

39. "The Minerva Controversy," *Social Science Research Council*, accessed February 18, 2018, http://essays.ssrc.org/minerva/.

40. According to the Reporters Committee for Freedom of the Press (2011, par. 1), "The reporter's privilege has been extended to include research analysts and academics. See, e.g., Cusumano v. Microsoft Corp., 162 F.3d 708 (1st Cir. 1998) (extending the privilege to the prepublication manuscripts of a distinguished academic); Summit Tech., Inc. v. Healthcare Capital Group, Inc., 141 F.R.D. 381 (D. Mass. 1992) (holding that the reporter's privilege applied to the report of an independent researcher and analyst hired by an institutional investor); U.S. v. Doe (In the matter of Falk), 332 F. Supp. 938 (D. Mass 1971) (finding that professors who publish books and articles are protected by the reporter's privilege)."

a growing number of data-gathering, data-analyzing, research, academic, and special interest activist organizations."[41]

Citizen Journalism

As seen earlier in this work, Western institutional GNNs are simultaneously losing their capacities and resources while non-Western institutional GNNs fill the void. Part of the contemporary debate in the news-gathering profession revolves around the rise of technology, increased transparency, low barriers to entry for journalistic enterprises, and instantaneous access to wide distribution and audience potential. The rise of the citizen journalists[42] is heralded by many as a possible substitute for the previously top-heavy institutional GNNs, with nimble movement, speed, and freedom from institutional constraints heralded as positive change.[43]

If this is the case, then why are contemporary human GNN capacities so important? What is it they do or did that cannot be replaced by citizen journalism or the new aggregating systems and big data crunching automations, such as the GDELT project?[44] In particular, there is a difference between citizen journalism's performance and that of institutional GNNs when it comes to geopolitical and geostrategic issues. As the interviews for this work as well as previous research found—up until the Trump

---

41. Downie and Schudson 2009, par. 112.

42. Citizen journalism or participatory journalism has been studied in a wide variety of settings, from Sweden (Holt and Karlsson 2015) to Syria (Al-Ghazzi 2014), from the United States (Fico et al. 2013) to Egypt (El-Nawawy and Khamis 2016), and from a wide variety of perspectives. For overviews, see the volumes edited by Allan and Thorsen (2009); Thorsen and Allan (2014); and the special issue of *Journalism Practice* edited by Wall (2017, nos. 2–3). Recent studies focus on citizen journalism and social media.

43. Reich 2008. This systemic study of citizen journalism "suggests that ordinary citizens can serve as a vital complement to mainstream journalism, however not as its substitute" (739).

44. GDELT holds great promise at contextualizing the news media written data worldwide, creating the possibility of grander connections between seemingly disparate events and how they are described. "Much of the true insight captured in the world's news media lies not in what it says, but the context of how it says it. The GDELT Global Knowledge Graph compiles a list of every person, organization, company, location, and over 230 themes and emotions from every news report, using some of the most sophisticated named entity and geocoding algorithms in existence, designed specifically for the noisy and ungrammatical world that is the world's news media" (GDELT Project, GDELT Global Knowledge Graph).

administration and the unconventional media diet of President Trump—decision makers limit their information intake to traditional media and established GNNs with their legacy means of information navigation (in newspapers, the importance of the front page; in broadcast, the urgency of the lead story) and predigested data and analysis via a layered and filtering editorial process. In this policy-making environment, the GNN takes primacy and maintains credibility among the elite.[45] The promise of institutional GNN use of new technologies and tools is great, but many non-GNN players confuse the tools with the content and output with analysis. The multiplicity of sources and blogs, tweets and posts, creates a noise problem that institutional GNNs cut through. "This only amplifies the noise. Thus, it's hardly surprising that we are prone to see trends and developments that only exist in the minds of our local interlocutors. Learning from foreign blogs is a long and tedious process; it is largely useless in times of a crisis—who has time to read and translate blog posts when people are dying in the streets?"[46]

Arising news institutions are entering the realm of foreign corresponding, but their products are focused more on the ephemeral and the sensational than the analytical and strategic reporting typical of institutional GNNs. As one of the fastest-growing news organizations online today, *Vice* has shown less interest in reporting on geopolitical issues and more of an affinity for the sensational. The description of the product on Google Play states, "The online den for nefarious activities, investigative journalism, and enlightening documentaries. *Vice* is a global media channel focusing on investigative journalism and enlightening videos about everything from world news, travel, art, drugs, politics, sports, fashion, sex, and super cute animals."[47] World news makes the cut but usually only when it also includes some or all of the other topics listed. The audience skews young. As Al Brown, the head of content at *Vice News* in London, put it, "It's made by young people for young people. If our journalists are

---

45. "Prior studies show that opinion leaders depend on mass media, particularly 'elite media' as well as 'outside sources'" (Meraz 2007, 115).

46. Morozov 2009, 12.

47. Description on Google Play, https://play.google.com/store/newsstand/news/VICE ?id=CAowis8w&hl=en.

scared, that makes it into the film. What our journalists are feeling is a huge part of our vernacular."[48]

Vice is still a young institution and it is already showing ambitions of becoming part of the GNN constellation as it gains funding,[49] reach, and seriousness of purpose and product. Particularly notable are the documentaries it has developed on Libya, as well as Syria and ISIS.

GNNs service a spectrum of audiences, but their domestic and international foreign affairs policy formation and intelligence clientele are predominantly within an elite policy-making and policy-influencing circle. As such, GNNs' intelligence gathering has not only great potential to influence elites, but an equally high degree of exclusive, high-level access. GNNs' systemic approach to data collection is credible and provides seasoned and informed analysis that goes through an established course of refining, prioritization, vetting of sources, follow-up on accuracy, confirmatory (and discomfirmatory) critical processes, pattern recognition, lateral linkage, scenario probability, editing, serendipity, and gut instincts—as well as prepublication alerting and second-sourcing prior to publication and distribution. This is a highly refined, multigenerational system that is proven, if not flawless.[50]

Access and Credibility

GNNs have unique institutional characteristics that give them privileged access to popular sources, elites, institutions, governing bodies, industrial and communal leaders, regions, sites, and other nonpublic venues where institutionally unaffiliated researchers and journalists are not welcome. Journalism scholars ask whether blogger or citizen journalist access to

---

48. Martinson 2015, par. 23

49. At the end of 2015, Walt Disney Company invested $400 million in Vice Media, bringing the current valuation of Vice to $4 billion (Shaw and Palmeri 2015). In 2016, Vice Media also launched the cable channel Viceland in the United States, Canada, Britain, and Australia. Since 2016, Vice News also has a nightly news program in the United States on cable channel HBO titled *Vice News Tonight*.

50. In the course of conversation with Valerie Plame Wilson, she made clear that one of the reporting strengths of institutional GNNs prior to and during the Iraq War was the accurate and fair work done by the McClatchy news organization. (I am currently contracted as a foreign affairs columnist for McClatchy).

decision-making elites is available. The answer is usually in the negative: "Bloggers . . . are still the relative upstarts. There is still an outsider quality to their content and their approach to politics."[51] Unaffiliated or independent reporters or news sites are often excluded from high-level or elite access. One unaffiliated blogger confided that he had tried and failed for years to get an interview with Germany's prime minister, Angela Merkel, and felt he "was discriminated against because I don't wear a tie."[52]

Without a history of institutional relations or a body of work with longevity and elite demographic appeal or respect, the newer, less institutional, otherwise unaffiliated reporter may have significant ability to move freely through daily life in a foreign venue with occasional exclusive or opportunistic reporting moments but seldom if ever gains access to the highest levels of society or government. As interviews with elite GNN institution staff and unaffiliated bloggers show, the level of access afforded to noninstitutional journalists is increasing, but primarily for those unaffiliated individuals who have regularly received the imprimatur of acceptance by the elite institutional media, that is, those who have received institutional awards for their reporting, are regularly quoted or sourced in conventional and established press reports, or who also work for established and branded news institutions.[53] Regardless, even with institutional validation, all the interviewees in this book reported a gross disparity between access afforded institutional representatives and nonaffiliated ones.

Institutional GNNs have comparatively unfettered access to a political and societal elite. For example, in the United States, established Sunday talk shows (e.g., *Meet the Press* and *Face the Nation*) have their pick of the political litter, with opposition leaders, legislative lobbyists, and administration officials clambering for exposure and access. The same is true of

---

51. R. Davis 2012, 54.

52. Personal communication, 2014.

53. An example of one former blogger whose website is now seen as an institutional player is a former employee at the *Washington Monthly*, Joshua Michael Marshall, who publishes the highly trafficked and recognized *Talking Points Memo* (TPM). Marshall won a Polk Award for his TPM work, but it should be noted that his rise in credibility and access was concurrent with regular recognized work within the institutional GNN framework. (I served as the president and publisher of the *Washington Monthly* during Marshall's contracted employment.)

leading GNN print institutions, with even greater access due to the lower threshold for participation (no need for travel or early Sunday morning prep time prior to performance). A call from the *New York Times*, for example, is nearly always returned as quickly as possible, unless the subject is actively avoiding the press, knowing that the call will translate into a highly visible, widely distributed quote or, if the call goes unreturned, a line indicating the subject was unavailable for comment. This is not the case for noninstitutional journalistic outlets and individuals.[54] They are rarely, if ever, granted press passes or access to the highest levels and offices in government.

For most of the twentieth century, Western GNNs had access worldwide because their resource base and distribution networks were unrivaled in size and breadth. As such, the access to a global elite was unparalleled and often invited, matched only by domestic newsgathering organizations, often state-run. This brought them elevated status, professional standards, constitutional protections, institutional training, and editorial structures reinforcing fairness and accuracy, as well as an aura of objectivity,[55] allowing them to engage directly in agenda setting and influence of elites.

GNN Institutional: Formal Intelligence Gathering

The most straightforward definitional relationships between GNNs and the intelligence-gathering and analysis community are contractually established, financially dependent, and publicly disclosed. While the public disclosure may have been forced or revealed after declassification of secret government documents, significant empirical evidence over long periods of time has established the interconnectedness of GNNs and the intelligence community of Western (and, as discussed in following chapters, non-Western) GNNs, with a more public record for those

---

54. Reich (2008, 739) "develops a version of the 'news access' theory, which sees citizen journalists as hindered by their inferior access to news sources, unlike mainstream journalism, where the problem is seen as the superior access."

55. W. Bennett 1996.

in liberal democracies as a result of publicly responsive and transparent states.

As pointed out previously, the CIA directly funded, directed, and promoted[56] the work of Radio Free Europe and Radio Liberty. The main work of Radio Free Europe (RFE) was to disseminate news into countries where information sovereignty prevented a domestic state-run news organization from presenting views or news that created a dissonant understanding of ruling regimes. RFE viewed itself as a surrogate domestic news agency and relied on being able to penetrate geographical borders and territory, circumvent authorities and censors, cut through electronic interference and jamming, and achieve a level of audience penetration so that the message—whose credibility was enhanced by the taboo around it, its scratchy and near unintelligible reception, and its subversive message—was able to counter a regime's narrative, inspiring opposition and forming the basis for shared knowledge and action.[57] RFE did not operate strictly as an output-oriented institution, however, but also engaged in intelligence gathering and analysis, employing native speakers, often dissidents or oppressed locals who had managed to escape from their homelands, to collect, analyze, and deliver reports back to the CIA.

This history has created ongoing suspicion in nations where RFE/RL continues to operate and where the organization's reporters and staff engage in journalism. Host nations where Prague-based RFE/RL employs journalists and stringers often harass and shadow its personnel. In 2014, for example, a number of RFE/RL employees were arrested on charges of espionage in the course of what could just as easily be considered straightforward performance of journalistic duties.[58]

---

56. A. Johnson 2010.

57. A. Ross Johnson is a Hoover Institution colleague, and this summary of goals was garnered from dialogue and interviews conducted in 2013 and 2014 and supplemented with detailed conversations held with another head of RFE/RL, S. Enders Wimbush.

58. "Azerbaijan's 'Spy Network' Charge Escalates Pressure on RFE/RL Journalists," Radio FreeEurope/RadioLiberty press release, February 18, 2014, accessed March 5, 2015, www.rferl .org/content/azerbaijans-spy-network-charge-escalates-pressure-on-rferl-journalists/25268641 .html.

More formal still was the creation of the British Broadcasting Company's World Service and its relationship to the MI6 foreign intelligence service.[59] From establishment to funding, execution, and performance, the BBC World Service has had a storied relationship with its country's intelligence and defense community. The BBC has faced a dramatic funding challenge, moving its underwriting base from a long and reliable government funding source to the vagaries of the marketplace[60] and, further, underwriting by foreign states and their non-Western state broadcasters in exchange for participation in thematic and topical production decisions.[61] Showing some signs of changing tides, in 2015 the British government decided to grant the BBC World Service £289 million in the 2015–20 period,[62] allowing it to launch eleven new language services, in its "biggest expansion since the 1940s."[63] At the same time, the BBC (not the BBC World Service) is now in full partnership with Chinese production institutions and jointly developing documentary work, with critics charging co-option of BBC journalistic standards and practices.[64] The general practice of co-opting media organizations is of growing Western concern. One interviewee for this work expressed direct knowledge of changes made by an American GNN in order not to offend the participating partners, while asserting that a curbing of intelligence gathering was also at play.

59. Dorril 2002. The long history of the relationship between British intelligence and the formal underwriting of the World Service by the state has provided many documented instances of the hierarchical workings, financial arrangements, and established agreements regarding collection and dissemination of intelligence material. Further, Dorril states that "the IRD [Information Research Department] maintained a strong relationship with the BBC" (78).

60. Geniets 2013.

61. House of Commons Foreign Affairs Committee 2011.

62. Conlan 2015.

63. "BBC World Service Announces Biggest Expansion 'since the 1940s,'" *BBC News*, November 16, 2016, accessed December 28, 2017, www.bbc.com/news/entertainment-arts-37990220.

64. Philipson 2013. Philipson considers the increased reliance upon production partners, quoting Mark Reynolds, director of Factual at BBC Worldwide: "CCTV is really quite an important partner in terms of factual programming now. We are going to talk to them about other projects coming up in the future because with the cost of these big productions we are always looking to bring in new partners where it's the right editorial fit for them" (par. 5).

In 2010, one of the more brazen uses of a journalistic organization involved the Pentagon contracting a newly formed corporation, International Media Ventures (IMV), ostensibly to report on the situation in Afghanistan. IMV qualifies as an institutional Western GNN, with a witting management and unwitting reportorial personnel. The Defense Department's head of this program, Michael D. Furlong, had extensive experience in the psychology operations (PSYOPS) world and used the subcontracting relationship with IMV to gather directly actionable intelligence in the field. As one IMV executive, Robert Young Pelton, explained in a *New York Times* article on the changing nature of the IMV-Pentagon relationship, "We were providing information so they could better understand the situation in Afghanistan, and it was being used to kill people."[65] The IMV story was independently corroborated but with the explanation that this operation is atypical, if not rogue, and that it would never be officially condoned, unlike in "countries like Russia or China."[66]

GNN Institutional Formal Intelligence Gathering: Corporate Entities

Formal relations between news organizations and other institutions that make up GNNs have decisively entered the digital age and spread to new media corporations that have yet to define whether they are aggregators, media companies, advertising organizations, or big data companies. Suffice it to say that the business and information juggernauts Google, Facebook, Twitter, Yahoo!, Skype, Apple, and subcorporate entities such as

---

65. Filkins and Mazzetti 2010, par. 17. This revelation is perhaps the single most important recent story on not only the formal intelligence-gathering relationship between an American-based news organization and the military but, going one step further, collusion between the organization and the state in the setup and funding of IMV so that subcontracted journalists for IMV could operate primarily as unwitting intelligence gatherers. Along with Mr. Young, a high-ranking former CNN vice president, "Eason Jordan, a former television news executive, had been hired by the military to run a public Web site to help the government gain a better understanding of a region that bedeviled them" (par. 18). IMV had journalistic legitimacy and access as a result of the credibility of the executive leadership and reporter corps but was used primarily for situational awareness and actionable intelligence.

66. I received this information from conversations with active duty US military conducted in 2013 and 2014.

YouTube and Gmail, which all belong among contemporary GNNs, have been formally engaged in global intelligence gathering and analysis for the state, regardless of GNN type, as revealed in documents and accompanying graphics of the top-secret PRISM program[67] that were made public as part of the Edward Snowden data dump and later confirmed by the US government.[68]

The ubiquitous nature of these corporate entities and their dynamically changing roles in the GNN firmament make it difficult to assess the import of signals intelligence (SIGINT), which they are able to gather efficiently and nearly instantaneously, as opposed to the traditional labor-intensive, individual-focused in-the-field and on-the-ground GNN reporting and analysis of human intelligence (HUMINT). Future study of the geopolitics of GNNs could use this subset of GNN structures as a focus to explore the relationships that the evolving SIGINT GNN capacities bring to their interactions with GNN HUMINT resources. The increasingly important role that aggregators, portals, ISPs, and other providers play in the information-gathering and delivery system makes them a larger and more integrated part of GNN structures, in particular as they increasingly develop their capacities for data collection, original content development, and—due to their financial heft—greater corporate power.

Thomas Fingar, currently a Stanford University professor of international studies, has held a series of US government positions, including first deputy director of national intelligence for analysis and, concurrently, chairman of the National Intelligence Council (2005–8). Shifting global GNN resources and increasing capacities—though, he argues, not credibility—of non-Western GNNs were, he notes, a worrisome phenomenon during his time working in the intelligence community. During his tenure in government, he advocated establishing formal reportorial roles, both in an official governmental context—via embassies and other official missions—and outside official missions, with support for underwritten assignments of external newsgathering sources. "I proposed this,

---

67. "NSA Prism Program Slides," *Guardian*, November 1, 2013, sec. US news, accessed January 10, 2018, www.theguardian.com/world/interactive/2013/nov/01/prism-slides-nsa-document.

68. Savage, Wyatt, and Baker 2013.

without success, years ago as print media was cutting back the information it was gathering around the world," said Fingar.[69] The goal was to
increase the human intelligence coming to the United States from overseas and to make up for diminishing open-source inputs and capacities.
Fingar confirmed that the journalistic approach was effective and worthy
of state support, something for which he advocated. One proposal was
the creation of a "reporting officer" within these missions, with a goal of
235 officers. The other was external to these missions: to make resources
available to have journalists around the world with "no more obligation
than to be a journalist."[70]

GNN Formal Intelligence Gathering:
International Nongovernmental Organizations

The formal intelligence-gathering relationship with GNNs in their
broadest sense, as referred to earlier in this book, includes not only
journalistic newsgathering organizations but also academia, nationally
identifiable corporate entities, and increasingly, nongovernmental organizations (NGOs). The increased importance of NGOs in the international reporting world is widely noted in the journalism profession, in
particular as some formerly traditional news organizations change their
structures to move from market-based systems to nonprofit organizations
with more defined relationships to their funders than the broader-based,
more anonymous relationship previously established with advertisers
and subscribers. In the contemporary Western world of reporting and
news dissemination, the NGO role[71] is becoming dominant in areas
where nonbreaking news, remote locations, humanitarian crises, political
stalemates, chronic economic challenge, and the perceived lack of mass
audience interest are concerns.

Certainly, the perception of Western NGOs as state agents by Russian and Chinese authorities has limited their activities and relationships
to civil society and made suspect those who work with foreign NGOs,
resulting in their collaborative work being labeled as foreign agent

---

69. Personal communication, 2014.
70. Thomas Fingar, personal communication, 2014.
71. Nieman Journalism Lab 2009.

performance.[72] This book demonstrates a mostly informal collaboration of NGOs, academics, and other GNNs with the state and its intelligence-gathering apparatus. Confirming the existence of such a nexus brings to light some highly controversial and potentially damaging protected relationships.[73]

Non-Western powers have acted to proscribe Western NGO activity regardless of validating data on this issue and have increased their pressure on NGO practices and programs. In Russia[74] and China,[75] the assumption is that NGOs are operating as active subversive and intelligence-gathering organizations.[76]

The sudden rise of NGOs within the GNN framework is cause for concern[77] by many who submit that NGOs, like industry and journalists, need to maintain impartiality and independence from governments.[78] However,

---

72. Famularo 2015. In a 2015 speech in Australia, former White House national security advisor Stephen Hadley stated that Vladimir Putin has personally warned China's Xi Jinping that the United States and its Western allies are actively using GNNs to destabilize their respective countries. According to the *Diplomat*, Hadley said the Russian argument is "that the agents of this Western effort are civil society groups, NGOs, free media, and dissidents; that these 'agents of foreign influence' must be stamped out in both Russia and China" (Famularo 2015, par. 18).

73. Specific NGO relationships and their manifest formal relations must remain confidential due to ethical respect for their ongoing nature and any security pressures that may arise from their divulgence.

74. "Russia's Putin Signs NGO 'Foreign Agents' Law," *Reuters*, July 21, 2012, accessed January 10, 2018, www.reuters.com/article/2012/07/21/us-russia-putin-ngos-idUSBRE86K05M20120721.

75. Wan 2015.

76. In 2014, after Russia's parliamentary elections and the protests that followed, "Putin . . . pointedly said that some foreign powers attempted—through their 'foreign agents' in Russia—to use NGOs to disrupt the elections. Putin said that some 'opposition politicians are just like jackals and scavengers, obtaining funding from foreign embassies and consulates.' He stated that these anti-Russian people want to turn Russia into a destabilized problem country" (as reported in the *People's Daily*, cited in Famularo 2015, par. 8). More recently, other countries, such as Israel and Hungary, have also passed laws against NGOs that receive foreign funding (Times of Israel Staff 2016; Simon 2017).

77. Journalism's growing reliance on NGOs in Africa, for example, is creating a false picture of the state of the continent, according to critics of NGOs' undue influence on foreign correspondents. They lament the NGO role in journalism because "even with shrinking resources, journalists can do better than this. For a start, they can stop depending so heavily, and uncritically, on aid organizations for statistics, subjects, stories, and sources" (Rothmeyer 2011, par. 24).

78. DeMars 2001. The questions that arise in this article by DeMars concerning intelligence and formal relationships between states and NGOs are twofold: "Both NGOs and intelligence agencies face (1) transparency questions of what information to make public, share discreetly, or conceal; and (2) operational questions of how they influence the policies of governments and warriors" (193).

NGOs are, in specific Western instances (and nearly all non-Western cases), directly engaged with and formally related to state operations, many of which involve intelligence gathering in both its narrow and broad senses.

Unique data acquired for this work showed direct engagement between NGOs and the state, further reinforcing the contention that GNNs and their institutional structures work to enhance and extend state power. In three cases, the involvement has led to direct access to some of the highest levels of Western governments, including one case in which the NGO had a direct line to the deputy secretary of defense, Paul Wolfowitz, and was involved in an Iraq postinvasion reconstruction partnership effort of which the State Department was unaware. The Western NGO representatives in this book who worked with international organizations emphasized that such relationships, while they do occur, are the exception rather than the rule and that most NGOs have no formal relationship with the state other than providing public, open-source reports or private reports to funders, some of whom are state agencies.

The abundance of empirical data regarding formal relationships between GNNs and the state is but one aspect of the interdependence of these institutions. Beyond institutional relationships, there are individuals who operate outside their formal roles within a GNN context, a recognized feature of those journalistic, academic, aid-working, civil-society-promoting, industrial, and trade professions where successful intelligence-gathering agents operate under nonofficial cover (NOC) and where the individual is neither suspected nor forthcoming about his or her official acts. The better the NOC, the less likely the public is to know about the actors' activities. The following section briefly reviews the research and empirical data on this activity. This work has had access to some individuals who have acted in this capacity in the past, while others can only be identified as potential NOCs, with some suspicions expressed by more than one interview subject.

GNN Personnel: Formal Intelligence Gathering

Individuals working in all three types of institutional GNNs participate in formal state intelligence-gathering operations for any number of personal reasons, drawing on the panoply of human motivations that range from parsimony to patriotism, liquidity to love, revenge to redemption. Their relationship to GNN institutions makes their work possible, gives them access, and increases their impact. The GNN is a force multiplier for their work and activity for the state, as well as the means by which their intelligence-gathering product credibly manifests itself. The history of such activity is long and the availability of narratives a testament that even a surreptitious activity cannot always be kept secret and that human beings just want to share.[79]

Individuals who are not driven by the need to be transparent about their activities, however, can also have their secrets shared in various, sometimes unintended, ways: the power of subpoena, the declassification of documents, the dissolution of a state, stolen data, stupidity. All those acts have led to individuals' activities being found out over time and, as a result, being further documented. The surprising part of the discovery is how prominent and public some of these earlier intelligence-gathering participants have been.

In the twentieth century, individuals like the author and journalist George Orwell freely participated in intelligence activity for the British while working for an institutional GNN. The activist, journalist, and political feminist Gloria Steinem worked for the CIA in the late 1950s and 1960s,[80] openly telling the *Washington Post* in 2008 that in her experience the agency "was completely different from its image: it was liberal, non-violent and honorable."[81] Her involvement came about only because of her direct relationship first with an NGO and then with a larger, national GNN news organization.

Radio Sweden (my employer in the early 1980s) hosted one of the more active CIA employees: Austin Goodrich. Goodrich was an active journalist who, once his identity was revealed by the Church Commission,

---

79. Nicholson 1998. As Nicholson puts it in his introduction, "According to evolutionary psychology, people today still seek those traits that made survival possible then: an instinct to fight furiously when threatened, for instance, and a drive to trade information and share secrets" (135).

80. M. Kounalakis 2015b.

81. Kazin 2008.

retired and wrote the book *Born to Spy: Recollections of a CIA Case Officer* (2004). Goodrich recognized the unique character of journalism as a cover and later shared the most important aspect of the role with his wife, Mona Goodrich: "What I remember him saying is that it was a great cover because it allowed you into places that normally you might not be able to get into."[82] Radio Sweden gave him access everywhere Goodrich sought to enter.

Intelligence-gathering operations in nearly every country that fields an intelligence establishment reach into GNNs to find participants who are ready to engage formally. Israelis have a long tradition of using journalists as NOCs and creating journalism cover for NOCs.[83] Israel actively creates fake journalist credentials for its Mossad agents.[84] A NOC can often bring a fake journalist or other GNN personnel close to a subject for which there is more than a mere intelligence goal. Sometimes the NOC has used the access accorded to him or her as a cover for something more pernicious, as in the case of General Ahmad Shah Massoud, an anti-Taliban Afghan leader and anti-Soviet occupation war hero who was assassinated by a fake journalist and his suicide bomber camera team on September 9, 2001.[85]

Archaeologists[86] and anthropologists,[87] businessmen[88] and bankers[89]— all perform intelligence-gathering functions and participate in an even more expansive GNN framework. For my purposes, however, the institutions and personnel who fall firmly within contemporary GNNs are journalists, NGOs, and academics, due to their long-standing and

---

82. Gores 2013.

83. "The Spy Cables: Israel's Mossad Using El Al as Cover." *Al Jazeera America*, February 15, 2015, accessed January 10, 2018, https://www.youtube.com/watch?v=-a8htQHZFXo.

84. Melman 2010. In this Haaretz article, the Danish-Israeli journalist Herbert Pundik explained his work for Mossad: "I traveled all over Africa under the cover of [being] a journalist," said Pundik. "In general, where is the boundary between espionage and journalism? For example, I wrote a detailed analysis of the tribes in Somalia and their attitude toward political parties, I investigated the political situation in northern Nigeria. These were things that the newspaper was also interested in" (par. 5).

85. T. Harding 2001.

86. Harris and Sadler 2003.

87. Moos, Fardon, and Gusterson 2005.

88. Williams 1996.

89. Matthews and Hong 2015.

	Informal	Formal
GNN Personnel	**Press corps at large, anonymous & confidential sources**	**Goodrich, Orwell, Steinem**
Institutional	***New York Times*, CNN, FAZ, BBC World Service**	**Xinhua, CCTV, RT, RFE/RL, BBC World Service**

Table 5. Intelligence-gathering ideal types

documented participation in GNNs' hard power attributes. Instead of enumerating and identifying each of the professions and activities who engage in intelligence gathering but whose main purpose is different, this book focuses on journalists' work in intelligence gathering, while aggregating data about NGOs and academics. Refining and expanding the GNN concept to include more categories of participants might be appropriate in a future study. In the meantime, this work focuses on the professions proscribed by non-Western, closed societies, which are, notably, currently expanding their own professional GNN engagement in other countries, primarily in journalism, academia, and the NGO world.

Table 5 shows a framework of GNN ideal types engaged in intelligence gathering, with individuals and institutions in this work identified within their category (individuals overlapping both formal and informal categories are not represented in this chart). In the first cell, where an informal relationship is paired with GNN individuals, the press corps at large engages at this level. Researched participants who corroborated this understanding of the role of the press or who have participated individually with the state on an informal basis requested anonymity, as they worried that their activity would blemish their career and credibility as news professionals. The individuals who have been discovered to have a formal intelligence-gathering role but who also worked professionally as news reporters, writers, or media professionals are in the second cell. The third cell comprises institutions; the numerous organizations that were found to have an informal relationship with the state are primarily Western GNNs, whereas institutions with a formal relationship to the state—where state and news institution are one and the same—are primarily though not exclusively non-Western GNNs.

GNN Institutional: Informal Intelligence Gathering

Intelligence analysts (be they in the intelligence, diplomatic, military, legislative, or administrative state structures) routinely, often exclusively, use news reports to inform their policy formation and policy making.[90] Beyond priming and framing the gathered and publicly presented news and information, the informal institutional intelligence-gathering function develops as a result of institutions' relationships with power elites. On the one hand, data that is made public via publication or broadcast is often a first look at breaking stories, with a first look at framing,[91] but on the other hand, the informal relationships allow for an ongoing dialogue with a GNN's leadership and personnel.[92]

Editorial board meetings are one way this dialogue is conducted at the institutional level, but it continues with ministerial interaction and the sharing of information with corporate executives. These publisher-level conclaves between states and GNNs allow for an informal sharing of strategies and a reaffirmation of shared values and goals. Some of the GNN protocols give an advantage in intelligence via tipping; a GNN usually contacts a political entity to request input on a story, either

---

90. Gendron 2005.

91. It is typical for political leaders and policy makers to keep a television screen tuned to a news source such as CNN running in the background for breaking items that might not reach them otherwise or in as timely a fashion.

92. Google, while part of the formal institutional intelligence-gathering state operation, also has an informal role to play, as do other GNNs. A manifestation of that informal relationship is the open door afforded its executives at the White House, as revealed by the *Wall Street Journal*: "Since Mr. Obama took office, employees of the Mountain View, Calif., company have visited the White House for meetings with senior officials about 230 times, or an average of roughly once a week, according to the visitor logs reviewed by the Journal" (Mullins 2015, par. 4).

for confirmation of facts or to make sure there are no national security issues with the release of the information. While not a prepublication censorship process per se, the conventional practice has led, in numerous instances, to the equivalent of a de facto prepublication withholding of information.[93]

The cases in which a news organization has withheld information from the public at the informal request of state authorities are significant, but it is worth noting that such requests do not have the force of law in many Western societies,[94] with cooperation being proffered voluntarily, if not always happily. At the same time, non-Western GNNs institutionally have a formal state relationship in nearly every case, making any informal institutional relationship superfluous. The same is true of Western type III (state-sponsored) GNNs, with the exception that there is a greater tradition of dissent and whistle-blowing, as well as a long legal precedent of challenges to prepublication censorship.

Open-Source Intelligence

Beyond the process by which informal national cultural, social, political, and economic interests shared between GNNs and the state feed a state's intelligence-gathering needs are the informal means by which the work product of journalists, and GNNs in general, serves an intelligence-gathering purpose. This is generally referred to as

---

93. Farhi 2005. When the NSA was engaged in Bush administration–authorized surveillance, the *New York Times* agreed with the intelligence services to defer publication of the story. The *Times* said it agreed to remove information that administration officials said could be "useful" to terrorists and delayed publication for a year "to conduct additional reporting." (Farhi 2005, par. 3). The case of James Risen and his eventual publication of this data led to legal action against the reporter and his source, not only freezing his journalistic actions and sources but having a "chilling effect" on other journalists, leakers, and whistle-blowers. His case was finally resolved, and after a seven-year legal fight, he was not ultimately required to testify before a court. For other examples, see Sullivan 2014.

94. Kimball 2013. A notable difference from first amendment protections in the United States is a system of prepublication censorship in many other Western allied nations, first and foremost in the United Kingdom. In the case of Edward Snowden and the release of secret information, the authorities acted directly to destroy the data: "After the Guardian published a series of articles revealing British-complicity in US-led mass telecommunications surveillance, Downing Street began to turn up the heat on the London-based newspaper, forcing its editor, Alan Rusbridger, to destroy computer hard drives under the threat of legal action" (par. 2).

open-source intelligence (OSINT). It is the dominant method of intelligence gathering, as "most of the information referred to as 'intelligence' is obtained from open sources, but some of it is derived from secret intelligence; that is, actionable intelligence obtained by covert means, through collection rather than operations."[95] Analysts consume public news reports, white papers, situation analyses, field studies, and other media productions, regardless of whether that material was intended for their private consumption. One key function of any embassy is compiling news clippings in the host nation for the benefit of leaders in the mission's home country. Intelligence agency reading of newspapers, for example, is an expected, understood, and conventional approach to conducting intelligence gathering[96] and analysis formulation.

GNN Personnel: Informal Intelligence Gathering

Institutions maintain informal high-level state relationships, but GNN personnel as well as individuals perform the unwitting intelligence-gathering function in an informal fashion. Whether *Los Angeles Times* correspondent Carol Williams reporting on the rape of women in Bosnia[97] or BBC and other GNN photojournalists documenting the starvation of children in Sudan[98] or Somalia, such coverage affects the decisions of governments to get involved and engage the policy-making apparatus directly—regardless of the "CNN effect's" established impotency in the strategic policy-making process, at times referred to as "the myth of news, foreign policy and intervention."[99]

The data reporters collect on the ground informs the process to a large degree, often because that data would not be available otherwise and can provide an impetus in decision making where there is policy ambiguity. The detailed data received by policy makers, which may not be publicly distributed, is supplemental and can be critical in decision

---

95. Gendron 2005, 398.
96. Mansfield 2010.
97. Williams 1992.
98. MacLeod 2001.
99. Robinson 2002.

making, not because of any wider public effect or pressure but because the data is unique, confirmable, and otherwise unavailable. Embassy officials and intelligence operatives are often shut out of grassroots-level investigations, for reasons concerning personal and situational security, surveillance realities, and official restrictions on movement. Journalists, however, have much greater freedom of movement than officialdom, and that freedom often translates into a broader spectrum of inputs in creating a final reporting and analysis product.[100]

That was certainly the case in the Gulf conflicts, when eyewitnesses and reporters came back with information that directly informed intelligence analysis, leading to policy decisions. Such details can go all the way to the president's daily brief (PDB), which is described by journalist Bob Woodward as "the TOP SECRET/CODEWORD digest of the most important and sensitive intelligence."[101]

Of course, this is simply what journalists routinely do in the course of their work. There is nothing here that can be construed as a conscious or unconscious act of intelligence gathering—other than for the public at large. It is not intended to serve a narrower audience. The published or broadcast work, however, is a key part of daily intelligence analysis that is incorporated in the daily routine of intelligence-gathering analysts. The dominance of Western GNNs in the twentieth century has meant that the facts, insights, analyses, and figures presented in their reports have been dominated by a Western approach to fact-finding and implications, with a focus on Western popular audiences, shared value systems, news relevance, topicality, political sensitivity, elite impact, and popular appeal.

Former secretary of state George P. Shultz gives some insight into how this system works. Shultz said he relied on the traveling press, in particular reporters from the *New York Times* and the *Washington Post* who accompanied him overseas and were "extremely helpful" in supplementing his understanding of foreign situations, political personalities, and popular societal and economic pressures. Such informal collaboration

---

100. Dover and Goodman 2009. A part of Dover and Goodman's anthologized volume describes CIA reliance on open-source intelligence garnered from public media sources—for example, in the analysis and policy formulation regarding Libya's nuclear program.

101. Woodward 2002, 39.

or coordination at the highest levels has rarely been corroborated.[102] In a personal interview with ninety-four-year-old Secretary Shultz, he said that he "relied" on information that he would "otherwise not have." Former secretary of state Condoleezza Rice expressed similar thoughts in a presentation in 2017: "I used to go the Soviet Union a lot as a young Soviet specialist and especially as the Gorbachev era was unfolding, I would first go to see the journalists. People like [*New York Times* correspondents] Phil Taubman, who is here at Stanford, or Felicity Berringer, or Bill Keller because they knew the place and could get out to the places where American diplomats couldn't. . . . I hope that when those decisions are being made in newsrooms these days that they're actually investing in people who can be out in these countries and know them."[103]

While the direct admission of an informal relationship with individuals is rare, the WikiLeaks cables released by Julian Assange and his organization revealed the role played by GNN institutions and individuals in both formal and informal diplomacy and intelligence gathering.[104] Aside from the substantial data and insight garnered from the WikiLeaks cables, showing the extensive informal relationships between journalists and state officials, in some cases the information brought serious personal and professional repercussions for journalists who were seen as collaborators with foreign governments.[105]

WikiLeaks as a website and a distributed organization relied on GNNs for distribution of the previously classified materials it received. Whether WikiLeaks acted on behalf of or in spite of a state is not currently

---

102. George P. Shultz, personal communication, 2014. George P. Shultz is a former US secretary of state during the Reagan administration and currently the Thomas W. and Susan B. Ford Distinguished Fellow at the Hoover Institution.

103. "World Class: Condoleezza Rice, Michael McFaul, Larry Diamond and Francis Fukuyama," Freeman Spogli Institute, Stanford University, 2017, audio recording, https://soundcloud.com/fsistanford/condoleezza-rice, flagged and noted by Janine Zacharia, Stanford journalism lecturer and former Jerusalem bureau chief for the *Washington Post*.

104. Chatriwala 2011. This article details some of the WikiLeaks cables regarding Al Jazeera and states: "There have been longstanding accusations that Al Jazeera serves as an arm of its host nation's foreign policy, and earlier leaked documents referred to the news organization as 'one of Qatar's most valuable political and diplomatic tools,' which could be used as 'a bargaining tool to repair relationships with other countries'" (par. 3).

105. Associated Press 2011. In this case, the cables reference a cooperative opposition journalist who had shared information about a source: "The Committee to Protect Journalists (CPJ)

known, and the responsible party is in diplomatic exile. Regardless of any relationship to a state, WikiLeaks was leveraged by states to distribute misinformation as well as embarrassing data. The question of whether WikiLeaks might be some sort of stateless GNN with no national affiliation or headquarters is an open one, but there certainly is a potential for GNNs to evolve out of their current three national typologies and be all or none of the three, given the ethereal, supranational nature of cyberspace.

Westerners are prominently featured in Ulfkotte's book, *Gekaufte Journalisten* (2014), a volume that includes names of individuals who informally cozy up to state officials and enjoy perquisites of international travel, access, conferencing, research, and publishing opportunities by dint of their close but informal ideological orientations and intelligence-sharing habits. A former US NOC, Valerie Plame Wilson, expressed deep curiosity as to why Ulfkotte went public with this book—questioning his motivation in identifying those who work either directly and formally as NOCs, as well as those who gather and share intelligence unwittingly and informally.[106] The implication is that Ulfkotte did this on behalf of a state entity working to discredit individuals and institutions and discourage them from continuing their work with Western allied states.

In a reporter's notebook, of which only 5 to 10 percent on average is used for a story, there is usually 50 to 90 percent useful intelligence in the form of names, quotes, and contacts—information that stays in the notebook until it is shared informally, perhaps at an embassy cocktail party or lunch or at a prearranged meeting with an official or unbeknownst NOC, where the goal is engaging and trading information or ideas.[107]

---

said reporter Argaw Ashine fled at the weekend after being interrogated over the identity of a government source mentioned in a leaked 2009 US cable. Argaw was the local correspondent for Kenya's Nation Media Group" (par. 5).

106. Valerie Plame Wilson, personal communication, 2015. This personal communication with Valerie Plame was during an informal conversation and not an organized or planned interview with the celebrity subject.

107. The high percentage of data, contacts, and analysis that remains unpublished in a reporter's notebook is an estimate based on interviews with foreign correspondents and personal experience.

One journalist I know well frequently engaged in informal sharing of information with Western embassies and state officials, both during and after the Cold War, primarily in Central Europe, where original reporting by Western GNNs and individuals was limited but social and political controls on Western reporters were rapidly diminishing. In at least three cases, the journalist shared with the US embassy and other Western diplomatic officials information that did not ultimately make it into his reporting. The information was shared informally, without expectation of remuneration and without agreement, but as a result of accepted journalistic practices of information trading, data confirmation, individual identification, credibility checking, and the search for new leads.[108] While such an admission is rare, the practice is broadly practiced and acceptable, albeit usually undisclosed publicly. The journalist's experiences have been corroborated by other journalists interviewed in this book.

This key journalist recounted in deep detail, with previously unpublished and undisclosed evidence, his informal intelligence gathering, information sharing, and state interactions. Details regarding his news organization, currently living individuals with whom he engaged and interacted, and other identifying traits or characteristics have been withheld. No details have been changed nor are any composite characters or details presented.

As explained by this journalist, in 1990, while he was a news reporter running the Prague bureau of a prominent institutional news organization, he was a frequent guest of US ambassador Shirley Temple Black at the Petschek Villa, her official residence. He always felt welcome, and she always made it a point to introduce him around, as he was one of the few American correspondents living in Prague immediately after the Velvet Revolution. One of the individuals he became acquainted with was the defense attaché at the embassy.

In the course of his reporting in Eastern Europe, prior to moving to the Soviet Union, this journalist came across three stories, at different times during his tenure, that he shared with either the attaché or, in some cases, the ambassadors of other Western nations. In each case, he was

---

108. Personal communication, 2015.

trying to get either a confirmation or a lead to advance his story "as well as to let embassy officials know about a suspicious or dangerous threat to individuals or national security."[109] He and others who engaged in this activity in the course of their work report that this is a professional tactic of information bartering.

One story this journalist was pursuing involved the explosive plastique Semtex, made in the Czechoslovak town of Semtin. His interest in this particular explosive was that it was the material suspected to have been used in blowing up Pan Am 103 over Lockerbie, Scotland. In the course of his reporting, he investigated Palestinian training camps located near Semtin, attended a meeting and press conference—and had a testy confrontation— with Palestine Liberation Organization leader Yasser Arafat, interviewed an individual who worked at the Semtex facility, and most important, "[came] across a shadowy figure who gave me photographs of Semtex testing on the fuselages of aircraft located outside of Prague."[110] Whether those photographs showed tests to check weak points on a fuselage or simply to destroy used aircraft was never ascertainable, but the photographs (see Figure 2) were clearly important, required technical interpretation, and could be evidentiary documents in the Pan Am case. "My journalistic instincts led me both to a non-American but Western embassy to ask general questions about the issue and also directly to the American defense attaché to show him the photos."[111] At that meeting, the attaché shared a lead and discussed the potential involvement of the Russian "Spetsnaz" forces—a term for "special forces" the journalist did not know—and the Palestinian presence in pre–Velvet Revolution Czechoslovakia.

In the process, the journalist said that the attaché was also open to sharing technical details and professional insights. He went on to say that in the course of the discussion with the attaché, this professional news correspondent

also revealed to him that I had discovered that a few diplomatic license plates from American embassy vehicles had been stolen. Not both front and back license plates, but only one of

---

109. Personal communication, 2015.
110. Personal communication, 2015.
111. Personal communication, 2015.

Figure 2. Semtex testing on the fuselage of an aircraft (original document from anonymous journalist)

the two plates on a car, albeit on more than one car. I was later told that Ambassador Black had altered her plans to attend an event celebrating the American soldiers' liberation of the western Czech town of Pilsen, my source informing me that the missing license plates may have been part of a plot to crash the event without being stopped at a checkpoint by virtue of the diplomatic plates that allow for free and unhindered passage. The source further claimed that the plates were possibly set to go into a car loaded with Semtex explosives and were to attack the embassy event.[112]

This means that the information gathered by this journalist and shared with US officials may have prevented an attack on Ambassador Shirley Temple Black. This is a clear case of a GNN intelligence-gathering function possibly preventing a terrorist attack.

In neither of these cases was the information disclosed publicly before now. In the case of the Semtex and the photographs, the large institutional news organization the journalist worked for kept him pursuing the story for a reasonable amount of time, but the level of speculation and the

---

112. Personal communication, 2015.

security implications imposed a higher than usual threshold for publication. What the embassy did with the information can only be guessed. That an informal intelligence-gathering relationship existed, however, is not speculative in the least. Whether sharing information over cocktails at an embassy reception or casually talking about contacts and sources at the bar in the embassy basement, the correspondent affirmed that "information that never made it out of my notebook and into my public reporting was regularly and informally shared with state officials."[113] This is a common experience. Multiple interviews with other correspondents and editors confirm that informal information sharing and "notebook dumps" are customary, and that it works both ways in the pursuit of information and source exchange.

A final instance of investigative reporting that led to intelligence sharing had to do with highly sensitive documents received by a journalist, which revealed a significant potential security threat. In this case, he was privy to a document that had formulas for a weaponized material known as red mercury that was rumored to be important in the manufacture of nuclear weaponry (see Figure 3). Red mercury was reported in the international press, and a supposed black market for the material was emerging, though its composition and import were unclear. Again, the journalist shared this document with a number of individuals in Western embassies and, in one case, was tipped off that the material in question might be a hoax intended to flush out less sophisticated individuals who were operating in the underground gun-running trade. "The official source had always seemed honest and credible to me, so I continued to pursue the story, a few sources, and a specific lead who was trying to purchase red mercury, but maintained a wariness about the material and the shadowy forces seeking it."[114] The story never ran publicly and is presented for the first time here.

One journalist recalled the process of informal cooperation in intelligence gathering, as noted in the foreword. NBC Radio journalist Peter

---

113. Personal communication, 2015.

114. Personal communication, 2015. It is still unclear whether red mercury was a hoax. "If the intention of the Russian and Western intelligence services was to concoct a disinformation campaign designed to entrap terrorist cells trading in the black market for nuclear arms and materials, then they could not have done a better job of placing the stories than in those prestigious professional and media journals and outlets" (Farrell 2009, 142).

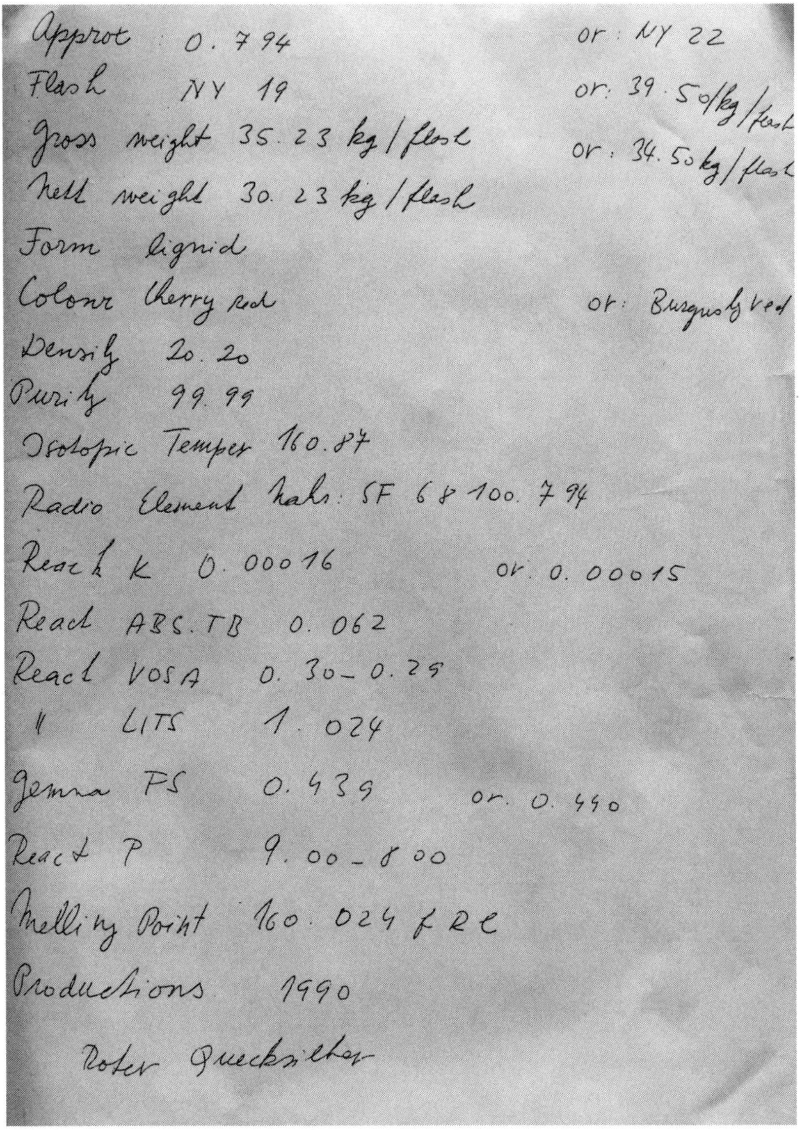

Approx : 0.794   or : NY 22
Flash   NY 19   or : 39.50 kg/flask
Gross weight 35.23 kg/flask   or : 34.50 kg/flask
Nett weight 30.23 kg/flask
Form   liquid
Colour   cherry red   or : Burgundy red
Density   20.20
Purity   99.99
Isotopic Temper 160.87
Radio Element nahs: SF 68 100.794
Reach K   0.00016   or. 0.00015
React ABS.TB   0.062
React VOSA   0.30 - 0.25
   "   LITS   1.024
Gemma FS   0.439   or. 0.440
React P   9.00 - 8.00
Melting Point 160.024 f R C
Productions   1990
      Roter Quecksilber

Figure 3. Red Mercury formula (original document from anonymous journalist)

Laufer recounted a visit he and a colleague made to the US consulate in Peshawar, Pakistan, during the Soviet war in Afghanistan in 1981.[115] He was on a reporting trip to the border region between Pakistan and Afghanistan and needed to stop at the consulate to have some documents authenticated and notarized for a home purchase in California.

In the course of his visit, he was invited to join the consul general for a meal, a great opportunity for him to get a background briefing on the situation from the US government perspective.

After dinner and dessert, over tea, as the discussion came to his planned reporting in the rebel areas, the government official did not mince words about some intelligence sought by the United States: Did the Soviets use plastique antipersonnel mines, previously only confirmed anecdotally?[116]

The government official told him that they had no hard evidence to date on these types of mines and implored Laufer to bring back such evidence. Photos, material, markings, or anything that would allow the United States finally to confirm the existence of these devices and press their case against the Soviets both in international bodies and back home.

Ultimately, Laufer found no evidence during his reporting trip, but years later, upon reflection, he questioned whether he would have delivered such evidence if he did, in fact, come across it. He asked rhetorically, "Would I have passed along data that proved that a bunch of bad guys were maiming kids? That an offensive system and state should answer for its crimes?"[117] Laufer found it difficult to admit he would pass along information to state officials.

Individual engagement in state intelligence gathering has more formal manifestations in non-Western GNNs, but the informal individual relations of Western GNNs are sometimes almost indistinguishable from formal state ties. During my tenure as the NBC-Mutual Radio news

---

115. Peter Laufer, personal communication, 2015.

116. These mines were popularly referred to as butterfly mines because they were dropped by Soviet helicopters and fluttered to the ground, where their bright colors and toy shape were meant to appeal to children, unaware that they would lose a limb or worse by playing with this dangerous device (personal interviews and observations, Afghanistan, December 1991)

117. Peter Laufer, personal communication, 2015.

correspondent in Moscow, expatriate American reporters enjoyed the privilege of using the US embassy cafeteria, a regular venue for the press corps in a city where American food and hamburgers were few and far between. Reporters were given special identification badges and could pay a small fee to become members of the embassy community, which included privileges at the gymnasium, swimming pool, and workout room, check-cashing privileges (unavailable in Moscow banks), a large lending library of English books (unavailable in the local marketplace), and access to the cafeteria that often served as American journalists' meeting place and hangout at lunchtime and where it was common to see the US ambassador having a quick bite or to run into the political officer or station chief (though it was not always apparent who that was). Invariably, the tables were a mix of journalists and embassy personnel, and conversations regularly focused on situational analyses, sources, and stories. As Terry Phillips put it, he could casually mention to a staff member, "Oh I've just been in Afghanistan," and the comment would provoke a friendly, informal conversation: "After all, you've just had this intense experience and you would love to talk about it. So, it happens that your interlocutor is a political officer who thoroughly mines your thoughts and feelings about that country as well as your observations along the way in Uzbekistan and Tajikistan."[118]

In conclusion, it is clear that in multiple instances, in various ways, and for a variety of reasons, GNNs provide an intelligence capacity to the state that is nontrivial and at times critical. This hard power intelligence capacity has been the nearly exclusive purview of Western GNNs by dint of their near monopoly in the last century. Those state-power-enhancing capacities are still available, though at a much diminished level, in the West. Further, those Western capacities have diminished due to the rapid rise and relative strength of the new type III (non-Western) GNNs and their structural central operating rationale, which aims to directly leverage GNNs' inherent and potential diplomatic and intelligence-gathering functions.

---

118. Terry Phillips, personal communication, 2015. Phillips was CBS Radio correspondent in Moscow (1991–94).

CHAPTER 4 | NON-WESTERN GLOBAL NEWS NETWORKS
Diplomacy and Intelligence Gathering

The previous two chapters established that Western nonstate GNNs perform the hard power functions of diplomacy and intelligence gathering, both formally and informally. Further, these GNN performances, while not central to their professional raison d'être and in direct contravention to their codes and standards of professional ethics when performed formally, are nonetheless critical to supplementing a diplomatic and intelligence-gathering system that has developed a state reliance on these GNN practices and products.

The predominant informality of Western GNNs' performance forms a striking contrast to the nearly exclusive formality of non-Western type III GNNs, where diplomacy and intelligence gathering are not an ancillary, peripheral, or epiphenomenal aspect of their performance but rather central to it.

This chapter investigates the varied aspects of these performances by examining the practices typical of Russian and Chinese GNNs. Both China and Russia are currently expanding their GNN structures, adding financial resources, personnel, and bureaus, and legitimizing distribution structures to their publicly expressed growth strategies and trajectories, which are supported by state leadership. This, too, stands in stark contrast to the media ecology once dominated by Western GNNs and now characterized by their rapid demise—and in certain cases (e.g., the newspaper industry) near collapse.

As noted earlier, type I GNN structures are under enormous pressure. The question is not only how they will continue to provide the state with adequate OSINT and diplomatic performance but how they will survive at all. "For twenty years, intelligent people at the papers have been hoping and praying for 'a new business model.' It has not arrived. Very likely it's not hovering in the wings. . . . The destruction or self-destruction of high-profit journalism is guaranteed."[1]

Despite the emergence of nontraditional journalistic GNN institutions—whether NGOs or academics—to fill the resulting information vacuum, the traditional reliance on firmly established, socialized news organizations is another diminished hard power capacity for the West. One former American undersecretary of state put it bluntly: "This is frightening."[2]

Loss of relative hard power, however, means that others are gaining relative GNN intelligence-gathering and diplomatic capacities. Non-Western countries, in particular the Russians and the Chinese, are working hard to develop these capacities in the early twenty-first century. Most of the publicly expressed Western official criticism of these GNNs is aimed at their attempts to propagandize a foreign public, with a critical emphasis on GNNs' soft power effects. Although in 2015 Victoria Nuland, then the senior American diplomat responsible for Europe and Russia, derided Russian efforts to influence foreign public opinion,[3] privately members of the Western diplomatic corps and intelligence communities recognized soft power GNN tools as expressions of state power. As one former German politician with experience dealing with Russia put it, "Putin's a former KGB guy. He'll use whatever he's got to get what he needs."[4] He went on to say that the Russians see the GNNs as another tool in their "hybrid warfare" strategies. In 2017, this interpretation of the expanding Russian media network dominated American public discourse about RT. In addition, RT and Sputnik have faced allegations that they tried to interfere with the US presidential election in 2016, playing a role in the election of Donald Trump.

---

1. Gitlin 2013, par. 14.

2. Personal communication 2016.

3. Nuland said, "All you have to do is look at RT's tiny, tiny audience in the United States to understand what happens when you broadcast untruths in a media space that is full of dynamic, truthful opinion" (Hudson 2015, par. 3). Nuland was speaking at the Brookings Institution on the Ukrainian conflict and RT efforts to counter the narrative of Russian military involvement. When asked by a reporter if RT should be banned in the United States, she responded, "We believe in freedom of speech, freedom of media in this country" (par. 4).

4. Personal communication and author translation, 2015.

The media component of "hybrid warfare" is generally considered a soft power resource, with emphasis on its use in psychological operations during conflict and strategically to sow doubt in a global audience about Western governing institutions and GNNs. One article published as the Kennan Institute's "Kennan Cable" on Russia's hybrid warfare in 2015 argued that Russia's GNNs' effectiveness was limited to its own sphere of influence: "Some fear that because information warfare is part of Russia's operations against Ukraine, other places where Russia's broadcasting and messaging can be felt may be future targets for 'hybrid war' operations."[5] This sanguine report then went on to say that "there is a vast gulf between Russia's global broadcasting and public diplomacy goals and its operational goals."[6] At the same time, many expressed fears about Russia's plans for hybrid warfare and its GNN component.[7] Such fears were given official confirmation in early 2017, when a report prepared by the CIA, the FBI, and the NSA on Russian activities and intentions in the 2016 presidential election was declassified. The report states that "Russian President Vladimir Putin ordered an influence campaign in 2016 aimed at the U.S. presidential election."[8] The report then goes on to detail RT's programming, writing that RT conducted "strategic messaging for [the] Russian government, . . . aimed at undermining viewers' trust in US democratic procedures."[9]

Regardless of public perceptions around non-Western GNNs— whether they are perceived as public diplomacy institutions or as institutions possessing and expressing hard power—it is generally understood that their current expansion will give them greater capacities to meet

---

5. Kofman and Rojansky 2015, 5.

6. Kofman and Rojansky 2015, 5.

7. Not even the Kennan Institute was uniform in its opinion on Russian hybrid war and the role of GNNs. Maxim Trudolyubov, the editor at large at the business newspaper *Vedomosti*, writes the *Russia File* blog for the Kennan Institute. In a *New York Times* opinion piece, he states: "It is not by crude force alone that Russia twists events to its advantage. By using its total control over the Russian news media to sow confusion in the West, Mr. Putin has managed, in the words of the journalists Peter Pomerantsev and Michael Weiss, to 'weaponize' information. In a report published in late 2014 by the New York–based Institute of Modern Russia, they outlined how the Kremlin manipulates the media, ethnic tensions and trade and financial transactions abroad to further its own ends" (Trudolyubov 2016, par. 3).

8. National Intelligence Council 2017, ii.

9. National Intelligence Council 2017, 7.

growing soft and hard power ambitions. For RT of Russia, this includes building new broadcast facilities, launching a multilingual service — which includes, as of December 2017, English-, Arabic-, Spanish-, and most recently, French-language channels — and the development of new broadcast, social media, or streaming productions, as Andrey Bukashkin, chief director of RT, described it in a satellite broadcast industry interview. "We have also been quick to embrace new platforms, in particularly social media. RT was the first Russian TV channel to create a YouTube channel back in 2007. Today we are the first TV news channel ever, worldwide, to cross the billion-views mark on the platform. We've created an award-winning Facebook app; we're constantly engaged with our audience."[10]

RT is also expending the financial resources to upgrade and expand its presence and productions. While official figures are hard to come by, Ioffe reported in 2010, "The channel's budget was just $30 million the first year, but it grew in subsequent years before taking a hit during the global economic crisis that began in 2008. RT officials won't provide specifics on the current budget, but the Kremlin has announced that it intends to spend $1.4 billion this year on international propaganda."[11] The BBC reported that in 2015 the Russian government increased the budget for RT by more than 50 percent, to $300 million.[12] According to the *Moscow Times*, in 2016, the Russian state budget allocated about $307 million to RT.[13]

China's newest GNN institution, CCTV (now called CGTN, China Global Television Network), has also received an enormous injection of cash, estimated by Nye to be "$8.9 billion in 'external publicity work,' much of it focused on the new 24-hour news operations."[14] However, Nelson adds, "This figure is hard to confirm, and appears to include the costs of hundreds of international Confucius Institutes as well as media

---

10. Quoted in Holmes 2013, par. 4.

11. Ioffe 2010, par. 22.

12. Ennis 2015.

13. "Russia Cuts State Spending on RT News Network," *Moscow Times*, October 11, 2015, accessed December 28, 2017, http://themoscowtimes.com/articles/russia-cuts-state-spending -on-rt-news-network-50194.

14. Nye quoted in A. Nelson 2013, 17.

operations."[15] To put this into perspective, the total for American type III GNNs run by the Broadcasting Board of Governors was $752 million in 2016.[16] In each of these cases, little revenue was generated by either Western or non-Western type III GNNs. The difference in the amount spent by the non-West compared to America's GNN budgets is one sign that there is a disproportionate and recent shift in the relational capacities of institutions that are built for and intended to enhance state power. A Western senior diplomat expressed the interest of the non-Western states to expand their GNN capacities: "They see them as another tool in an ongoing struggle against America."[17]

Non-Western GNNs' Formal Relationships to the State

The Chinese have long had a firmly established systemic process by which GNN institutions and individuals have an established protocol for providing raw and processed intelligence directly up the chain of command to the highest level of the governmental and party hierarchy. This system was acknowledged in the US government's *Intelligence Threat Handbook*,[18] in ongoing work by Chinese intelligence analyst Nicholas Eftimiades,[19] in Doug Young's authoritative work (2013) — an important

---

15. Nelson 2013, 17.

16. Broadcasting Board of Governors 2016. "The President's budget request for Fiscal Year 2017, sent to Congress on February 9, 2016, includes $777.8 million for the Broadcasting Board of Governors (BBG)," according to the BBG website, only a slight increase from 2014–16 (after a 4.2 percent decrease in 2013 compared with 2012) rather than an attempt to match the non-Western Type III GNNs' expenditures and rapid capacity building.

17. Personal communication, 2016.

18. While the US government's *Intelligence Threat Handbook* does not identify China's GNNs per se as intelligence-gathering structures, it does identify the categories of institutions and individuals who make up GNNs. "A large portion of the PRC's [intelligence] collection efforts against common targets like technology is conducted directly by PRC students, delegations, and commercial enterprises" (Interagency OPSEC Support Staff 2004, 18). This unclassified document was written prior to China's development of an outward-focused CCTV/CGTN and before its larger, structural GNN took shape, but the elements of the state's intent and the intelligence-gathering capacities inherent in every asset with analytical skill is understood.

19. Chapter 4 of his book *Eftimiades* (1994) looks at the Ministry of State Security (MSS) and provides one of the ministry's few published organizational charts. He writes that "a sampling

inside look at the relationship between reporters and the Chinese state directly established via the formal systemic practice known as *neican*[20]— and in the interviews and data collected here.

Neican is a critical component of how intelligence formally travels up the chain of command in the Chinese state and party apparatus. *Neican* reports are secret internal documents with circulation limited to top officials, "designed to inform party and government officials about key policy matters deemed too sensitive for the general public."[21] As Young notes, the system was officially established in 1951 and "is largely based in Xinhua, but reporters at all publications are also expected to write up their own *neican* reports when they come across information that might be useful to government leaders."[22]

In the course of this research, one highly placed Chinese media consultant was able to provide a confidential organizational chart that expresses the formalized relationship between the newsgathering Chinese institutions and the state party and governing apparatus (Figure 4). The document reflects two levels of information and intelligence flow within the formal Chinese type III GNN system. The figure also shows the direct *neican* structure that delivers reports and responds to directions from the highest levels of the state and party apparatus.

The general outlines of this previously unpublished organizational chart have been confirmed by a second confidential source working within CCTV. The attestation to its accuracy is presented with the following caveats regarding reporting relationships between the GNN and the state:

---

of the world press further indicates the wide reach of China's overseas clandestine espionage operations. Such operations have been uncovered—and publicly exposed—in the Sudan in 1964, Malawi in 1965, Kenya in 1965, the Central African Republic in 1966, Brazil in 1964 and 1977, France in 1983, and the United States in 1985 and 1987. In each case, the intelligence officer operated under the cover of a New China News Agency journalist, official trade representative, military attaché, or accredited diplomat."

20. Young's book (2013) is described in a blurb as an inside look at "the role of the press in China and how the Chinese government uses the media."

21. Bandurski and Hala 2010, 121.

22. Young 2013, 65.

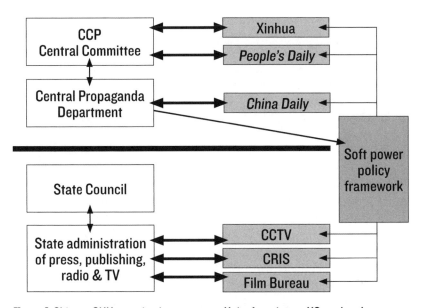

Figure 4. Chinese GNN organization structure: Units focusing on US marketplace

For Xinhua although I have it reporting directly to the CCP, it may be that this is a dotted relationship and it is primarily under the State Council. The head of Xinhua is on the CCP Central Committee so this is why I had it reporting to just the CCP but in other places I see it under the State Council. Not clear if he is on the Central Committee as an individual or in his capacity as Xinhua president. For the *China Daily*, I have it just reporting to the Central Propaganda Department.[23]

The organizational chart is broken into two distinct relationships, with the Chinese state (State Council) and the Chinese Communist Party (CCP), separated by a solid line. The complex and deep relationship between the state and the party has been thoroughly researched in the literature on Chinese power and formal governing structures. For the purposes of this book, however, the reporting relationships are presented as distinct and do not reflect the interdependence of the two structures. The chart is designed to represent Chinese GNN structures operating in

---

23. Personal interview with CCTV consultant, November 2014.

the context of the United States, but the structural specifics are typical of Chinese organizational operations worldwide, according to two individuals I interviewed.

In the top part of the organizational chart, the reporting relationships between GNN news organizations *China Daily*, *Xinhua*, and *People's Daily* all feed into the party operational and propaganda apparatus, which in turn defines the soft power policy framework, which then dictates the strategies and editorial approaches and priorities of all the GNN institutional news structures, including CGTN, CRIS (Chinese Radio International Service), and the state Film Bureau. It is a flow that harkens back to and reflects the introductory chapter's power flowchart, showing the interlocking relationships between information, intelligence, operational capacities, and the state.

Africa is a unique case where Chinese GNNs have an established presence and are increasing their footprint.[24] Most analyses look at this increasing presence on the African continent as a soft power effort on the part of the Chinese.[25] The expanding media presence and growth of the CGTN center in Nairobi provide a substantial narrative of development but also provide Beijing with "the pulse of the African public"[26] via GNN reporting and analysis. This is key, as "China is steadily expanding its military footprint in Africa,"[27] as it deals with new diplomatic challenges[28]

---

24. To get a sense of how quickly Beijing is using its multibillion-dollar global GNN expansion effort, a look at the media component shows that "in April 2011, the Xinhua news agency partnered with a Kenyan network operator to provide news for mobile phones. That was followed nine months later by CCTV Africa in Nairobi, the first broadcast hub to be established by China Central Television (CCTV) outside Beijing" (Shek 2013, par. 3).

25. While analysis of media often acknowledges the full panoply of tools and institutions that make up a GNN in the Chinese push into Africa, the analysis generally stays on the level of soft power justification, as in this Canadian article: "From newspapers and magazines to satellite television and radio stations, China is investing heavily in African media. It's part of a long-term campaign to bolster Beijing's 'soft power'—not just through diplomacy, but also through foreign aid, business links, scholarships, training programs, academic institutes and the media" (York 2013, par. 3). Another example is the important volume edited by Zhang, Wasserman, and Mano (2016), *Chinese Media and Soft Power in Africa*.

26. Personal communication with Ugandan research assistant Jawoko, 2015.

27. Olander 2015a, par. 1.

28. For example, the "full scale diplomatic crisis" originating from "the Kenyan government's consent to a Chinese request for the deportation of dozens of alleged cyber and telecom fraud" (Olander 2015a, par. 1).

and looks to the potential markets and economic opportunities of the continent so that when "African policy makers scan the globe in search of inspiration on how to structure their economies, that search often leads to Beijing."[29]

While the flow of information and intelligence from these type III GNNs interacts directly with the state party and governing apparatus, there is also an important soft power component in the operations of these GNNs. The soft power policy framework is the policy-aligned ideological framework developed and implemented by the PRC's Central Propaganda Department. All GNN flows are affected and shaped by this framework. As my source pointed out, the framework does not constrict the free flow of information but does exert editorial parameters on that flow so that information assembly and collection is understood to be strategically aligned with state plans, supportive of state goals, and profitable for state policies, industry, and the face the PRC presents to the world. My source concluded that the various GNN entities exist for one purpose: "CCTV and Xinhua exist to serve the state. Period."[30] He went on to say that the structural hierarchies and systems for regulating the flow of information and intelligence support GNNs' singular charge.

Non-Western NGOs

Russia[31] and China approach Western INGOs with the assumption that their performance and work product are directed by and directly serve the state. This assumption matches the assumption in the West that non-Western NGOs are surely engaged in state-sponsored and under-written activities, and nearly always include intelligence gathering in

---

29. Olander 2015b, par. 1.

30. Personal communication, 2014.

31. A Latvian report (Jemberga 2015, par. 1) studied the detailed relationships between the Kremlin holds and various NGOs it sponsors abroad with the intention of extending Russian foreign policy goals and keeping the Russian intelligence services informed. It asserts that "with one hand, Kremlin strangles non-governmental organizations in Russia. With another, it generously supports the defenders of its interests in the Baltics. Russia's President Vladimir Putin knows what poses the greatest threat to the domestic stability in his country: it comes from foreign-sponsored nongovernmental organizations (NGOs) who serve as agents of Russia's enemies."

their operations. One organization, the International Fund for Animal Welfare (IFAW), prominently proclaims its advocacy and intelligence work, touting its ability to share its findings with Chinese officials in the pursuit of illegal poaching and sale of ivory.[32] Less successful examples of cooperation between international NGOs and the state abound and can create or increase tension between states.[33]

The rise of Chinese NGOs as part of a larger type III GNN institutional structure has been relatively rapid. Already, Chinese NGOs are following the lead of some Chinese GNN news organizations and expanding operations in Africa and Asia. Notably, "state actors are not the only ones involved in China's internationalization. Chinese nongovernmental organizations (NGOs), too, have begun to 'go abroad,' setting up in Africa and Southeast Asia.[34] They are funded in part by Chinese state-owned enterprises and the Chinese state (in the form of 'government-organized NGOs' or GONGOs) further muddying the difficult distinction between state and non-state actors in China's overseas presence."[35] While NGOs are, by definition, nongovernmental, they often receive substantial funding and direction from the government and coordinate with the state to form part of Western GNNs' hard power capacity. "In the Chinese case, however, the NGOs doing the teaching were born, socialized and evolved in an authoritarian institutional environment, in which they have adapted to tight state supervision and limitations."[36]

At the same time as China is spreading its newly established NGO presence globally, it has imposed onerous new restrictions and laws on INGOs operating inside China. "Beijing is already suspicious of foreign and Chinese nongovernment organizations that receive funding from outside sources deemed politically suspect, like the National Endowment for Democracy and the Open Society Foundations, both based in the

---

32. International Fund for Animal Welfare 2012.

33. Herman 1996.

34. The rapid rise of Chinese NGOs does not mean that as of yet they are successful. A case study of Malawi and Ethiopia found that "irrespective of regime type, Chinese NGOs have yet to make a substantial impact" (Hsu, Hildebrandt, and Hasmath 2016, 423).

35. Hasmath 2016, par. 4.

36. Hasmath 2016, par. 11.

United States. Groups that operate here with any financing from those sources will be even more vulnerable under the new law."[37]

China: Diplomacy

As discussed earlier in this book, a unique feature of Xinhua's 107 foreign bureaus is that they are sometimes located on the property of diplomatic missions, confounding the differences between independent journalistic functions and state-underwritten and operational functions. Until 1997, for example, the Xinhua bureau in Hong Kong was the de facto PRC diplomatic mission in the unrecognized British territory.[38] This is a formal diplomatic representation that manifests the dual role of Xinhua. Further, in 1958, Xinhua news agency was China's only permanent presence in Peru and served as the de facto embassy, hosting functions and acting as a plenipotentiary much like any other ambassador of a sovereign nation. Peru's official recognition of the People's Republic of China came much later, on November 2, 1971.

Aside from performing diplomatic duties at times, Xinhua correspondents actively develop alternative public narratives. They create factual stories that have no relevance to intelligence collection, reporting on issues that are primarily relevant to the Chinese state. Targeted reporting allows the reports to maintain relevance to their sponsors. In states that once had reporting resources on the ground in areas where Xinhua is now predominant, not only are non-Chinese policy makers deprived of relevant data but they are denied access to undistributed information that Xinhua personnel maintain within their organization. Xinhua aims to serve its audience, the Chinese state, with facts and reporting

---

37. Wong 2016, par. 30. Curbing the civil society work of INGOs in China is certainly one aspect of the state's legal action. However, reports did not mention if part of the goal was to curtail any intelligence-gathering capacities of Western type II GNNs operating within China.

38. Lai 2007. According to Lai, the Liaison Office of the Central People's Government in the Hong Kong Special Administrative Region is the PRC's representational office to Hong Kong, originally established in 1947 as the Xinhua News Agency and renamed in January 2000. Xinhua played a direct diplomatic role, with the chief of its news organization operating as ambassador to a country it did not officially recognize.

oriented toward this audience rather than secondary audiences' needs and interests.

A feature of GNN foreign correspondence is that reporters often take a national (and nationalistic) perspective in their approach to their topics. In the most extreme cases, as in wartime, the correspondents interact intimately with their national forces and militaries and lose objectivity, as for example, when Bob Bazell of NBC reported on the first night of battle in the first Gulf War that "we only lost one casualty." The well-known American news reporter Dan Rather ended his interview with an American general by vigorously shaking the general's hand and saying, "Congratulations on a job wonderfully done!"[39] The examples continue in that war, including a US colonel passing out American flags to pool reporters and telling them, "You are warriors, too!"[40]

The same relationships hold true for those who are now employed by the evolving Chinese news and information networks, with varied levels of awareness of these biasing pressures. In Nairobi, where the Chinese established a large television network in January 2012, there has been high-level hiring of native broadcast and journalism talent to collect, gather, edit, and present news on television for African audiences using familiar and credible African news presenters. A longitudinal but informal content analysis done by me of the news product on this network reflected an uncritical approach toward stories where the topic is China or involves a Chinese subject. This has been confirmed in content analysis carried out by Vivien Marsh.[41]

China has focused much of its early GNN expansion efforts in countries with high favorability ratings, welcoming leaders, and a possibility

---

39. *CBS Evening News*, February 1991, cited in Craige 1996, 115.

40. These and other examples from the first Gulf War are cited by Naureckas (1991). For an analysis of the "patriotism" of US GNNs during the first Gulf War, see Craige 1996.

41. Marsh 2016. This analysis compares *Africa Live* on CCTV and BBC's *Focus on Africa* over two weeks in 2014. It finds that the two media outlets' coverage of the same events was rather different. Most important, the researcher notes the "relentlessly positive reporting on Chinese investment and development projects" (Marsh 2016, 63) on CCTV's program, in marked contrast to its other reporting. Marsh concludes that in general the narrative promoted by CCTV is not so much "Africa rising" but rather "China rising."

to leverage its substantial financial heft to gain access and favor.[42] China also focuses disproportionately on countries that maintain diplomatic relations with and continue to recognize Taiwan.[43] "The Chinese efforts often result in helping authoritarian governments expand control of their local media, while working to undermine the Western model of a free and independent media."[44] China's GNNs extend the state's power to achieve its policy objectives, an accepted function for non-Western type III structures.

The case of Africa was investigated in depth, revealing the high level of access accorded to the new Chinese GNNs on the continent. Research showed the Chinese GNNs to be pursuing soft power goals, while also achieving diplomatically relevant engagements and relations, leading to access at the highest levels of African governments. According to the director of the African Media Research Center, Yanqui Zhang,

China's media is much more visible in Africa, not only the state-owned media like CCTV Africa, *China Daily, Africa Weekly, Beijing Review* as well as with Xinhua News Agency, China Radio International (CRI), but also private media companies, like Star Times, the private Chinese digital pay TV operator. Meanwhile, over the last decade, as Africa's largest trade partner, China has also invested in building communications infrastructure in Africa, providing technical upgrades for state broadcasters and training journalists from across the continent.[45]

The first Forum on China-Africa cooperation (FOCAC), held in 2000, focused on countering criticism from the West, dealing in part with

42. Farah and Mosher 2010. This report looked at Chinese GNN presence and expansion and stated, "A great deal of emphasis is placed on forming alliances that are anti-Western and on promoting an anti-Western media model to combat what the Chinese regularly portray as part of an imperialist plan to distort the truth" (4).

43. Taiwan remains a high-priority policy issue for the PRC. "A secondary but important purpose in China's new emphasis on media outreach is to demonstrate the benefits of a relationship with the PRC to those nations that still have diplomatic relations with Taiwan. The diplomatic isolation of Taiwan remains a high priority for the PRC, and the bulk of the countries that recognize Taiwan are in Latin America and Africa" (Farah and Mosher 2010, 4). For example, China recently reestablished ties with the tiny sub-Saharan country of Gambia, one of the small number of states that had recognized Taiwan (Bloomberg 2016; Browne 2016).

44. Farah and Mosher 2010, 4.

45. Y. Zhang 2014, 3.

how China was portrayed as a neocolonial power.[46] China promised to build a media relationship promoting a positive African image worldwide. "Cooperation in the media sector was one of the eight principles of the Chinese policy of cooperation with Africa that was announced during the first FOCAC [promoted at] . . . the first China-Africa Media conference in Nairobi, and the first China-Africa Media forums in August 2012 in Beijing."[47]

FOCAC was a catalyst for new Chinese companies aimed at African-Chinese cooperation: Xinhua Mobile started the first-ever mobile newspaper in sub-Saharan Africa.[48] Chinese GNNs are complemented by numerous media products developed in the last few years, including the African CGTN channel in Nairobi and the inauguration of Chin-Africa Media and Publishing (Pty) Ltd. in Pretoria (owned by the larger Beijing-based China International Publishing Group, CIPG), which produces *ChinAfrica*, an English- and French-language magazine. In Nairobi, the company started a weekly African edition of China's most important state English-language print publication, *China Daily*. Chinese GNNs' presence in Africa is further enhanced by expanding from eighteen Xinhua News Agency bureaus to twenty-five in 2013. Further, an academic GNN component was added to the constellation of Chinese media structures with the creation of the first institute for African media research, the Africa Communication Research Center at the Communication University of China.[49] The aim of this institute is to be "a first-class academic platform for research of and cooperation between Chinese and African media," according to the director of the African Communication Research Center, Yanqui Zhan.[50] This center represents Chinese GNNs' engagement in Africa's media landscape and encourages GNNs to present a positive relationship between China and Africa, or, according to Liu

---

46. Forum on China-Africa Cooperation 2013.

47. Chichava, Côrtes, and Orre 2014, 3.

48. Xinhua 2011.

49. This complements academic elements of Chinese influence over Africa. The number of African students studying in China has risen exponentially, from 2,757 in 2005 to 49,792 in 2015 (Gu 2017). FOCAC also grants scholarships for academic exchange; in 2009–15, 34,500 scholarships were awarded (Gu 2017).

50. Xinrui 2013, par. 15.

Guangyuan, China's former ambassador in Kenya, "[to] tell the world the true 'Chinese story' and the true 'African story.'"[51] Chinese GNNs continue to grow in Africa:

CCTV launched its first overseas news production center, CCTV Africa in Nairobi in January 2012, which has been hailed as a new voice of Africa. The launch of CCTV Africa is a milestone in the sense that CCTV has become the first international media to establish a news production center in Africa. CCTV Africa is responsible for gathering news from the continent and distributing to a global audience through the CCTV News platform. In addition, CCTV has become the first international media to dedicate more time to Africa through CCTV Africa programs such as Africa Live, Talk Africa and Faces of Africa. On average it can be noted that CCTV has a minimum of 10 hours in a week for Africa to tell its story to the world.[52]

CGTN and other Chinese GNNs, like *China Daily*, are tasked with carrying out China's grand plan for Africa. As Newton Ndebu of CGTN Africa noted, China's journalism model is based on portraying Africa in a "new positive light"[53] as a place of resourcefulness, entrepreneurship, and innovation.[54] Ndebu dismisses fears about China's likely influence on professional standards in the media. He says the entry of Chinese media into Africa poses no threat to the practice of journalism in Kenya and Africa and that "as the world transitions from the information age to the knowledge era, there is hunger in Africa to bridge the knowledge gap that currently exists between it and the rest of the world. Many Africans are eager to be part of a new intelligent narrative that acknowledges the challenges in Africa but does not reduce these challenges into simplistic explanations. Overall, CCTV is attempting to do that."[55]

Bob Wekesa, a former journalist and journalism research associate at the University of the Witwatersrand, South Africa, focuses on soft power effects and argues that when it comes to content on CGTN, there

---

51. Guangyuan 2011.

52. Y. Zhang 2014, 4.

53. This "positive light" has been called "positive reporting" (Gagliardone 2013) or "constructive journalism" and argued to be a new journalistic paradigm introduced by Chinese media in Africa (e.g., Zhang and Matingwina 2016).

54. Personal communication from Kennedy Jawoko, December 2, 2014.

55. Personal communication from Kennedy Jawoko, December 2, 2014.

is "hardly a bent towards a communist persuasion. . . . Rather, one sees Chinese media on a public diplomacy mission, angling stories to show the benefits of China-Africa relations while avoiding narratives that cast China in a negative light."[56]

From December 27, 2014, to January 22, 2015, my research assistant, Kennedy Jawoko, conducted content analysis of CCTV's *Talk Africa*, a thirty-minute weekly talk show that covers current affairs in Africa on the platform of CCTV Africa. He summarized his findings and identified strategic geopolitical GNN engagement by corroborating Wekesa's analysis. He finds that *"Talk Africa* [is] a deliberate and ideologically loaded program," exemplified by what Wekesa describes as an undercurrent of West versus non-West frames:

The overwhelming majority of Kenyan episodes are about the country's electioneering and political leadership. . . . On the surface, these episodes may seem domestic to Kenya and therefore not worth the extensive coverage by a CCTV Africa that conceives of itself as a continental broadcaster. Closer examination reveals the geopolitical underpinnings informing this selection in that the presidential candidacy of Uhuru Kenyatta and his running mate William Ruto (and their eventual triumph at the ballot) was mired by their indictment by the International Criminal Court (ICC) — seen as a Western tool used to target African leaders — for crimes against humanity.[57]

Wekesa here presents Western GNNs as actively promoting a negative political outcome for the Kenyan presidential race and sees Chinese GNNs as a counter to that narrative as well as a successful diplomatic tool.

Access to leaders is necessary to perform diplomatic functions or achieve higher-order intelligence gathering. Chinese GNNs have successfully achieved a high level and frequency of access to the continent's political leadership, in this case for CGTN.

The high number of exclusive interviews with African presidents was telling: Sudan's Hassan Omar El-Bashir; South Sudan's Salva Kiir Maryadit; Ghana's John Dramani Mahama;

---

56. Wekesa 2014a, par. 5.
57. Wekesa 2014b, 12.

Burundi's Pierre Nkrunziza; Somalia's Hassan Sheikh Mohamoud; Kenya's Uhuru Kenyatta; Nigeria's Goodluck Jonathan; Gabon's Omar Bongo Odimba; Malawi's Joyce Banda and Peter Mutharika and Seychelles's James Michel. The number of presidential interviews is a feat given that securing presidential interviews is often a difficult journalistic task for many seasoned African journalists. In addition, there is quite a good number of interviews with high ranking officials at the levels of diplomats and statesmen including former UN secretary general Kofi Annan and former Nigerian president Olusegun Obasanjo to mention but two. Contingent on the fact of CCTV Africa securing these top-level-official-guests, often in their state houses/palaces, most of these prized interviewees have a kind word for China's role in their countries or the continent at large. Interestingly, the high level guests speak in favor of China on their own volition but when they don't, the anchor is more likely than not to directly or indirectly nudge them towards their commenting on China.[58]

CGTN journalist Ndebu believes that there is a lot of freedom working for a Chinese GNN and that criticism of "positive reporting" as a sign of poor CGTN journalism is unwarranted, saying that African journalists are not "trained" to follow the Chinese policy script.[59] Ndebu acknowledges, however, that there is an understanding at CGTN that the way Western media covers China in Africa is biased and that it needs to be challenged. He notes that as a line-up producer, he is one of the key people who decide what to put out. The CGTN staff in Nairobi meet each morning at 9:30 a.m. to plan the news day and get input from Beijing and Washington, DC, CGTN's main newsgathering arms. "But we also have to balance what everybody else is putting out. We watch all our competitors and see how we can make a story fit our model," says Ndebu. "We prefer stories where we have our own outlook on things. So we do not rely very much on the wires. We send our own reporters where we can but we have a long leash because there is a lot of freedom."[60]

---

58. Wekesa 2014b, 17–18.

59. At the same time, the Communication University of China (CUC) has reportedly "trained or educated more than a hundred journalists or government officials from Africa through its Radio and Television Newsgathering and Editing for African Countries Program" (Xinrui 2013). The alumni include Bob Wekesa, who earned his PhD at CUC.

60. Directed personal communication with Kennedy Jawoko, 2014.

Ndebu says there are some instances when they take guidance from Beijing. He says that coverage of the 2014 visit to Africa by China's president was all dictated by Beijing. "On some foreign policy issues related to China, we get guidance from Beijing," said Ndebu, but he did not elaborate, saying he had little information on the details. Ndebu, who was one of the journalists sent to Beijing on a "familiarization tour," points out that in the management structure of CGTN, all the senior managers (managing editor, deputy editor, and bureau chief) are Chinese.[61] Chinese GNNs are involved in nearly every stage of the news and information-gathering process, in an environment that often seems neglected by the rest of the world.

Moses Wasemu, a Kenyan freelance journalist covering China in Africa, pointed out that African countries receive scant coverage from international Western media, and that CGTN and Al Jazeera are "a breath of fresh air—giving Africa a positive face" but also portraying the challenges the continent faces "in [a] more humane way rather than the doom and gloom of the Western media's coverage of Africa."[62] Wasemu believes that African audiences relate better to non-Western GNNs.

Jonathan Mueke, the deputy governor of Nairobi City County, suggests that apart from the symbolic political cum public diplomacy projects in which Chinese GNNs participate, much more takes place at both official and unofficial levels to buttress Chinese soft power.[63] This is why, he argues, "media play a key role" in any society as information sources on what is happening not only within the local environment but also beyond. In this regard, Mueke argues, "Chinese media is doing what every other country's media does. "It is serving as the face of China in Africa by playing a key role in shaping African attitudes towards the Chinese people and products. China has strategically made investments in media, and CCTV is one of those investments."

---

61. Marsh also observed that at the time of her research, much of the offscreen workforce of (then) CCTV was Chinese (Marsh 2016, 64).

62. Directed personal communication with Kennedy Jawoko on November 24, 2014, January 10, 2015, and January 20, 2015. Other researchers have made similar observations (e.g., Zhang and Matingwina 2016).

63. Personal communication with Kennedy Jawoko on November 26, 2014, January 10, 2015, and January 20, 2015.

Another way GNNs engage with African media is through the China-Africa Reporting Project in the University of Witwatersrand's Journalism Department, which focuses on developing journalism on Africa-China issues. Whether through academic institutions such as these or news outlets like CGTN or *China Daily*, GNNs actively blur the line between the Chinese government and other Chinese state and quasi-private entities that seek African market prominence, if not outright dominance. Christine Nagujja, digital television communication manager for Star-Times (Uganda), gave an example of that strategic market dominance strategy by sharing that China's StarTimes is leading the market in East Africa (Kenya, Tanzania, Rwanda, Burundi, and Uganda), with an 80 percent share in the Ugandan market, for example. The StarTimes mission: "To enable every African family to afford digital TV, to watch digital TV, and to enjoy digital TV."[64]

The Chinese state currently expends considerable resources to establish Confucius Institutes worldwide. Africa is no exception. These government-funded institutions promote Chinese language, culture, and understanding and serve as centers for outreach to local media, with the first Confucius Institute established in Kenya in 2005 at the University of Nairobi. These institutes resemble Western nonprofit educational institutions and find their homes within academic institutions, but they are funded and managed by the Chinese state. Confucius Institute personnel and instructors are selected and paid by the Chinese state.

In a speech on December 1, 2014, at the Confucius Institute at the University of Nairobi, Wang Zheng, director of the Institute of West-Asian and African Studies at the Chinese Academy of Social Sciences, insisted that China and Africa must speak more to each other through Chinese and African media.[65] Zheng believes that media outlets such as CCTV are key to securing a more cooperative relationship between the two regions. This cooperative relationship between Chinese GNNs and a host region reflects not only the level of access accorded these GNN institutions but also a deep intermingling of resources and personnel,

---

64. StarTimes 2016, par. 5.
65. Kennedy Jawoko in attendance; personal communication, November 30, 2014.

training that reinforces policy proximity, collaborative information research, analysis, and distribution—and all within a practical and professional GNN context that aligns cultural attitudes, political interests, perspectives, and policies. Chinese GNNs have found welcoming entry points in the developing world, but their expanding operations are not limited to these regions.

In the United States and other developed countries, CGTN/X has begun serious efforts to develop a news and information infrastructure in capital cities. Western employees' awareness of bias varies here too, but in a seemingly candid moment, Barbara Dury, a former CBS producer for *60 Minutes* who worked for CCTV-America developing and producing its news magazine broadcast *Americas Now,* said that she was "keenly aware of the issue" of sensitivities that may affect CCTV-America—even though there had been no explicit attempt at censorship. She said she "believes that it could happen, for example, on topics such as Taiwan or Tibet."[66]

The relationship between states and news organizations can also be viewed as interdependence. States rely on news organizations, just as policy and security analysts depend upon reporting from a region. Diplomatic, military, and intelligence agency analysts, whether they are at foreign embassy missions or in their national capitals, spend much of the day following the media reports of what is happening on the ground. They spend a considerable part of their time analyzing, comparing, and distilling the meaning of events abroad based on media actualities and analyses.[67]

Another part of this GNN–foreign policy intelligence nexus is the informal relationship between journalists and policy makers or diplomats. This informal relationship is as important as it is conventional. It is most

---

66. Quoted in Hille 2012, par. 15. Time and again, CGTN is shown to display such "sensitivities." Recently, for example, the *Washington Post* noted that CCTV-America's coverage of the Panama Papers failed to include any of the powerful Chinese individuals named in the documents (Rauhala 2016). At the same time, Marsh (2017) and others find that in its reporting on areas with low Chinese interest, CGTN's approach is often very similar to that of Western news outlets.

67. As Kingsbury (2008, par. 5) notes in a magazine piece, "The use of nonclassified information, whether news accounts or other publicly retrievable information, is gaining credibility within the intelligence community."

casually represented in the form of the cocktail party but exists in more structured forums, including organized debriefs, think-tank lectures, background conferencing, notebook dumps, and personal blog entries. The informality of the engagement does not mean that these information exchanges have little significance for policy analysis and formation. Oftentimes, the information gathering done by foreign correspondents reaches into parts of foreign societies and cultures that are inaccessible to more traditional intelligence-gathering institutions and often unique and of high value.[68] GNNs' institutional and individual access and their credibility open doors that are often closed to non-GNNs, freelancers, and other individuals not affiliated with institutions.

Research into these otherwise inapparent aspects of newsgathering organizations and networks indicates that the current trends in resource allocation for global reporting result in increased capabilities for non-Western GNNs. If this is the case, then not only are Chinese capacities increasing, putting them in a constantly improving position to gain or provide key elements of stories and analyses, but at the same time, non-Chinese analysts and policy makers are being deprived of one of their traditional sources of informal intelligence gathering.[69]

Russia: Diplomacy

Russia has a direct relationship with its state-owned GNNs but has not elevated this relationship to fully credentialed diplomatic status. Russia's news services play a highly visible and active role, but they do not issue visas or sign treaty documents. However, that does not preclude these institutions from acting as intermediaries or mediators, nor does it diminish the close relationship between Russian GNNs and the diplomatic corps of their nation.

---

68. As posited in Kaiser's Brookings Institution essay (2014, par. 3), which looks at the business market challenge for Western GNNs to produce high-quality, high-level access information, "there is no right to reliable, intelligent, comprehensive journalism. We only get it when someone provides it. And if it doesn't pay someone a profit, it's not likely to be produced."

69. See Figure 1 in chapter 1, depicting how intelligence gathering and analysis are a determined aspect of GNNs' functions.

Highly visible news vehicles in the United States include not only the RT video news product, ubiquitous on YouTube, but the nationally distributed newspaper section insert "Russia beyond the Headlines"[70] (RBTH), now called "Russia Beyond." Operated by the government-owned *Rossiyskaya Gazeta*, this eight-page supplement is added to major non-Russian newspapers in twenty-six countries and sixteen languages. In the United States, it appears within the pages of the *Wall Street Journal*, the *New York Times*, and the *Washington Post*. According to its website, "RBTH's **mission** is to contribute to a better understanding of Russia in the world, be it ordinary citizens, public officials, opinion experts or entrepreneurs."[71]

RBTH is based in Washington, DC, and forms part of the Russian GNN firmament. It employs and engages non-Russian personnel to report, write, and edit the material, proclaiming itself to be "in compliance with standards of journalism, editorial polices and traditions of countries in which the content is published."[72] In the course of researching this work, I made multiple attempts to engage with various Russian GNN representatives, to little avail. The only response came as a result of the direct diplomatic engagement of the Russian Consulate General of San Francisco and the intervention of press attaché Evgeny Avdoshin, who elicited a response from Olga Guitchounts, the RBTH representative in Washington, DC. In an email on October 27, 2014, Mr. Avdoshin made clear the line of command and the relationship his diplomatic mission has with RBTH: "I want to make sure that they do get back to you, so let me know if anyone got in touch with you already. If not, I will make sure they are reminded :)." While many news organizations enjoy friendly relations with their domestic diplomatic corps, only state-owned media understand that they are a part of a chain of command. Mr. Avdoshin was solicitous of my efforts and was able to get direct results.

The organization structure of news agencies in Russia and China is pyramidal: the hierarchy leads up to the upper echelons of political or

---

70. Shafer 2007.
71. *Russia Beyond*, https://www.rbth.com.
72. *Russia Beyond*, https://www.rbth.com.

party leadership, as with Cai Mingzhao,[73] a former Chinese Communist Party State Council leader, or, in Russia, Kremlin loyalist Dmitry Kiselyov as head of RT.[74] While the state-run organizations might operate semiautonomously and have specific missions that are not directly related to state operation, these organizations always serve under the authority (or at the very least, subject to the benevolence) of the state.[75]

Formerly, the Soviet Union's practice of using TASS reporters as part of the *legal rezidentura* employee structure of the USSR[76] provided journalists with official diplomatic cover for their activities and a chain of command that was officially recognized, if somewhat obfuscated. This official diplomatic relationship is no longer a Russian state practice. Russian GNN journalists, in whatever capacity, now operate officially outside the confines of official embassy structures.

Non-Western GNNs: Intelligence Gathering

Congressman Dana Rohrabacher has used his role in the Foreign Affairs subcommittee to point out, in specific terms, some of the institutional and individual intelligence-gathering roles performed by Chinese journalists. He stated that of the hundreds of Chinese nationals sent to the United States every year, some may be real reporters but many function as intelligence officers; they report on what is happening in the United States regarding issues of concern to Chinese leaders—including the movements of Tibetan activists and Chinese dissidents—and write secret cables accessible only to a select few.[77]

---

73. Pinghui 2014.

74. Associated Press 2013. According to the *New York Times*, the appointment of Kiselyov, previously a television program host, came as a shock to many RT employees. Kiselyov then set out to define RT's editorial policy to the staff as "love for Russia" (Rutenberg 2017).

75. Schudson 2002. In this broad review of media institutions, Schudson identifies ownership and behavior of news institutions as a means of study that differentiates practices between relatively liberal and relatively repressive states, in this case, Russia and China.

76. Gruntman 2010, 17. As Gruntman points out in his analysis of KGB activities in California, Soviet journalists operated directly out of or in direct relation to Soviet embassies responsive to the *legal rezidentura*: "Most Soviet KGB and GRU intelligence officers commonly operated in the United States and other countries under official diplomatic cover. They posed as staff members of embassies and consulates or as journalists" (17).

77. Rohrabacher 2013.

According to Rohrabacher, the U.S.-China Economic and Security Review Commission, the congressional body responsible for monitoring national security issues between the two countries, reported in 2009 that "China's official Xinhua state news agency also serves some of the functions of an intelligence agency, gathering information and producing classified reports for the Chinese leadership on both domestic and international events."[78] Furthermore, "the Ministry of State Security [a Chinese ministry roughly equivalent to the CIA and FBI] also makes extensive use of the news media covers, sending agents abroad as correspondents for the state news agency Xinhua and as reporters for newspapers such as the *People's Daily* and *China Youth Daily*."[79] In its 2017 report, the commission stated that "Xinhua serves some of the functions of an intelligence agency by gathering information and producing classified reports for the Chinese leadership."[80] According to CNN, it recommended that all US-based staff of Chinese media organizations be registered under the Foreign Agents Registration Act.[81]

Institutionally, Chinese GNNs—and CGTN/X specifically—are, in essence, an extension of the intelligence-gathering services. Given the highly sensitive nature of this relationship, it appears in few public reports. In one, a Canadian reporter, Mark Bourrie, left the Xinhua agency because of demands that he perform intelligence duties.[82] This formal institutional relationship between China's GNNs and the state intelligence apparatus was investigated by the international organization Reporters without Borders and, while the report focused on the propaganda aspects of Xinhua, it established traditional as well as contemporary ties.[83]

---

78. Bartholomew 2009, 153.

79. Bartholomew 2009, 151. The congressman wrote this piece for *Foreign Policy* to attract attention to the practice and to advocate for a restriction on working visas for Chinese reporters in the United States.

80. US-China Economic and Security Review Commission 2017, 475.

81. Shane 2017.

82. Green 2012. Bourrie told the reporter that, for example, he was instructed "to collect names of all present at Falun Gong press conferences" (par. 3). Further, Falun Gong's Ottawa spokesperson Lucy Zhou said it was "not unusual for . . . Xinhua staff . . . to collect names and take an unusual number of close-up pictures at protests" (par. 3).

83. The report found that "with more than 8,000 employees and 105 branches worldwide, the official news agency, Xinhua, is at the heart of censorship and disinformation put in place by the communist party" (Reporters without Borders 2005, par. 1).

One of the more detailed reports came from a Chinese Foreign Ministry defector who has lived in Australia since 2005. Chen Yonglin was extensively quoted in the *Epoch Times*, saying of reporters' propaganda roles that they play a critical systemic role in formal institutional intelligence gathering: "In addition, they play the role of a spy because Xinhua is actually an outreach organ of CCP's intelligence agencies. The nature of their work means they must use all means to infiltrate and obtain intelligence."[84] Chen elaborated, "As part of an intelligence network, Xinhua reporters are often under two different bosses, maybe even three different bosses, mainly CCP officials. . . . If they were sent by the Ministry of State Security (MSS), then they report to the MSS, if they were sent by PLA (People's Liberation Army) General Staff Department, then they answer to the PLA General Staff Department; they all have secret missions. At the same time, they help the Consulate with political and propaganda work."[85]

As for Russia, the Soviets recruited the investigative reporter and journalist gadfly I. F. Stone and, as revealed in KGB files available for a brief moment after the collapse of the USSR, even engaged the journalist and author Ernest Hemingway, under the codename "Argo." Hemingway reportedly may not have done much, if any, work for the KGB but was enthralled by the idea of espionage.[86] The number of NOCs in Europe and the United States formally working for the Soviets, some directly for the KGB, specifically in journalism positions was said to be at least 150 just prior to the empire's collapse, according to Yuri Yarim-Agaev. Yarim-Agaev found out about the number of NOCs during discussions with former Russian acting prime minister Mikhail Kasyanov.[87]

Academics are also often part of the GNN intelligence-gathering network. A Chinese example of this GNN practice was recently brought to light when, in a case of academic espionage, the American Department

---

84. Luo 2011, par. 10.
85. Luo 2011, par. 12.
86. Haynes, Vassiliev, and Kehr 2009.
87. Yuri Yarim-Agaev, personal communication, 2014. Yarim-Agaev was part of the Moscow Helsinki Group and a leader of the human rights movement in Russia who was invited by the Yeltsin government to develop a system securing the exchange of free information in Russia. He was recently a Hoover Institution visiting fellow.

of Justice charged "six Chinese citizens, including three professors who trained together at the University of Southern California" with stealing "sensitive wireless technology from U.S. companies and spirit[ing] it back to China."[88]

The Chinese Ministry of State Security (MSS) considers open-source intelligence to be an important informal means of institutional data collection. Here the direct intelligence relationship is complemented by an informal system of data aggregation and reporting that, according to Western intelligence analysts and individuals familiar with CGTN/X protocols, is a focused and active practice. As described in the *Intelligence Threat Handbook*, "Other MSS activities, however, would not normally be conducted by a Western service. 'Strategic Intelligence,' for example, consists of culling information from sources such as People magazine, talking to pundits about prognostications, and then combining the two into a classified intelligence product for consumption by PRC leaders. The MSS considers it to be worthy of assigning intelligence resources to this product. In the West, this would be considered only news or news analysis."[89] Likewise, "unregistered agents" of the Russian government have been found sending open-source intelligence back to Moscow. In a 2010 case where the Russian effort seemed vastly disproportionate to the hoped benefit, a "spy ring" of eleven people, placed in the US suburbs, were instructed "to collect routine political gossip and policy talk that might have been more efficiently gathered by surfing the Web."[90]

The Soviet Union and its successor state, Russia, have always used news organizations as intelligence-gathering operations with direct links to the KGB.[91] As Julia Ioffe puts it, "In the Soviet era, a journalist was understood to be a Kremlin trumpet, and journalism was simply another

---

88. Grossman 2015, par. 1. In recent years, there have been a number of high-profile arrests for espionage of ethnic Chinese and Chinese nationals in the United States, raising the concern that American law enforcement is "racially profiling" (Guillermo 2015).

89. Interagency OPSEC Support Staff 2004, 22.

90. Shane and Weiser 2010, par. 3.

91. Haynes, Vassiliev, and Kehr 2009. Haynes and his coauthors write, "A 1941 KGB summary report broke down the occupations of Americans working for the spy agency in the prior decade. Twenty-two were journalists, a profession outnumbered only by engineers (forty-nine) and dwarfing economists (four) and professors (eight)" (331).

government job."[92] Ioffe claims the tradition has continued in Russia, through the KGB's successor intelligence organization, the Russian Foreign Intelligence Service (SVR): "In post-Soviet Russia, the idea that the press is essentially a branch of the government never truly went away."[93] That Russian journalists work as Russian foreign intelligence agents is a basic assumption in the industry.[94]

The highest-profile case to date is the New York "spy ring" case involving the ITAR-TASS news agency,[95] officially denied by both the news agency and its government sponsor. In the case, a Manhattan banker named Evgeny Buryakov, recruited by accused Russian spy Igor Sporyshev, was asked by Sporyshev to come up with questions "to put in the mouth of a journalist for a Russian news outlet, who is apparently interviewing someone with privileged knowledge of the New York Stock Exchange."[96] It was confirmed that the Russian news outlet was ITAR-TASS. Buryakov formulated questions about how the automated trading in the NY Stock Exchange works and what forces might be disruptive to trading. Oleg Kalugin, an ex-KGB general who ran operations in the United States, admitted that TASS was involved in spying: "Tass has long been a den of spies. 'At least half if not more [of Tass employees] were involved in the intelligence business' during the Cold War."[97]

The Russian news organization's relationship with the Russian state intelligence-gathering operation exemplifies the formal relationships between institutions. The individuals involved in the operations are not always engaged in a formal relationship, often working as unwitting

---

92. Ioffe 2015, par. 5.

93. Ioffe 2015, par. 6. Ioffe goes on to say that socialized in this tradition, lots of Russians suppose that American media work the same way: "When I was traveling around Siberia a couple of years ago and introduced myself to people as an American journalist, many of them immediately assumed I was a C.I.A. agent" (par. 6).

94. S. Harris 2015. This was best summarized in a report regarding Russia's TASS news agency: "The agency has a long history of giving cover to Russian spies, current and former intelligence officials say" (par. 1).

95. S. Harris 2015.

96. Ioffe 2015, par. 2.

97. S. Harris 2015, par. 11. I met with Kalugin at the NBC Moscow bureau on Gruzinsky Pereulok during my time living and working in Russia, specifically while reporting on a story in 1992 regarding the assassination of President John F. Kennedy and the relationship between Lee Harvey Oswald and the KGB.

agents or suppliers of news, information, and data. However, in the ITAR-TASS New York case, Evgeny Buryakov was accused of formally working for Russian intelligence. This high-profile case revealed an elaborate use of non-Russian nationals who were involved in a scheme with Russian officials to use multiple state institutions, from trade offices to journalistic organizations, to gather strategic information. Buryakov eventually pleaded guilty, was fined and sentenced to thirty months in prison, and finally deported to Russia in April 2017.

The prevalence of both institutional and individual direct engagement is, by its very nature, difficult to discern, and I am unable to draw definitive conclusions on collusion at institutional or individual levels. At the same time, there is evidence of this in past cases, and certainly this was true in the Buryakov affair.

Much of the data on formal Russian intelligence has been garnered via congressional investigation, judicial inquiry, law enforcement arrests,[98] or by defectors. Colonel Stanislav Lunev, who defected to the United States in 1992, identified a system by which Russian journalists worked as spies, as he had done prior to his defection: "He worked out of the National Press Building and filed hundreds of stories back to Moscow. Being a Tass correspondent provided perfect cover for Stanislav Lunev, Soviet spy."[99]

---

98. For example, of the ten suspected Russian spies arrested by the FBI in June 2010 in the United States, one had been working as a journalist. The *Washington Post* reported, "The defendants, eight of whom are married couples, held jobs in fields such as finance and media. One, Vicky Pelaez, was a reporter for a Spanish-language newspaper in New York" (Markon 2010, par. 12).

99. Loeb 2001, par. 1.

CHAPTER 5 | CONCLUSION

Foreign correspondents are neither spies nor diplomats. Regardless, they perform both intelligence-gathering and diplomatic functions, whether formally or informally, as the empirical and historical data of the preceding chapters indicate. The larger GNN framework in which they function makes their work and the work product materially relevant to the states they serve or the structures of the states in which the GNNs are based. For those in the journalism profession, this performance is uncomfortably counterintuitive; for most public diplomacy and agenda-setting analysts it is at most epiphenomenal and counterintuitive; and for states where GNNs are headquartered it is counternarrative with ambiguous legality.

The material nature of the work that GNNs do goes beyond the predominant understanding in the academic literature, which considers GNNs to be performing a public diplomatic practice and providing a source of power within a smart power framework that is limited mostly to the soft power side of the smart equation.

GNNs operate, in the broadest sense, not merely as institutions targeting foreign audiences to make their national sponsors or affiliated nations appear more attractive, as a soft power argument would assert, but also as sources and expressions of national hard power. Regardless of their type—type I (nonstate), type II (hybrid), or type III (state)— they all perform, formally or informally, hard power functions. The geo-political question that remains is what the dynamic changes in the GNN constellation of individuals and institutions might presage as this material resource of hard power weakens in states that dominated this resource in the twentieth century and as new and, in the case of China, rising powers overtake other states in the presence and, perhaps eventually, the performance of this resource.

The collection of empirical data for this research redirected the book from a focus on the relative shift of GNN resources from Western to non-Western states, with the hypothesis that this shift could indicate a shift in soft power capacities and lead to strengthened state counternarratives regarding ideologies, such as the ideological shift from a formerly dominant Washington consensus to an evolving Beijing consensus. Indeed, it was the search for narratives and counternarratives that led to my paper, "The Press and Pressure," in the *Brazilian Journalism Research Journal*.[1] That study focused on Chinese media and the discourse surrounding sovereignty versus responsibility to protect. I concluded that the Chinese type III (state) GNNs promoted PRC state policy preferences more faithfully and in a perfectly aligned manner. In this case, Chinese GNNs presented a unified voice critical of the policy of responsibility to protect (R2P) interventions in Syria while upholding a unified legal argument for maintenance of international norms bolstering the case for sovereignty.

The Chinese rising narrative combined with an equally prevalent Russian GNN voice to counter the Western call to action and provided an alternative argument that was used during the United Nations' Security Council attempts to gain support for intervention in the Syrian crisis.[2]

The new non-Western counternarratives create increasingly sophisticated, widely distributed, increasingly sourced, and financially underwritten type III GNN messaging to effectively counter a diluted, diminishing, relatively fragmented, and sometimes faltering Western narrative. The soft power dynamic of this contemporary worldwide GNN development is well documented in the academic literature. Nonetheless, there is not only a transfer of GNN soft power from the West to non-Western states, but also Western loss of GNN capacities—in particular, the relative loss of both diplomatic and intelligence-gathering capacities—which has a significant effect on hard power. For example, the combination of GNN power and the policy preferences of non-Western countries prevented

---

1. M. Kounalakis 2015a.
2. M. Kounalakis 2015a.

direct, multilateral, internationally sanctioned, collective humanitarian and interventionist actions in Syria.

Whether such an intervention would have changed the outcome of the Syrian conflict is beyond the scope of this work, which is focused on analyzing the way state capacities and policy preferences are manifested via different GNN types. In Syria, Western narratives and policy preferences at the United Nations were blocked, and non-Western policy narratives and policy preferences prevailed. GNNs contributed to that outcome.

While the earlier study of multiple GNN-type narratives and counternarratives proved intriguing and rich, unanticipated and, in many ways, culturally, socially, politically, and professionally taboo practices dominated the data regarding these dynamics. Most discomforting was the realization that I myself, in the course of a full career as a foreign correspondent,[3] had engaged directly, if informally, in practices that both supported the soft power equation in multiple Western countries and—albeit to an individually limited degree—underwrote the hard power material strengths of Western states while remaining unaware of this act and of its potential effects.

In the course of researching this work, it became ever more apparent that this taboo needed to be addressed as significant to the contemporary shift in GNNs, but that those admitting to this taboo mostly demanded to remain anonymous. On the one hand, the story needed to be told; on the other, those telling it wanted to remain in the shadows.

This need for anonymity resulted from a desire for self-protection as well as a broader professional concern for the protection of those continuing to serve GNNs as reporters, NGO workers, or academics. There are increasing numbers of Western GNN personnel around the

---

3. I have been a GNN foreign correspondent for much of my career, covering the wars and revolutions of Central Europe in the late 1980s and early 1990s for *Newsweek* as well as the dissolution of the Soviet Union from a position as NBC-Mutual News Moscow correspondent from 1991 to 1992. I later became the publisher and president of the *Washington Monthly*. My work in the GNN international shortwaves and with global broadcasters include work for Radio Sweden International, Deutsche Welle, Radio New Zealand, and MonitorRadio.

world who are currently being held hostage or facing trial for spying. Until recently, Jason Rezaian of the *Washington Post* was one of those threatened individuals.

Rezaian was detained for 544 days in Tehran in 2015[4] and convicted on charges of espionage. The findings regarding GNNs' inherent and developed hard power capacities and their role in intelligence gathering, if popularized, could jeopardize current and future cases brought against correspondents like Rezaian — as well as those working at INGOs and universities — and make credible serious charges of espionage, while undermining the credibility of the accused and their GNN institutions. Rezaian's release was not tied to a finding that his GNN actions and activities were innocent and unrelated to building hard power capacities for the West; rather, he was released after conviction as a result of a deal made between the United States and Iran, potentially bolstering a previously exclusive non-Western argument that foreign correspondents are, in fact, extensions of state power and authority.

The *Washington Post* reported, "White House officials confirmed that the swap was clinched during months of secret talks that gained momentum in the days before the nuclear pact was formally implemented."[5] This means that the release was part of direct state-to-state negotiations that focused on nuclear weaponry and state secrets but concluded with what Iran presented as a spy exchange, where four Iranian-Americans (including Rezaian) were released in return for seven Iranian nationals held in the United States who were allegedly part a spy ring.[6] Western GNN personnel are regularly detained or arrested in multiple nations, from Azerbaijan, where Radio Free Europe's Khadija Ismayilova was imprisoned and sentenced to 7.5 years, later reduced to a suspended term of 3.5 years,[7] to North Korea, where reporters travel at their own risk.

Despite ongoing threats to GNN workers' safety and security (predominantly non-Western threats), my work has benefited from the help

---

4. Holley 2015.

5. Morello et al. 2016, par. 11.

6. Read 2016.

7. "RFE/RL Journalist Ismayilova Released from Custody," *RadioFreeEurope/RadioLiberty*, May 25, 2016, accessed December 29, 2017, https://www.rferl.org/a/azerbaijan-ismayilova-khadija-supreme-court-appeal/27756276.html.

of a few individuals who were willing to go on the record with personal and professional experiences that confirmed what initially seemed counterintuitive. Those individuals, whom I have known for many years, helped to identify, isolate, and formalize these wider GNN practices and performances as providing state hard power functions.

Following the establishment of these practices, the data collection and interviews conducted for this work focused on understanding how widespread these practices are. My research indicated that the practice of diplomacy and intelligence gathering, in their broadest sense (informally unselfconscious)—but also in a narrow and self-conscious manner when done formally—was a behavioral norm in a profession that publicly denies most such activity and, at times, actively denounces it as counter to its interests, ethics, and professional standards. This work has often been personally and professionally uncomfortable.

My conclusion is that, indeed, GNNs do perform hard power functions and consequently enhance state power. The central research question in its early stages questioned the reasoning of states to expend extraordinary financial resources to pursue national GNN development. If I had focused on state behavior, I might have concluded that states expended such resources in an attempt to expand their hard power capacities, with GNNs as one more manifestation of hard power. But instead I chose to address the more fundamental question of what type of power GNNs contingently possess and how they form and express that power. I hope my work may open the door to further research and analysis of the implications of these hard power GNN practices.

Some geopolitical consequences can be drawn from this work. Rising non-Western powers are deploying their GNNs to enhance their global power. They do this by expending unprecedented resources to develop their production and distribution infrastructure, choosing strategic sites (Washington, DC; Nairobi, Kenya; cyberspace) to focus their expanding content options and narrow their target audiences, while making sure that the target sites are strategic centers for intelligence-gathering operations and diplomatic activity.

Further, these non-Western type III GNNs are working to develop greater efficiencies to improve the signal-to-noise ratio inherent in intelligence gathering and analysis by developing big data analysis capacities in their IT infrastructures, thus keeping undesirable information away from the population while allowing critical information to reach policy-making and leadership levels of the state and party.[8]

The non-Western type III GNNs employ more and better intelligence-gathering nationals in the field, no longer limiting themselves and their organizations to their own nationals. This has the effect of engaging native individuals with foreign institutional experience, training, and access to accomplish GNN-assigned reporting and information-gathering tasks. There are multiple benefits associated with using Western nationals who have been institutionally trained and professionally developed in the accepted adversarial role of the press. Western journalists in the employ of non-Western GNNs apply their honed adversarial practices, leverage their power relationships, and are deployed to challenge the open societies within which they freely work. A less generous critique would be to suggest that the Western fourth estate is being turned into a fifth column. The Western practice of holding the powerful accountable, when combined with the resources and editorial direction to investigate and uncover an open society's social, political, and economic weaknesses, can be a very powerful tool, both from soft power and hard power perspectives. These practices are highly constrained within media or civil society circles in China. Type III GNNs do not function as national watchdogs. Instead, they focus their critical eye on nations other than the sponsoring nation's allies and serve the state's strategic interests.

These capacities were not available to non-Western GNNs in the twentieth century, when Western journalism was financially healthy and Westerners employed by Chinese or Russian state organizations

---

8. Symon and Tarapore 2015; Akhgar et al. 2015. As Symon and Tarapore put it, "Consider the conflicts that flared in Ukraine and Iraq in 2014. In both cases, irregular forces—Russian-backed separatists and Islamic State militants, respectively—made rapid advances against their adversaries, not only deploying effective military force but also documenting their campaigns in social media platforms such as Twitter and YouTube. Exploiting the content and metadata of these sources, fused with data from traditional intelligence, surveillance, and reconnaissance (ISR), could yield significant data about those forces' tactics, social networks, and geolocation at particular times" (8).

were seen as spies. In the twenty-first century, it is common practice to fill the ranks of non-Western GNNs with employees who have years of experience in Western GNNs but are unemployed or unemployable within Western GNNs. This book has focused on how GNNs operate, analyzing a component of diplomacy and intelligence gathering that is inherent in non-Western type III GNNs in order to bring attention to an otherwise obscure practice: "China's intelligence services have long been underanalyzed as major bureaucratic organizations and components of state power. This may have mattered relatively little during China's inward-looking and under-developed years."[9] China's rising power and its exploitation of its material hard power resources are important in the world today.

Diplomatically, non-Western GNNs are increasingly using their institutions to perform multilevel diplomatic practice. From working closely with state enterprises to propagating an ideological orientation, state sponsors leverage these non-Western GNNs as one more tool in a policy toolbox that gives them greater reach, improved access, and more points of engagement in the work of political, educational, commercial, and military diplomacy. Type III GNNs understand this as part of their mandate, as reflected in their organizational structures, and aggressively fulfill this role, particularly in regions within their perceived spheres of influence, whether geographically, politically, militarily, or economically. For China, this means an active GNN presence in Africa and Asia, but also in parts of the world where nations continue to recognize Taiwan as the legitimate Chinese state. For Russia and China, neutralizing Western GNNs is critical. The tools available for this practice are intimidation tactics, including nonaccreditation, censorship, legal registration, physical threat, or arrest. Both nations also deny visas and access for journalists, INGOs, and academics who possess good linguistic skills and can easily access Chinese or Russian dissenters or data. Autocratic non-Western countries recognize the undesirability of GNN entities and individuals with experience, language skills, or a history of critical reporting and

---

9. Mattis 2012, 54.

deep investigatory abilities. Those institutions are forced to leave the country—for example, by creating onerous conditions for their continued presence. In some cases, both Russia and China have outlawed GNN institutional activities.

Finally, non-Western type III GNN bureaus and offices overseas may be used as operational bases for official and formal diplomatic performance and state power extensions. This is a historical practice that continues to find expression, particularly in areas without consulates or embassies. The increasing number of non-Western type III GNN bureaus, offices, and employees around the world gives the state greater reach and deeper diplomatic resources.

Overall, non-Western countries are building their hard power capacities by leveraging relatively inexpensive, seemingly open-source GNN systems to enhance state power. Russia and China have increased the resources they allocate to type III GNN institutions, allowing them to deploy targeted, effective and cost-effective, plausibly deniable intelligence-gathering institutions aligned perfectly with the state's strategic—as well as soft power—goals. The result is a formidable non-Western GNN intelligence agency and worldwide diplomatic service with little pretense that it serves freedom of speech or any other Western GNN type I and II values.

As the non-West exponentially expands its reach and capacities, the West and its GNNs continue to decline and retrench. In 2016, the third-largest American newspaper chain, McClatchy-Tribune, closed all of its foreign bureaus.[10] The type I GNN broadcasters that remain economically viable do so by refocusing their reporting and production interests away from foreign news and replacing coverage and analysis with more profitable and less resource-intensive domestic political reporting, health stories, business news, and dramatic shared footage of extreme weather stories. This trend leaves a Western GNN void around the world. The result is a diminution of this category of once formidable Western hard power capacities, further diminishing the intelligence collection and

---

10. I am a foreign affairs columnist for the McClatchy-Tribune media group.

analysis from both informal open-source assets and formal intelligence and diplomatic resources.

Further, the vacuum is increasingly filled by type III non-Western GNNs, which have a presence where Western nations have little or none. Chinese CGTN footage filled the screens of Western GNN broadcasters when an attack on a Kenyan university in the countryside was covered more thoroughly by Nairobi-based Chinese television. Google News, in its early iteration before algorithms had the ability to tailor news delivery to individual tastes and interests, was an active distributor of Xinhua reports, particularly from developing Latin American countries and in Asia. Xinhua was suspected of exploiting metadata tricks to game the Google algorithm and bring its stories to the fore, putting news and analysis from Western GNNs at a disadvantage.[11]

Credible work done to exacting standards following Western traditions and norms has been important for generations of policy makers and leaders. In the twentieth century, there was a general reliance on Western GNN capacities, in particular on robust and widespread GNN foreign corresponding resources. This reliance went all the way to the White House, for instance during "the Vietnam war, when Kennedy . . . confid[ed] in Schlesinger that he learned more from their dispatches than he could from his generals and ambassadors."[12]

Western analysts and policymakers are now denied the hard power GNN capacities that were once ubiquitous. They now face an environment where information flow and GNNs' diplomatic engagement are hindered or entirely blocked by non-Western states that actively proscribe their operations. Western GNNs lack resources they once had, including traditional GNN training, tradition, and nonadvocacy systems of analysis and intelligence gathering that INGOs or academics are not always able to replace.

Given the rapid rise of non-Western GNN capacities and the power they represent—and the concomitant drop in Western GNN

---

11. Personal communication with former Google employee, 2012.
12. Halberstam 1993, 169.

capacities—Western policy makers and leaders should be raising a red flag just as they would if other hard power attributes, such as military capacities or formal intelligence and diplomatic resources, were disappearing. In the West, however, GNNs have no public constituencies to fight for them nor do states generally recognize the hard power aspect of their work, giving them insufficient public financial support to survive the crisis in the business model for type I and II GNNs or the flat investment funding type III GNNs receive from the state. Most recently, in the United States, President Donald Trump's hostile relationship with American GNNs further complicates the situation, by making foreign correspondents even less important from a news business perspective, degrading American GNNs' already diminished stature overseas by calling them purveyors of "fake news," and undermining all institutions and individuals that he does not fully authorize or personally perceive as respectful. President Trump actively questions the relevance and authority of GNNs. At the same time, a whole bureaucratic system (including embassies, intelligence agencies, military commanders, and congressional delegations) rely on these sources and networks. At the end of 2017, it is unclear if the entire administrative branch has disregard for these networks or if it is only President Trump personally.

This book has identified and categorized GNNs and delineated the way they enhance state power. It has shown that non-Western states recognize this power, incorporate it into their governing and party structures, and are aggressively investing in it. The West is falling behind. The first thing the West must do is to recognize the importance of this GNN resource, but the reality seems far from this imperative. Instead, the opposite seems to be the case.

Ben Rhodes, former president Barack Obama's deputy national security advisor for strategic communications, has explained why it was easy to manipulate GNNs into the White House narrative regarding the recent Iran nuclear deal. Rhodes said, "All these newspapers used to have foreign bureaus. Now they don't. They call us to explain to them what's happening in Moscow and Cairo. Most of the outlets are reporting on world events from Washington." Rhodes went on to disparage not only GNN institutions and their systems but those who work for those institutions:

"The average reporter we talk to is 27 years old, and their only reporting experience consists of being around political campaigns. That's a sea change. They literally know nothing."[13]

This attitude suggests that the state is unlikely to seek out Western GNNs' unique knowledge and analysis, upon which policy-making, intelligence, and military institutions have relied in the past. If Rhodes is correct, those GNN institutions and capacities are effectively gone.

---

13. Samuels 2016, par. 48.

APPENDIX 1 | INTERVIEW WITH TERRY PHILLIPS[1]

MARKOS KOUNALAKIS: The United States had prepared Operation Uphold Democracy, a military operational plan to invade Haiti, remove the regime installed by a military coup, and restore the elected government of President Jean-Bertrand Aristide. You and I directly intervened in the process, participated in the diplomatic process, and helped precipitate the conditions for a peaceful resolution to the Haiti crisis. Recount the details. . . .

TERRY PHILLIPS: It was the summer of 1994. I had just returned to the United States from having spent about five years in the Soviet Union and then in the new Russian Republic following the breakup of the USSR. I was looking for my next great gig, and CBS called me back to ask whether I would be willing to sit in temporarily in Port-au-Prince, waiting for whatever came next. It was a bit of a lull in the events in Haiti. And I said, sure. So I managed to get on the last commercial flight from the United States to Haiti. We had a connection to make in San Juan, Puerto Rico, and then there was the very last commercial flight actually scheduled to land in Haiti, and I got bumped off that flight, so CBS chartered a small plane . . . a small private plane to fly me and a couple of other people into the country. And then I kind of hunkered down for a little while, getting the lay of the land, doing some reporting, but primarily in a caretaker role as what amounted to acting bureau chief for Port-au-Prince. And then things started to cook and we had more and more staff come in. At one point I think there were about fifty of us from CBS in Haiti, including the anchor, Dan Rather, and a lot of senior correspondents for the evening news. . . .

MK: Fifty people. That is a large contingent by today's standards.

---

1. Interview in San Francisco, September 23, 2013. Edited by Markos Kounalakis for clarity on May 9, 2015.

TP: About fifty CBS News employees. And a large technical staff, we had a big satellite uplink—I mean it became a big operation. Not the first time these people came in. We'd had an ongoing presence in Haiti. But as I said, there had been a little bit of a lull while we waited to see what would happen next in diplomatic relations and in relations internationally in general. At that time there was a military junta, the leader was Lt. General Raoul Cédras, and he and his entourage had forcibly evicted Jean-Bertrand Aristide, the elected president, who was then in exile in the United States—I think he was living in Washington. And there was an effort by the US government to put him back in power. And so part of our job while I was there was to do the daily rounds, to find the bodies that were littering the streets of Port-au-Prince, to cover the various other activities, do scene-setters. It was kind of a normal . . . a "normal" day-to-day type of operation.

Then it became clear that the United States was going to use force. They had tried to do that once before. They had sent in a warship, and there was a huge response by the Haitians in protest of this arrival, and so they left, there was no direct interaction.[2] Well, the American government had gotten fed up, and things were getting worse and worse, and so they finally made it clear that they were going to use all necessary force. In fact I think there was a UN resolution.[3] Anyway, they made a commitment to use whatever military force was necessary to put an end to the junta and to put Aristide back in power. So one day, I was making my rounds, I went to the . . . to the . . . it wasn't the palace, it wasn't the main government center, it was the place, the building where the junta was operating—I'm sorry, I can't remember the name of the building, but the headquarters for the military. And one of Cédras's underlings approached me and asked whether I knew anybody in Washington to whom I could transmit a message from them.

Now, keep in mind that at this time there was an active United States embassy in Port-au-Prince, but there were no direct contacts

---

2. USS *Harlan County*, October 1993.
3. UN Security Council Resolution 940, 1994.

between the embassy . . . at least no formal, public contacts between the embassy and the junta. I don't think there was an ambassador at the place, but I think there was a chargé d'affaires, but I've forgotten that detail. But anyway, they didn't have a normal relationship. So this military officer asked me whether I could communicate a message from them to Washington. . . . Well, I wasn't in the government, I didn't have deep connections with the United States government, but I did have a couple of friends who had some connections at cabinet level and at congressional level offices. . . . And so I contacted you, and you put me in contact with the chair of the House Foreign Affairs Committee. . . .

MK: Yeah, so you called me and we talked at length about the situation. You said that US military action seemed imminent and that this Haitian contact was making a last-minute appeal to keep the military invasion from happening. I remember it all having a great deal of intensity and immediacy and that we had to decide on that phone call if I was going to go further and act. It was clear to me that if I made that call, I would be intervening directly in events. But it was also clear that I would act because the stakes were so high, the risk of violence and the death of American soldiers very real. So we hung up the phone, and I called my good friend, Chris Kojm, who at the time served as the coordinator for regional issues in Congress on the staff of the House International Relations Committee, under ranking member Lee Hamilton.

TP: That's right. That's right. And so that led to a conference call with me on one end of the line and Lee Hamilton and several other members of Congress and staff at the other end of the line. And for, I think, about a half an hour, they essentially interrogated me to find out what I knew, what really was said and what might happen, and you know, what could this really mean. So I told them everything I knew.

Now, I should back up a couple of steps and say that I did not do this on my own initiative. As I mentioned, my boss, the anchor—CBS anchor Dan Rather—was there also. So he and I also had a lengthy conversation beforehand. I told him what I had been asked to do and I asked him about the propriety of a reporter getting involved in a process like this. And we examined it in various ways. Of course, the example of the Cuban missile crisis came up, where a similar opportunity presented itself, but that time from the American side wishing to communicate with the Soviets. . . . And so there was precedent for it, and as long as there were clear boundaries about what I was willing and able to do, he as my putative boss did not have a problem with me serving in this role. I couldn't be involved in the negotiations, and I couldn't take a position, but simply transmitting a message from one party to the other, in his view, was not a problem. By the way, I don't know whether Dan Rather talked to anybody else about this; I had the impression this was his decision. And he was the managing editor of the evening news, so this probably was the point of decision for CBS.

And so, with that, with those guidelines I then had this telephone conversation with Lee Hamilton and the others. And the upshot of it was that rather than sending in military force, the Clinton administration dispatched Colin Powell, Sam Nunn, and Jimmy Carter to Haiti, where they negotiated not just an end to the crisis but an end to the junta. And they provided a way for these military leaders to leave the country, to go to a place [Panama] that was comfortable for them, and to allow for a peaceful transition of power back to the elected president.

MK: And one of the really more telling moments of the role that you and Rather played was when that delegation arrived in Haiti. . . .

TP: Oh, right [*laughing*]. So suffice to say that we had a slight advantage in access to this story. We knew we made it possible, we knew it was going to happen. It was not a quid pro quo, but we were in a very fortunate position. We also were staying at a hotel . . . *hotel* is not exactly the right word for it, there were a number of hotels in town where people were staying; we stayed at a compound that was not just very comfortable and with great facilities, but it was also the place where things happened. And one of the things that happened at this place was a meeting between these officials who came and the representatives of the military junta.

MK: You were in the middle of the mediation. . . .

TP: Since we were the only news agency staying at this place, I mean all fifty of us had rooms at this place, when they arrived we were on the inside and everybody else of the press corps was on the outside suddenly scratching their heads wondering how come we got this story [*laughing*]. . . . I don't know that we ever explained it to them. At least I didn't ever explain it to them. So yes, that was kind of a tasty result of this exercise.

MK: And weren't you guys also on the tarmac welcoming the delegation?

TP: I was not there. That might be true. I've forgotten that. But yeah, I think Dan Rather did. . . . Yeah, it's right [*laughing*]. I'd forgotten this, but yeah, I think it was Dan Rather who welcomed them as they got off their flight. Yeah. Yeah, we had a . . . well, to call that a scoop doesn't begin to do it justice, we owned this story. We became very close to making news, very, very close.

MK: So if you were to postulate, you know, and parts of this are all speculation at this point, if you did not make that connection with the US government through my contacts, and then the engagement of congress and Lee Hamilton, who was very focused on this issue, do you think the likelihood of a nondiplomatic outcome was high? . . . I mean, of course, I'm asking retrospectively, how do you think it could have evolved? Because it was really an eleventh-hour call. . . .

TP: As far as I know, there was no other prominent, credible alternative at that moment to full-blown military invasion. It's not impossible that the junta would have found somebody else to deliver its message. Could have happened. It's unlikely, but possible, that they would have found some third party, nonjournalist third party, such as another embassy, for example, or some businessperson, because there were a few businesspeople still there. . . . Keep in mind a lot of people had left. People were leaving Haiti in droves because of genuine fear that there was going to be a massive military conflict. But there wasn't another obvious alternative at that moment. So I suppose that if . . . 'cause it wasn't just that they had somebody to communicate the message but someone who was fortunate to know somebody, who could then put these wheels into motion. It was—in a positive way—it was a perfect storm. We had all of these pieces lined up very nicely. So I would not have been shocked, if I had the perspective of God to look down on this and say, well, this didn't happen, I wouldn't be shocked if the alternative would have been in fact, for the United States to send in military force. And of course, down the road that ended up happening—the deal didn't collapse, but the government failed and there was a lot of violence and eventually international troops did go in, and Haiti has just been, some might say, a cursed place, for a long time, but especially in the wake of all of this. But I believe we saved lives. I'd put it that way. I believe we saved lives in avoiding—or at the very least forestalling—direct conflict between the military junta of Haiti at the time and certainly the United States. I think we saved lives.

MK: I acted very much with that premise in mind when I made my call to Washington, DC. I acted knowing that if we were successful in helping to bring about the conditions for a negotiated solution, we would be saving lives. Anything else you want to add?

TP: Yeah, there's one other thing I want to say, which is that I was in a fortunate position not to need a specific outcome. I didn't have an agenda here. I was doing what I did professionally: I was telling a story. And I think the fact that I had the support of my boss at that time, to tell this story to this audience without compromising our journalistic integrity, was the sort of thing that I believe journalists ought to do more often. We are often in a position to know things that other people don't know, to have connections with people that other people don't have, and I think we oftentimes either ignore or deliberately avoid serving in other capacities, and I think it's unfortunate. We can clearly do some good when these opportunities arise. And I wish that there was some training, or some element of the so-called code of ethics for journalism that would enable, and facilitate and encourage, such behavior. This is not, and this shouldn't be, a one-off. And you know, you can make this as broad as you want and go from something as simple as the question whether a reporter should help somebody who is being harmed, rather than just report the event that's happening, to something as large as the international stage I happened to be on at that time. We're not oriented to think this way, and I was very lucky to have been in the right place, to have had the support, the encouragement, and the collegial help that I did. I wish we would do this more deliberately and more often.

MK: So do you know of any other instances, either yourself or others, where there has been a direct engagement with the US government in some way, or any government, to perform what is a quasi-diplomatic effort because of this privileged access, or because of a request, or because of unique knowledge of a story or individuals or networks? I mean I'm recounting one of my own in this, regarding the Semtex story in Czechoslovakia.

TP: Right.

MK: But maybe you have knowledge of some other ones.

TP: Well, of course, I've mentioned the famous case of the reporter who served as an intermediary between the United States and the Soviet Union at the height of the Cuban missile crisis. Because there wasn't a hotline at the time, and so he was delivering messages between the White House and the Soviet embassy. And I give you one other personal example. When I was in Armenia in 1990s, I was approached one day by someone I didn't know, who told me that he knew that there was a conspiracy to overthrow the president of Armenia. And he asked me whether I would deliver that message to the president of Armenia. And I said to him, "I'm a reporter, I cannot play an interventionist role in a story. What I can do is report the story." He said, "No, no, no, no, no, I don't want anybody to know about this, you have to do this secretly." And I said, "I'm not a spy. I do things publicly. I report the news. Now, I report to a small audience or a large audience; I don't report to an audience of one." And so he refused to give me the details. Now is that a difference with a distinction compared to the Haiti situation? I believe it is. Because in the Haiti case, I wasn't playing a role in trying to stop something from happening or start something happening, I was delivering a message from one person to the government, from one government, not from one person, from one government to another government. And as it turned out, by the way, apparently that story was either false or stopped in other ways, the Armenian story. But I felt that the distinction was that I was being asked to be a player in a developing situation.

MK: Other cases where you know journalists who have been players in a specific situation?

TP: I have a strong belief, you know, I think, you might have been in the room when this was said, that there was a reporter in, I think it was in Czechoslovakia, who was accused of carrying credentials in addition to his journalistic credentials—the implication was that he was a spy. And I have strong belief that there was a guy operating in Tbilisi, Georgia, pardon me, not Tbilisi, in Baku, Azerbaijan, who was more than a journalist. He had very close relations with the United States embassy in that country, and he found himself—not that we all don't occasionally find ourselves in interesting places in unusual times, but it seemed to be a habit with him that things would happen around him. Now, can I tell you for sure that he was a player? No, but he started to behave more and more that way....

But when he and I spoke privately, his views—his political views—and his philosophy lent credence to my suspicion that he was in this for more than journalism. And I can tell you one last thing in that regard. When I was in Nagorno-Karabakh, which is a separatist part of Azerbaijan that's still legally part of Azerbaijan but that is effectively more Armenian and at the very least independent, I saw Soviet tanks. I don't know that anybody else knew that. But I was able to report this. And I was then asked about my reportage by someone from the American embassy in Yerevan. Now, I didn't feel compromised telling him what I had already told everybody else. But I presume that that information figured into a report somewhere. By the way, the person who asked me later turned out to be the CIA station chief in Armenia. I didn't feel compromised because I wasn't doing anything more than what I had already done. But did I play a role in the American assessment of the situation there and policy in some way? I don't know. Maybe. But I didn't do it deliberately. And I think that's an important distinction.

APPENDIX 2 | METHODOLOGY

This project is based on qualitative research on a small number of cases; that is, the methodology utilized is the intensive case study. Bennett and Elman summarize the advantages of such studies: "Suited to the study of rare events, they can facilitate the search for omitted variables that might lie behind contingent events, and they allow for the study of interaction effects within one or a few cases."[1]

The drawbacks are also clear, with the main one being that the results of case studies are hard to generalize: "The case study researcher gains leverage on internal validity, but only at the expense of external validity."[2] Scholars also emphasize that case selection bias and confirmation bias are real problems.[3]

The case study approach allows for an in-depth look at "complex and relatively . . . infrequent" phenomena[4] that "are more amenable to labeling by words rather than numbers."[5] GNNs fit the description. Using the case study approach, the research was able to gain insight into the vertical and horizontal functions of GNNs. The exploratory case study of GNN institutions and individuals, including RT and CGTN, looked at GNNs' organizational, editorial, and technological developments. For the CGTN research, two sites were examined: the Washington, DC, center and the Nairobi center—the only two full production and distribution centers outside the CGTN headquarters in Beijing. During

---

1. A. Bennett and Elman 2006, 259.

2. Levy 2002, 445.

3. Positivist scholars also question the scientific nature of the case study approach. Maoz (2002), for example, claims that case study approaches often mean an anything-goes attitude on the behalf of the researcher. G. King, Keohane, and Verba (1994, 5) call for case study approaches to be more "systematic and scientific."

4. A. Bennett and Elman 2007, 171.

5. Thies 2002, 352.

site visits to these centers, one I conducted in Washington, DC, and the other by my Ugandan research assistant, Kennedy Jawoko, to the Nairobi center, both in 2014, we engaged with the administration and employees of CGTN, then called CCTV, as well as colleagues outside the CGTN network who had either direct knowledge or a consulting relationship with the network.

Apart from the CCTV visits, research and observation during the course of this study took place in Prague, Czech Republic, at Radio Free Europe/Radio Liberty (RFE/RL) in 2012, with a visit to the facility, group discussion with the entire editorial management staff, private meetings with lead administrators, and a walk through the physical plant to observe the reportorial and editorial process. Prior to this research visit, my professional life in international broadcasting included corresponding, reporting, and producing, either on contract or as an employee, with Radio Sweden International, Deutsche Welle, Radio New Zealand, NBC–Mutual News Radio Network, National Public Radio, CBS, Hellenic Radio and Television, and Christian Science Monitor's *Monitor Radio*. I also interacted with reporters for the Voice of America. Herein lies a risk of confirmation bias, given the years of exposure to and employment in the broadcasting arms of multiple Western nations, which make up today's Western GNNs. Carrying out part of the research outside of the Western GNN structures was key to ensuring divergent points of view regarding GNNs and their relationship to the state and state power. I successfully gained access to non-Western GNNs, conducting observation and interviews. I was also able to access people working in non-Western GNNs who were willing to share information and insight into their organizations' operations, missions, and personnel, as well as larger strategic goals.

The research also borrowed a method from ethnography: participant observation of the creative process of the news production. Attendance at editorial meetings, review of program budgets, and interviews with personnel regarding attitudes, goals, and metrics of success were important elements of this research. In the course of the research, I engaged with a senior consultant at the highest levels of CCTV, who made available previously confidential data regarding operations and structural features.

Elite Interviewing

Although interviewing, and by extension, elite interviewing, can be viewed as part of the case study approach, it has played such an important role in my research that it deserves separate treatment, in line with Tansey's observation that "when interviewees have been significant players, when their memories are strong, and when they are willing to disclose their knowledge . . . , elite interviews will arguably be the most important instrument in the process tracer's data collection toolkit."[6]

The secrecy of political processes means that the only way to find this kind of information is by interviewing the participants. The fact that some of the research on the intelligence or strategic function of GNNs is highly confidential called for elite interviews as one of the only ways to get information on these issues.[7]

The interview method serves two purposes in research. First, it is used to gather facts and data that are impossible to uncover by different methods. For this goal, in a sort of triangulation,[8] it was necessary to interview a number of participants in the same event or to otherwise gain independent confirmation of the data collected.[9] Second, the interviews are useful in gaining insight into opinions, values, and interpretations of events. For these purposes, I conducted semistructured interviews.[10]

Confirmation bias is a great danger of any research, but is a particular threat in qualitative research methods. To avoid it, care was taken to select a wide range of interviewees. A firmly Western perspective, reinforced by a close relationship with US government politics and policies, has informed my approach to writing a syndicated foreign affairs column.

---

6. Tansey 2007, 767. Although Tansey discusses the role of elite interviewing for process tracing in particular, his observation is arguably valid for the broader case study approach as well.

7. Beamer 2002.

8. Davies 2001.

9. Lilleker 2013.

10. While Tansey (2007) elaborates on these goals by stating that elite interviews are useful to "corroborate what has been established from other sources," to "establish what a set of people think," to "make inferences about a larger population's characteristics/decision," and to "reconstruct an event or a set of events" (766), George and Bennett (2005) add two more theoretical goals of data collection such as interviewing: uncovering variables and hypotheses that were previously ignored as well as revealing causal processes.

This approach, if unchecked, might warrant suspicion of a Western bias. I have gone to extra lengths here to engage with non-Western readers and critics. I approached people who worked in non-Western diplomatic and journalistic organizations as well as at non-Western academic institutions. The non-Western participants were not primarily drawn from dissident ranks (although some, like the Russian Yuri Yarim-Agaev, were), but rather from the active Russian diplomatic corps, management and employees of CGTN/X, employees of Sina Weibo, and those on the receiving end of both Russian and Chinese GNN systems. Such an approach, which applies journalistic values and professional experience in fact-based reporting and fair and accurate writing and publishing, guided this project.

My unique position provided access to interviewees that are generally out of reach for other researchers. The interviewees were not selected at random;[11] rather, the goal was to include as many of the important actors as possible.[12] This was achieved via purposive or criterion-based sampling.[13] This kind of sampling ensures that in interviewee selection, "the purpose of the study and the researcher's knowledge guide the process."[14] Along with snowball sampling, this sampling method is often used to study hard-to-reach populations.

The interview subjects came from a wide range of professions related to the subject, though the largest segment, which included forty interviewees, came from the ranks of reporters, editors, producers, and publishers from mostly Western media, from the United States, Germany, the United Kingdom, Sweden, Mexico, Uganda, South Africa, Nigeria, Kenya, Canada, Spain, Italy, Greece, Hungary, Austria, Poland, and Denmark. In all but two cases, Terry Phillips and Peter Laufer, the interview subjects asked for confidentiality due to the sensitivity of the subject matter and potential ethical and legal challenges to the practices they described or in which they had directly participated. Most were

---

11. Ritchie et al. (2014, 107) state that qualitative studies rarely do; instead, they rely on nonprobability samples. See also Tansey (2007).
12. Tansey 2007, 769.
13. Ritchie et al. 2014
14. Tansey 2007, 770

concerned about their livelihoods; some feared for their lives and the lives of colleagues still working in the field. The current charged environment made the sensitivity of the information and data sharing even more important: right now, journalists are being held in foreign lands under accusations of espionage. In some countries, journalists have been threatened with expulsion in retaliation for unrelated diplomatic actions, such as the expulsion of a diplomat. Sometimes journalists are held by states as leverage in an exchange deal for accused spies or arrested NOCs. Despite the challenges, professional dangers, and in many cases, possible threats to personal safety, interview subjects were willing to share data, information, professional experiences, institutional relationships, structural insights, and processes either on the basis of a long personal or professional relationship or after being introduced through an acquaintance or trusted intermediary. In yet others, the interviews were conducted with individuals with whom I had no prior relationship. In two instances, an interview subject contacted me following publication of my work on GNNs[15] and once following academic publication of my work on soft power.[16]

Chinese and Russian GNN personnel constituted the main non-Westerners interviewed. I interviewed three Russians and fifteen Chinese. The Chinese were particularly difficult to interview because of legally binding nondisclosure forms and fears of personal reprisal—through pay, visa and work considerations, or family members still residing in the People's Republic of China. The nondisclosure agreement—which is, in my experience, less effective in technology and in the Silicon Valley, for example—was ironclad as regards the sharing of CCTV data. Only one confidential high-level source was willing to share crucial structural data regarding the workings of CCTV.

As GNNs comprise more than journalistic institutions, per this work's broader definition, individual employees, freelance personnel, administrators, and governing board members of eight NGO organizations were interviewed, shared data, or in some instances, engaged in

---

15. M. Kounalakis 2014a.
16. Kounalakis and Simonyi 2011.

less formal conversations regarding their activities overseas. A total of eighteen people in this field were part of the field research. Only one was willing to share his name and position.

The interviewees for this study include Thomas Fingar, the former deputy director of national intelligence, former secretary of state George P. Shultz, and a number of other senior former administration and foreign government officials, members of the diplomatic corps, public diplomacy specialists, and academics, all of whom, other than Fingar and Shultz, asked to remain anonymous due to the sensitive nature of this study. Most recently, in 2016, two former US undersecretaries of state were also interviewed to test the conclusions and observations of Shultz and Fingar.

In most instances, the recording method was handwritten note taking, though in a few instances where subjects were willing to go on the record, an audio recording device was utilized.

This study extended to Nairobi, Kenya, where I directed my research assistant, Kennedy Jawoko, to conduct interviews and collect data on the work of CCTV Africa and Xinhua.

REFERENCES

Aday, Sean, Robert M. Entman, and Steven Livingston. 2012. "Media, Power and US Foreign Policy." In *The SAGE Handbook of Political Communication*, edited by Holli A. Semetko and Margaret Scammell, 327–41. London: SAGE.

Adelman, Kenneth L. 1981. "Speaking of America: Public Diplomacy in Our Time." *Foreign Affairs* 59, no. 4 (Spring): 913–36. Accessed March 11, 2014. doi:10.2307/20040828.

Akhgar, Babak, Gregory B. Saathoff, Hamid R. Arabnia, Richard Hill, Andrew Staniforth, and Petra Saskia Bayerl. 2015. *Application of Big Data for National Security: A Practitioner's Guide to Emerging Technologies*. Oxford: Butterworth-Heinemann.

Al-Ghazzi, Omar. 2014. "'Citizen Journalism' in the Syrian Uprising: Problematizing Western Narratives in a Local Context." *Communication Theory* 24, no. 4 (November): 435–54. Accessed December 28, 2017. https://doi.org/10.1111/comt.12047.

Allan, Stuart, and Einar Thorsen, eds. 2009. *Citizen Journalism: Global Perspectives*. New York: Peter Lang.

Althaus, Scott L., and David Tewksbury. 2002. "Agenda Setting and the 'New' News Patterns of Issue Importance among Readers of the Paper and Online Versions of the New York Times." *Communication Research* 29, no. 2 (April): 180–207. Accessed May 2, 2015. doi:10.1177/0093650202029002004.

Altunışık, Meliha Benli. 2008. "The Possibilities and Limits of Turkey's Soft Power in the Middle East." *Insight Turkey* 10, no. 2: 41–54.

Arant, M. David, and Philip Meyer. 1998. "Public and Traditional Journalism: A Shift in Values?" *Journal of Mass Media Ethics* 13, no. 4: 205–18. Accessed April 18, 2015. doi:10.1207/s15327728jmme1304_1.

Arceneaux, Kevin, and Martin Johnson. 2013. *Changing Minds or Changing Channels? Partisan News in an Age of Choice*. Chicago: University of Chicago Press.

Archetti, Cristina. 2012. "Which Future for Foreign Correspondence?" *Journalism Studies* 13, nos. 5–6: 847–56. Accessed December 21, 2017. https://doi.org/10.1080/1461670X.2012.664352.

Arnett, Peter. 1998. "State of the American Newspaper: Goodbye, World." *American Journalism Review*, November. Accessed May 8, 2016. http://ajrarchive.org/article.asp?id=3288.

Associated Press. 2011. "WikiLeaks-Named Ethiopian Reporter in Unredacted Cable Flees Country in Fear." *Guardian*, September 15. Accessed May 5, 2015. www .theguardian.com/media/2011/sep/15/wikileaks-named-ethiopian-reporter-flees.

———. 2015. "Putin Appoints Homophobic Presenter to Head State News Agency." *Guardian*, December 9. Accessed May 16, 2015. www.theguardian.com/world /2013/dec/09/putin-appoints-homophobic-presenter-kiselyov-head-news -agency-homosexuals.

Auerbach, Yehudith, and Yaeli Bloch-Elkon. 2005. "Media Framing and Foreign Policy: The Elite Press vis-à-vis US Policy in Bosnia, 1992–95." *Journal of Peace Research* 42, no. 1: 83–99. Accessed March 13, 2014. doi:10.1177/0022 343305049668.

Axelrod, Alan. 2009. *Selling the Great War: The Making of American Propaganda*. New York: Palgrave Macmillan.

Bachrach, Peter, and Morton S. Baratz. 1962. "Two Faces of Power." *American Political Science Review* 56, no. 4: 947–52. Accessed November 7, 2013. doi:10.2307 /1952796.

Baker, Ray Stannard, John Maxwell Hamilton, Robert Mann, and D'Seante Parks. 2012. *A Journalist's Diplomatic Mission: Ray Stannard Baker's World War I Diary*. Baton Rouge: Louisiana State University Press.

Balci, Bayram. 2014. "The Gülen Movement and Turkish Soft Power." *Carnegie Endowment for International Peace*, February 4. Accessed December 23, 2017. http://carnegieendowment.org/2014/02/04/g-len-movement-and-turkish -soft-power-pub-54430.

Bandurski, David, and Martin Hala. 2010. *Investigative Journalism in China: Eight Cases in Chinese Watchdog Journalism*. Hong Kong: Hong Kong University Press.

Barboza, David. 2009. "China Yearns to Form Its Own Media Empires." *New York Times*, October 4. Accessed January 9, 2018. www.nytimes.com/2009/10/05 /business/global/05yuan.html.

———. 2010. "China Puts Best Face Forward with News Channel." *New York Times*, July 1. Accessed February 18, 2018. www.nytimes.com/2010/07/02/world/asia /02china.html.

Baron, Martin. 2015. "Full Statement on Jason Rezaian from Post's Executive Editor Martin Baron." *Washington Post*, April 20. Accessed May 4, 2015. www .washingtonpost.com/world/full-statement-on-jason-rezaian-from-posts -executive-editor-martin-baron/2015/04/20/1fbb97b2-e771-11e4-9767-627 6fc9b0ada_story.html.

Baron, Robert A., and Gideon D. Markman. 2000. "Beyond Social Capital: How Social Skills Can Enhance Entrepreneurs' Success." *Academy of Management Executive (1993–2005)* 14, no. 1: 106–16.

Bartholomew, Carolyn. 2009. *Report to Congress of the U.S.-China Economic and*

Security Review Commission. Washington, DC: US Government Printing Office.

Baum, Matthew. 2003. *Soft News Goes to War: Public Opinion and American Foreign Policy in the New Media Age.* Princeton, NJ: Princeton University Press.

Baum, Matthew A., and Tim J. Groeling. 2010. *War Stories: The Causes and Consequences of Public Views of War.* Princeton, NJ: Princeton University Press.

Baum, Matthew A., and Philip B. K. Potter. 2008. "The Relationships between Mass Media, Public Opinion, and Foreign Policy: Toward a Theoretical Synthesis." *Annual Review of Political Science* 11, no. 1: 39–65. Accessed February 8, 2013. doi:10.1146/annurev.polisci.11.060406.214132.

Beamer, Glenn. 2002. "Elite Interviews and State Politics Research." *State Politics and Policy Quarterly* 2, no. 1: 86–96. Accessed March 11, 2013. doi:10.1177/1532440002002200106.

Bebow, John. 2002. "Journalist or Diplomat?" *American Journalism Review,* April. Accessed April 14. 2015. http://ajrarchive.org/Article.asp?id=2502.

Bennett, Andrew, and Colin Elman. 2006. "Complex Causal Relations and Case Study Methods: The Example of Path Dependence." *Political Analysis* 14, no. 3: 250–67. Accessed March 6, 2013. doi:10.1093/pan/mpj020.

———. 2007. "Case Study Methods in the International Relations Subfield." *Comparative Political Studies* 40, no. 2: 170–95. Accessed March 6, 2013. doi:10.1177/0010414006296346.

Bennett, Daniel. 2013. *Digital Media and Reporting Conflict: Blogging and the BBC's Coverage of War and Terrorism.* New York: Routledge.

Bennett, W. Lance. 1996. "An Introduction to Journalism Norms and Representations of Politics." *Political Communication* 13, no. 4: 373–84. Accessed May 3, 2015. doi:10.1080/10584609.1996.9963126.

Bernstein, C. 1977. "The CIA and the Media: How America's Most Powerful News Media Worked Hand in Glove with the Central Intelligence Agency and Why the Church Committee Covered It Up." *Rolling Stone,* October 20, 55–67.

Bially Mattern, Janice. 2005. "Why 'Soft Power' Isn't So Soft: Representational Force and the Sociolinguistic Construction of Attraction in World Politics." *Millennium* 33, no. 3: 583–612. Accessed January 20, 2014. doi:10.1177/03058298050330031601.

Bloomberg. 2016. "China's Gambia Move Reminds Tsai of Power to Isolate Taiwan." *Bloomberg.com,* March 18. Accessed May 8, 2016. www.bloomberg.com/news/articles/2016-03-18/china-s-gambia-move-reminds-tsai-of-power-to-isolate-taiwan.

Bonsal, Stephen. 1944. *Unfinished Business.* New York: Simon.

Boynton, G. R., Jr., and Glenn W. Richardson. 2015. "Agenda Setting in the Twenty-First Century." *New Media and Society* 18, no. 9: 1916–34. Accessed December 23, 2017. https://doi.org/10.1177/1461444815616226.

Brewer, Paul R. 2006. "National Interest Frames and Public Opinion about World Affairs." *Harvard International Journal of Press/Politics* 11, no. 4: 89–102. Accessed March 23, 2014. doi:10.1177/1081180X06293725.

Broadcasting Board of Governors. 2016. "Budget Submissions." Accessed May 7, 2016. www.bbg.gov/about-the-agency/research-reports/budget-submissions.

Browne, Andrew. 2016. "Beijing's Gambia Gambit Feeds Suspicion across Taiwan Strait." *Wall Street Journal*, March 22, sec. World. Accessed May 8, 2016. www .wsj.com/articles/chinas-gambia-gambit-feeds-suspicion-across-taiwan-strait -1458624741.

Brüggemann, Michael, and Hagen Schulz-Forberg. 2009. "Becoming Pan-European? Transnational Media and the European Public Sphere." *International Communication Gazette* 71, no. 8: 693–712. Accessed March 20, 2013. doi:10.1177 /1748048509345064.

Bucci, O. M., G. Pelosi, and S. Selleri. 2003. "The Work of Marconi in Microwave Communications." *IEEE Antennas and Propagation Magazine* 45, no. 5: 46–53. Accessed May 10, 2015. doi:10.1109/MAP.2003.1252809.

Bullogh, Oliver. 2013. "Inside Russia Today: Counterweight to the Mainstream Media, or Putin's Mouthpiece?" *New Statesman*, May 10. Accessed May 6, 2016. www.newstatesman.com/world-affairs/world-affairs/2013/05/inside-russia -today-counterweight-mainstream-media-or-putins-mou.

Bunce, Mel. 2015. "International News and the Image of Africa: New Storytellers, New Narratives?" In *Images of Africa: Creation, Negotiation and Subversion*, edited by Julia Gallagher, 42–62. Manchester: Manchester University Press.

Burns, Alex, and Ben Eltham. 2009. "Twitter Free Iran: An Evaluation of Twitter's Role in Public Diplomacy and Information Operations in Iran's 2009 Election Crisis." In *Communications Policy and Research Forum*. Accessed February 18, 2018. http://vuir.vu.edu.au/15230/1/CPRF09BurnsEltham.pdf.

Canel, María-José. 2012. "Communicating Strategically in the Face of Terrorism: The Spanish Government's Response to the 2004 Madrid Bombing Attacks." *Public Relations Review* 38, no. 2: 214–22. Accessed May 9, 2016. doi:10.1016/j .pubrev.2011.11.012.

Carothers, Thomas. 2006. "The Backlash against Democracy Promotion." *Foreign Affairs* 85: 55.

Carpenter, Serena. 2007. "U.S. Elite and Non-Elite Newspapers' Portrayal of the Iraq War: A Comparison of Frames and Source Use." *Journalism and Mass Communication Quarterly* 84, no. 4: 761–76. Accessed April 9, 2015. doi:10.1177 /107769900708400407.

Chaban, Natalia, and Martin Holland. 2015. "Theorizing and Framing 'Normative Power Europe': Asian Journalists' Comparative Perspectives." *Asia Europe Journal* 13, no. 3: 285–96. Accessed May 9, 2016. doi:10.1007/s10308-015-0424-z.

Chalaby, Jean K. 2002. "Transnational Television in Europe: The Role of Pan-European Channels." *European Journal of Communication* 17, no. 2: 183–203. Accessed March 20, 2013. doi:10.1177/0267323102017002692.

———. 2005a. "Deconstructing the Transnational: A Typology of Cross-Border Television Channels in Europe." *New Media and Society* 7, no. 2: 155–75. Accessed March 20, 2013. doi:10.1177/1461444805050744.

———. 2005b. "From Internationalization to Transnationalization." *Global Media and Communication* 1, no. 1: 28–33. Accessed March 20, 2013. doi:10.1177/1742766505000100107.

———. 2006. "American Cultural Primacy in a New Media Order A European Perspective." *International Communication Gazette* 68, no. 1: 33–51. Accessed March 20, 2013. doi:10.1177/1748048506060114.

Chang, Tsan-Kuo, and Fen Lin. 2014. "From Propaganda to Public Diplomacy: Assessing China's International Practice and Its Image, 1950–2009." *Public Relations Review* 40, no. 3: 450–58. Accessed December 23, 2017. https://doi.org/10.1016/j.pubrev.2014.04.008.

Chatriwala, Omar. 2011. "What Wikileaks Tells Us about Al Jazeera." *Foreign Policy*, September 19. Accessed January 26, 2018. http://foreignpolicy.com/2011/09/19/what-wikileaks-tells-us-about-al-jazeera/.

Chichava, Sérgio, Lara Côrtes, and Aslak Orre. 2014. "The Coverage of China in the Mozambican Press: Implications for Chinese Soft-Power." Paper presented at the China and Africa Media, Communications and Public Diplomacy conference, Beijing, September 10–11. Accessed May 10, 2016. www.cmi.no/file/2954-.pdf.

Cho, Young Nam, and Jong Ho Jeong. 2008. "China's Soft Power: Discussions, Resources, and Prospects." Accessed March 11, 2014. doi:10.1525/as.2008.48.3.453.

Clausewitz, Carl von, and Wilhelm von Scherff. 1883. *Vom Kriege: Hinterlassenes Werk des Generals Carl von Clausewitz*. Berlin: R. Wilhelmi.

Clinton, Hillary Rodham. 2010. "Leading through Civilian Power: Redefining American Diplomacy and Development." *Foreign Affairs* 89, no. 6: 13–24.

Coe, Kevin, David Tewksbury, Bradley J. Bond, Kristin L. Drogos, Robert W. Porter, Ashley Yahn, and Yuanyuan Zhang. 2008. "Hostile News: Partisan Use and Perceptions of Cable News Programming." *Journal of Communication* 58, no. 2: 201–19. Accessed May 11, 2015. doi:10.1111/j.1460-2466.2008.00381.x.

Cohen, Bernard C. 1963. *The Press and Foreign Policy*. Princeton, NJ: Princeton University Press.

———. 1994. "A View from the Academy." In *Taken by Storm: The Media, Public Opinion, and U.S. Foreign Policy in the Gulf War*, edited by W. Lance Bennett and David L. Paletz, 8–11. Chicago: University of Chicago Press.

Cohen, Yoel. 1986. *Media Diplomacy: The Foreign Office in the Mass Communications Age*. London: F. Cass.

Conlan, Tara. 2015. "BBC World Service to Receive £289m from Government." *Guardian*, November 23. Accessed December 28, 2017. www.theguardian.com /media/2015/nov/23/bbc-world-service-receive-289m-from-government.

Conrad, David. 2013. "Underwritten or Undercut?" *Columbia Journalism Review*, July 1. Accessed November 21, 2013. www.cjr.org/feature/underwritten_or _undercut.php.

———. 2015. "The Freelancer–NGO Alliance." *Journalism Studies* 16, no. 2: 275–88. Accessed December 19, 2017. https://doi.org/10.1080/1461670X.2013.872418.

Conway-Silva, Bethany A., Christine R. Filer, Kate Kenski, and Eric Tsetsi. 2017. "Reassessing Twitter's Agenda-Building Power: An Analysis of Intermedia Agenda-Setting Effects during the 2016 Presidential Primary Season." *Social Science Computer Review*, July. Accessed December 23, 2017. https://doi.org/10 .1177/0894439317715430.

Cooper, Glenda. 2009. "When Lines between NGO and News Organization Blur." *Nieman Lab*, December 21. Accessed December 20, 2017. www.nieman lab.org/2009/12/glenda-cooper-when-lines-between-ngo-and-news-organi zation-blur.

———. 2011. "From Their Own Correspondent? New Media and the Changes in Disaster Coverage: Lessons to Be Learnt." *Reuters Institute for the Study of Journalism*. Accessed December 21, 2017. https://reutersinstitute.politics.ox.ac.uk /sites/default/files/2017-11/From%20Their%20Own%20Correspondent.pdf.

Cottle, Simon, and David Nolan. 2007. "Global Humanitarianism and the Changing Aid-Media Field." *Journalism Studies* 8, no. 6: 862–78. Accessed April 29, 2015. doi:10.1080/14616700701556104.

Craige, Betty Jean. 1996. *American Patriotism in a Global Society*. Albany: SUNY Press.

Cronkite, Walter. 2007. "Media Played Role in '70s Mideast Peace Process." *NPR .org*. Accessed April 7, 2015. www.npr.org/templates/story/story.php?storyId =6861044.

Crovitz, L. Gordon. 2011. "The VOA Is Losing Its Voice." *Wall Street Journal*, April 18. Accessed January 9, 2013. https://online.wsj.com/article/SB100014240527487 04495004576264880231253582.html.

Cull, Nicholas J. 2008. *The Cold War and the United States Information Agency: American Propaganda and Public Diplomacy, 1945–1989*. Cambridge: Cambridge University Press.

———. 2011. "WikiLeaks, Public Diplomacy 2.0 and the State of Digital Public Diplomacy." *Place Branding and Public Diplomacy* 7, no. 1: 1–8. Accessed May 21, 2013. doi:10.1057/pb.2011.2.

Dahl, Robert A. 1956. *A Preface to Democratic Theory*. Expanded edition. Chicago: University of Chicago Press.

———. 1961. *Who Governs? Democracy and Power in an American City*. New Haven, CT: Yale University Press.

Danielian, Lucig, and Stephen D. Reese. 1989. "A Closer Look at Intermedia Influences on Agenda Setting: The Cocaine Issue of 1986." In *Communication Campaigns about Drugs: Government, Media, and the Public*, edited by Pamela J. Shoemaker, 47–66. New York: Routledge.

Davies, Philip H. J. 2001. "Spies as Informants: Triangulation and the Interpretation of Elite Interview Data in the Study of the Intelligence and Security Services." *Politics* 21, no. 1: 73–80. Accessed August 26, 2015. doi:10.1111/1467-9256 .00138.

Davis, Aeron. 2009. "Journalist-Source Relations, Mediated Reflexivity and the Politics of Politics." *Journalism Studies* 10, no. 2: 204–19. Accessed May 3, 2015. doi:10.1080/14616700802580540.

Davis, Richard. 2012. "Blogging and the Future of News." In *The SAGE Handbook of Political Communication*, edited by Holli A. Semetko and Margaret Scammell, 49–61. Los Angeles: SAGE.

DellaVigna, Stefano, and Ethan Kaplan. 2006. "The Fox News Effect: Media Bias and Voting." Working Paper 12169. National Bureau of Economic Research. Accessed September 1, 2014. www.nber.org/papers/w12169.

Dell'Orto, Giovanna. 2013. *American Journalism and International Relations: Foreign Correspondence from the Early Republic to the Digital Era*. Cambridge: Cambridge University Press.

DeMars, William E. 2001. "Hazardous Partnership: NGOs and United States Intelligence in Small Wars." *International Journal of Intelligence and CounterIntelligence* 14, no. 2: 193–222. Accessed April 24, 2015. doi:10.1080/08850600130006 3154.

Demick, Barbara. 2015. "The Times, Bloomberg News, and the Richest Man in China." *New Yorker*, May 5. Accessed May 6, 2016. www.newyorker.com/news /news-desk/how-not-to-get-kicked-out-of-china.

Dizard, Wilson P. 2004. *Inventing Public Diplomacy: The Story of the U.S. Information Agency*. Boulder, CO: Lynne Rienner.

Dorril, Stephen. 2002. *MI6: Inside the Covert World of Her Majesty's Secret Intelligence Service*. New York: Simon and Schuster.

Dover, Robert, and Michael S. Goodman. 2009. *Spinning Intelligence: Why Intelligence Needs the Media, Why the Media Needs Intelligence*. New York: Columbia University Press.

Downie, Leonard, Jr., and Michael Schudson. 2009. "The Reconstruction of American Journalism." *Columbia Journalism Review*, November/December. Accessed

May 7, 2016. www.cjr.org/reconstruction/the_reconstruction_of_american
.php.

Dulles, Allen. (1963) 2006. *Craft of Intelligence: America's Legendary Spy Master on the Fundamentals of Intelligence Gathering for a Free World*. Lanham, MD: Rowman & Littlefield.

Eckel, Mike. 2017. "U.S. Radio Station Registers as 'Foreign Agent' for Russian Sputnik Broadcasts." *RadioFreeEurope/RadioLiberty*, November 17. Accessed December 27, 2017. https://www.rferl.org/a/us-russia-foreign-agent-sputnik-radio-station-washington-registration/28860508.html.

Eftimiades, Nicholas. 1994. *Chinese Intelligence Operations*. Annapolis, MD: Naval Institute Press.

Elhassani, Camille. 2011. "US Intelligence Success." *Al Jazeera Blogs*. May 8. Accessed May 3, 2015. http://blogs.aljazeera.com/blog/americas/us-intelligence-success.

El-Nawawy, Mohammed, and Sahar Khamis. 2016. *Egyptian Revolution 2.0: Political Blogging, Civic Engagement, and Citizen Journalism*. Berlin: Springer.

Enda, Jodi. 2011. "Retreating from the World." *American Journalism Review*. Accessed February 8, 2013. www.ajrarchive.org/article.asp?id=4985.

Ennis, Stephen. 2015. "Russia in 'Information War' with West." *BBC News*, September 16, sec. Europe. Accessed December 28, 2017. www.bbc.com/news/world-europe-34248178

Entman, Robert M. 1989. "How the Media Affect What People Think: An Information Processing Approach." *Journal of Politics* 51, no. 2: 347–70. Accessed May 15, 2015. doi:10.2307/2131346.

———. 2004. *Projections of Power: Framing News, Public Opinion, and U.S. Foreign Policy*. Chicago: University of Chicago Press.

———. 2008. "Theorizing Mediated Public Diplomacy: The U.S. Case." *International Journal of Press/Politics* 13, no. 2: 87–102. Accessed February 8, 2013. doi:10.1177/1940161208314657.

Evans, Alfred B. 2006. "Vladimir Putin's Design for Civil Society." In *Russian Civil Society: A Critical Assessment*, edited by Alfred B. Evans Jr., Laura A. Henry, and Lisa McIntosh Sundstrom, 147–58. London: Routledge.

Fakazis, Elizabeth. 2003. "How Close Is Too Close? When Journalists Become Their Sources." In *Desperately Seeking Ethics: A Guide to Media Conduct*, edited by Howard Good, 45–60. Lanham, MD: Scarecrow.

Famularo, Julia. 2015. "The China-Russia NGO Crackdown." *Diplomat*, February 23. Accessed May 1, 2015. http://thediplomat.com/2015/02/the-china-russia-ngo-crackdown.

Farah, Douglas, and Andy Mosher. 2010. *Winds from the East*. Washington, DC: Center for International Media Assistance. Accessed October 7, 2012. www.re-visto.de/wp-content/uploads/2010/09/CIMA-China-Report_0.pdf.

Farhi, Paul. 2005. "At the Times, a Scoop Deferred." *Washington Post*, December 17, sec. Nation. Accessed May 5, 2015. www.washingtonpost.com/wp-dyn/content /article/2005/12/16/AR2005121601716.html.

Farrell, Joseph P. 2009. *The Philosopher's Stone: Alchemy and the Secret Research for Exotic Matter*. Los Angeles: Feral House.

Fico, Frederick, Stephen Lacy, Steven S. Wildman, Thomas Baldwin, Daniel Bergan, and Paul Zube. 2013. "Citizen Journalism Sites as Information Substitutes and Complements for United States Newspaper Coverage of Local Governments." *Digital Journalism* 1, no. 1: 152–68. Accessed December 28, 2017. https://doi.org /10.1080/21670811.2012.740270.

Filkins, Dexter, and Mark Mazzetti. 2010. "Contractors Tied to Effort to Track and Kill Militants." *New York Times*, March 14, sec. World / Asia Pacific. Accessed May 4, 2015. www.nytimes.com/2010/03/15/world/asia/15contractors .html.

Flew, Terry. 2017. "CGTN: China's Latest Attempt to Win Friends and Influence People." *China Policy Institute: Analysis* (blog), May 1. Accessed December 21, 2017. https://cpianalysis.org/2017/05/01/cgtn-chinas-latest-attempt-to-win -friends-and-influence-people.

Forum on China-Africa Cooperation. 2013. "FOCAC ABC." April 9. Accessed May 10, 2016. www.focac.org/eng/ltda/ltjj/t933522.htm.

Franks, Suzanne. 2008. "Getting into Bed with Charity." *British Journalism Review* 19, no. 3: 27–32. Accessed December 21, 2017. https://doi.org/10.1177/0956 474808097346.

Fritzinger, Linda. 2006. *Diplomat without Portfolio: Valentine Chirol, His Life and "The Times."* London: I. B. Tauris.

Gabrielson, Ryan. 2014. "Intelligence Gap: How a Chinese National Gained Access to Arizona's Terror Center." *ProPublica*, August 26. Accessed May 10, 2016. https://www.propublica.org/article/lizhong-fan.

Gagliardone, Iginio. 2013. "China as a Persuader: CCTV Africa's First Steps in the African Mediasphere." *Ecquid Novi: African Journalism Studies* 34, no. 3: 25–40. Accessed December 29, 2017. https://doi.org/10.1080/02560054.2013.834835.

Garon, Jon. 2012. "Revolutions and Expatriates: Social Networking, Ubiquitous Media and the Disintermediation of the State." SSRN Scholarly Paper ID 2008024. Rochester, NY: Social Science Research Network. Accessed May 17, 2015. http://papers.ssrn.com/abstract=2008024.

Garthoff, Raymond L. 1989. *Reflections on the Cuban Missile Crisis: Revised to Include New Revelations from Soviet and Cuban Sources*. Washington, DC: Brookings Institution Press.

Gelder, Lawrence Van. 1995. "John A. Scali, 77, ABC Reporter Who Helped Ease Missile Crisis." *New York Times*, October 10, sec. US. Accessed April 7, 2015.

www.nytimes.com/1995/10/10/us/john-a-scali-77-abc-reporter-who-helped
-ease-missile-crisis.html.

Gendron, Angela. 2005. "Just War, Just Intelligence: An Ethical Framework for Foreign Espionage." *International Journal of Intelligence and CounterIntelligence* 18,
no. 3: 398–434. Accessed May 2, 2016. doi:10.1080/08850600590945399.

Geniets, Anne. 2013. *The Global News Challenge: Market Strategies of International
Broadcasting Organizations in Developing Countries.* Abingdon: Routledge.

George, Alexander L., and Andrew Bennett. 2005. *Case Studies and Theory Development in the Social Sciences.* Cambridge: MIT Press. Accessed August 26, 2015.
https://mitpress.mit.edu/books/case-studies-and-theory-development-social
-sciences.

Gerring, John. 2004. "What Is a Case Study and What Is It Good For?" *American
Political Science Review* 98, no. 2: 341–54. Accessed March 6, 2013. doi:10.1017
/S0003055404001182.

Gil, Jeffrey. 2017. *Soft Power and the Worldwide Promotion of Chinese Language Learning: The Confucius Institute Project.* Bristol: Multilingual Matters.

Gilboa, Eytan. 2000. "Mass Communication and Diplomacy: A Theoretical Framework." *Communication Theory* 10, no. 3: 275–309. Accessed March 12, 2014.
doi:10.1111/j.1468-2885.2000.tb00193.x.

———. 2001. "Diplomacy in the Media Age: Three Models of Uses and Effects."
Diplomacy and Statecraft 12, no. 2: 1–28. Accessed March 12, 2014. doi:10.1080
/09592290108406201.

———. 2002. "Global Communication and Foreign Policy." *Journal of Communication* 52, no. 4: 731–48. Accessed March 7, 2014. doi:10.1111/j.1460-2466.2002
.tb02571.x.

———. 2005a. "The CNN Effect: The Search for a Communication Theory of
International Relations." *Political Communication* 22, no. 1: 27–44. Accessed
September 30, 2012. doi:10.1080/10584600590908429.

———. 2005b. "Global Television News and Foreign Policy: Debating the CNN
Effect." *International Studies Perspectives* 6, no. 3: 325–41. Accessed February 8,
2013. doi:10.1111/j.1528-3577.2005.00211.x.

———. 2005c. "Media-Broker Diplomacy: When Journalists Become Mediators."
Critical Studies in Media Communication 22, no. 2: 99–120. Accessed December 27, 2017. https://doi.org/10.1080/07393180500071998.

———. 2008. "Searching for a Theory of Public Diplomacy." *Annals of the American
Academy of Political and Social Science* 616, no. 1: 55–77. Accessed January 6,
2014. doi:10.1177/0002716207312142.

———. 2016. "Digital Diplomacy." In *The SAGE Handbook of Diplomacy,* edited by
Costas M. Constantinou, Pauline Kerr, and Paul Sharp, 540–51. Los Angeles:
SAGE.

Gitlin, Todd. 2013. "The Washington Post Doesn't Need a New-Media Mogul—It Needs an Old-Fashioned One." *New Republic*, August 14. Accessed August 14, 2013. https://newrepublic.com/article/114286/jeff-bezos-washington-post -needs-old-fashioned-mogul.

Golan, Guy. 2006. "Inter-Media Agenda Setting and Global News Coverage." *Journalism Studies* 7, no. 2: 323–33. Accessed May 2, 2015. doi:10.1080/14616700 500533643.

———. 2013. "The Gates of Op-Ed Diplomacy: Newspaper Framing the 2011 Egyptian Revolution." *International Communication Gazette* 75, no. 4: 359–73. Accessed February 18, 2018. http://journals.sagepub.com/doi/abs/10.1177/17 48048513482264.

Golan, Guy J., and Josephine Lukito. 2015. "The Rise of the Dragon? Framing China's Global Leadership in Elite American Newspapers." *International Communication Gazette* 77, no. 8: 754–72. Accessed December 27, 2017. https://doi.org /10.1177/1748048515601576.

Goode, Luke. 2009. "Social News, Citizen Journalism and Democracy." *New Media and Society*, November. Accessed May 10, 2015. doi:10.1177/146144480934 1393.

Goodrich, Austin. 2004. *Born to Spy: Recollections of a CIA Case Officer*. New York: iUniverse.

Gores, Paul. 2013. "Goodrich Combined Journalism with Undercover Service." *Milwaukee-Wisconsin Journal Sentinel*, June 22. Accessed January 10, 2018. www .jsonline.com/news/obituaries/goodrich-combined-journalism-with-under cover-service-b9939614z1-212639361.html.

Grayson, Louise. 2014. "The Role of Non-Government Organisations (NGOS) in Practising Editorial Photography in a Globalised Media Environment." *Journalism Practice* 8, no. 5: 632–45. Accessed December 21, 2017. https://doi.org/10 .1080/17512786.2014.883124.

Green, Justin. 2012. "Journalist, or Spy? Xinhua Doesn't Distinguish." *Daily Beast*, August 24. Accessed April 11, 2015. www.thedailybeast.com/articles/2012/08 /24/chinese-agency-spying.html.

Greenwald, Glenn, Ewen MacAskill, and Laura Poitras. 2013. "Edward Snowden: The Whistleblower behind the NSA Surveillance Revelations." *Guardian*, June 11. Accessed April 26, 2015. www.theguardian.com/world/2013/jun/09 /edward-snowden-nsa-whistleblower-surveillance.

Griffith, Erin. 2017. "Memo to Facebook: How to Tell If You're a Media Company." *Wired*, October 12. Accessed January 11, 2018. https://www.wired.com/story /memo-to-facebook-how-to-tell-if-youre-a-media-company.

Grossman, Andrew. 2015. "U.S. Charges Six Chinese Citizens with Economic Espionage." *Wall Street Journal*, May 20, sec. US. Accessed May 10, 2015. www

.wsj.com/articles/u-s-charges-six-chinese-citizens-with-economic-espionage-1432046527.

Gruntman, Mike. 2010. *Enemy amongst Trojans: A Soviet Spy at USC.* Los Angeles: Figueroa.

Gu, Mini. 2017. "The Sino-African Higher Educational Exchange: How Big Is It and Will It Continue?" *World Education News and Reviews*, March 7. Accessed December 29, 2017. https://wenr.wes.org/2017/03/the-sino-african-higher-educational-exchange-how-big-is-it-and-will-it-continue.

Guangyuan, Liu. 2011. "Building a Better China-Africa Partnership." Presentation at the *Towards a New Africa-China Partnership* conference, Nairobi, March 28. Accessed February 18, 2018. http://www.fmprc.gov.cn/ce/ceke/eng/zkgx/t831021.htm.

Guillermo, Emil. 2015. "Calls for Investigation over Alleged Profiling of Chinese-Americans Scientists Grow." *NBC News*, November 24. Accessed May 10, 2016. www.nbcnews.com/news/asian-america/calls-investigation-over-alleged-profiling-chinese-americans-scientists-grow-n468736.

Guzman, Andrea L. 2016. "Evolution of News Frames during the 2011 Egyptian Revolution: Critical Discourse Analysis of Fox News's and CNN's Framing of Protesters, Mubarak, and the Muslim Brotherhood." *Journalism and Mass Communication Quarterly* 93, no. 1: 80–98. https://doi.org/10.1177/1077699015606677.

Haigh, Michel M., Michael Pfau, Jamie Danesi, Robert Tallmon, Tracy Bunko, Shannon Nyberg, Bertha Thompson, Chance Babin, Sal Cardella, and Michael Mink. 2006. "A Comparison of Embedded and Nonembedded Print Coverage of the U.S. Invasion and Occupation of Iraq." *International Journal of Press/Politics* 11, no. 2 (April): 139–53.

Halberstam, David. 1993. *The Best and the Brightest.* New York: Ballantine Books.

Hale, John R. 2009. *Lords of the Sea: The Epic Story of the Athenian Navy and the Birth of Democracy.* London: Penguin.

Hallin, Daniel C. 1989. *The Uncensored War: The Media and Vietnam.* Berkeley: University of California Press.

Hamilton, John Maxwell, and Eric Jenner. 2004. "Redefining Foreign Correspondence." *Journalism* 5, no. 3: 301–21. Accessed August 22, 2014. doi:10.1177/1464884904044938.

Hamilton, Keith, and Richard Langhorne. 2011. *The Practice of Diplomacy: Its Evolution, Theory, and Administration.* 2d ed. Abingdon: Routledge.

Harding, Luke. 2014. "Russia Expels US Journalist David Satter without Explanation." *Guardian*, January 13, sec. World. Accessed January 23, 2014. www.theguardian.com/world/2014/jan/13/russia-expels-american-journalist-david-satter.

Harding, Thomas. 2001. "Blast Survivor Tells of Massoud Assassination." *Telegraph*, October 26. Accessed January 10, 2018. www.telegraph.co.uk/news/worldnews /asia/afghanistan/1360632/Blast-survivor-tells-of-Massoud-assassination .html.

Harris, Charles Houston, and Louis R. Sadler. 2003. *The Archaeologist Was a Spy: Sylvanus G. Morley and the Office of Naval Intelligence.* Albuquerque: University of New Mexico Press.

Harris, Shane. 2015. "This Russian News Agency Doubled as a Spy Machine." *Daily Beast*, January 27. Accessed May 4, 2015. www.thedailybeast.com/articles/2015 /01/27/meet-russian-spies-best-friends-in-the-media-itar-tass.html.

Hashimoto, Kayoko, ed. 2018. *Japanese Language and Soft Power in Asia.* Singapore: Palgrave Macmillan.

Hasmath, Reza. 2016. "China's NGOs Go Global." *Diplomat*, March 23. Accessed December 29, 2017. https://thediplomat.com/2016/03/chinas-ngos-go-global.

Haynes, John Earl, Alexander Vassiliev, and Harvey Kehr. 2009. *Spies: The Rise and Fall of the KGB in America.* New Haven, CT: Yale University Press.

Herman, Michael. 1996. *Intelligence Power in Peace and War.* Cambridge: Cambridge University Press.

Herpen, Marcel H. Van. 2016. *Putin's Propaganda Machine: Soft Power and Russian Foreign Policy.* Lanham, MD: Rowman and Littlefield.

Hille, Kathrin. 2012. "Chinese State TV Tries to Woo US." *Financial Times*, February 13. Accessed May 10, 2015. www.ft.com/intl/cms/s/0/2d2c7cb8-5552-11e1 -b66d-00144feabdc0.html#axzz3ZkWYBDdH.

Hinsley, Francis Harry, and C. A. G. Simkins. 1990. *British Intelligence in the Second World War: Security and Counter-Intelligence.* Cambridge: Cambridge University Press.

Hodgson, Godfrey. 1987. "Yale—a Great Nursery of Spooks: Review of *Cloak and Gown: Scholars in the Secret War, 1939–1961* by Robin W. Winks." *New York Times*, August 16, sec. Books. Accessed May 7, 2016. www.nytimes.com/1987 /08/16/books/yale-a-great-nursery-of-spooks.html.

Holley, Peter. 2015. "Post Correspondent Jason Rezaian Sentenced to Prison Term in Iran." *Washington Post*, November 22. Accessed May 9, 2016. https://www .washingtonpost.com/world/post-correspondent-jason-rezaian-sentenced-to -prison-term-in-iran/2015/11/22/bfb5c112-912f-11e5-befa-99ceebcbb272 _story.html.

Holmes, Mark. 2013. "Bukashkin Talks Russia Today's Next Generation Growth Plans." *Via Satellite*, October 16. Accessed May 7, 2016. www.satellitetoday.com /publications/2013/10/16/bukashkin-talks-russia-todays-next-generation -growth-plans.

Holt, Kristoffer, and Michael Karlsson. 2015. "'Random Acts of Journalism'? How Citizen Journalists Tell the News in Sweden." *New Media and Society* 17, no. 11: 1795–1810. Accessed December 28, 2017. https://doi.org/10.1177/1461444814535189.

Horton, Scott. 2010. "The Trouble with Contractors." *Browsings: The Harper's Blog,* March 16. Accessed May 7, 2016. https://harpers.org/blog/2010/03/the-trouble-with-contractors.

House of Commons, Foreign Affairs Committee. 2011. *The Implications of Cuts to the BBC World Service: Sixth Report of Session 2010–11, Vol. 1: Report, Together with Formal Minutes, Oral and Written Evidence.* London: Stationery Office.

Howard, Philip N. 2015. *Pax Technica: How the Internet of Things May Set Us Free or Lock Us Up.* New Haven, CT : Yale University Press.

Hsu, Jennifer Y. J., Timothy Hildebrandt, and Reza Hasmath. 2016. "'Going Out' or Staying In? The Expansion of Chinese NGOs in Africa." *Development Policy Review* 34, no. 3: 423–39. Accessed December 28, 2017. https://doi.org/10.1111/dpr.12157.

Hudson, John. 2015. "Top American Diplomat Decries 'Lies' of Russian Media." *Foreign Policy,* January 27. Accessed May 7, 2016. https://foreignpolicy.com/2015/01/27/top-american-diplomat-decries-lies-of-russian-media.

Ichihara, Maiko. 2018. *Japan's International Democracy Assistance as Soft Power: Neoclassical Realist Analysis.* New York: Routledge.

Interagency OPSEC Support Staff. 2004. *Intelligence Threat Handbook.* Operations Security Information Series. Accessed February 18, 2018. https://fas.org/irp/threat/handbook/index.html.

International Fund for Animal Welfare. 2012. "NGO Intelligence Led to Ivory Bust in China." *IFAW.* August 12. Accessed May 5, 2015. www.ifaw.org/canada/news/ngo-intelligence-led-ivory-bust-china.

Ioffe, Julia. 2010. "What Is Russia Today?" *Columbia Journalism Review,* September/October. Accessed May 7, 2016. www.cjr.org/feature/what_is_russia_today.php.

———. 2015. "Spy vs. Nonspy in Putin's Russia." *New York Times,* January 30. Accessed April 22, 2015. www.nytimes.com/2015/01/30/magazine/spy-vs-nonspy-in-putins-russia.html.

Ipek, Pinar. 2015. "Ideas and Change in Foreign Policy Instruments: Soft Power and the Case of the Turkish International Cooperation and Development Agency." *Foreign Policy Analysis* 11, no. 2: 173–93. Accessed December 23, 2017. https://doi.org/10.1111/fpa.12031.

Iwabuchi, Koichi. 2015. "Pop-Culture Diplomacy in Japan: Soft Power, Nation Branding and the Question of 'International Cultural Exchange.'" *International Journal of Cultural Policy* 21, no. 4: 419–32. Accessed December 22, 2017. https://doi.org/10.1080/10286632.2015.1042469.

Iyengar, Shanto, and Kyu S. Hahn. 2009. "Red Media, Blue Media: Evidence of Ideological Selectivity in Media Use." *Journal of Communication* 59, no. 1: 19–39. Accessed October 7, 2012. doi:10.1111/j.1460-2466.2008.01402.x.

Jaramillo, Deborah L. 2009. *Ugly War, Pretty Package: How CNN and Fox News Made the Invasion of Iraq High Concept.* Bloomington: Indiana University Press.

Jemberga, Sanita. 2015. "Kremlin's Millions." *Re:Baltica, Baltic Centre for Investigative Journalism*, August 27. Accessed May 7, 2016. www.rebaltica.lv/en/investigations /money_from_russia/a/1257/kremlins_millions.html.

Johnson, A. Ross. 2010. *Radio Free Europe and Radio Liberty: The CIA Years and Beyond.* Washington, DC: Woodrow Wilson Center Press.

Johnson, A. Ross, and R. Eugene Parta. 2010. *Cold War Broadcasting: Impact on the Soviet Union and Eastern Europe : A Collection of Studies and Documents.* Budapest: Central European University Press.

Johnson, Loch K. 2007. *Handbook of Intelligence Studies.* London: Routledge.

Kaiser, Robert. 2014. "The Bad News about the News." *Brookings Institution*, October 16. Accessed May 17, 2015. www.brookings.edu/research/essays/2014/bad -news.

Kazin, Michael. 2008. "Dancing to the CIA's Tune." *Washington Post*, January 27, sec. Arts & Living. Accessed January 10, 2018. www.washingtonpost.com/wp-dyn /content/article/2008/01/24/AR2008012402369.html.

Keohane, Robert O., and Joseph S. Nye 1998. "Power and Interdependence in the Information Age." *Foreign Affairs* 77, no. 5: 81–94. Accessed January 8, 2014. doi:10.2307/20049052.

Khatib, Lina, William Dutton, and Michael Thelwall. 2012. "Public Diplomacy 2.0: A Case Study of the US Digital Outreach Team." *Middle East Journal* 66, no. 3: 453–72. Accessed December 11, 2015. https://muse.jhu.edu/journals/the _middle_east_journal/v066/66.3.khatib.html.

Kimball, Spencer. 2013. "UK Reporters Battle Pre-Publication Censorship." *DW.DE.*, August 21. Accessed May 5, 2015. www.dw.de/uk-reporters-battle-pre -publication-censorship/a-17037772.

King, Gary, Robert O. Keohane, and Sidney Verba. 1994. *Designing Social Inquiry: Scientific Inference in Qualitative Research.* Princeton, NJ: Princeton University Press.

King, Nathan. 2015. "CCTV's the Heat on Hillary Clinton's Presidential Bid." *CCTV America*, April 14. Accessed April 15, 2015. www.cctv-america.com/2015/04/14 /cctvs-the-heat-on-hillary-clintons-presidential-bid.

Kingsbury, Alex. 2008. "Spy Agencies Turn to Newspapers, NPR, and Wikipedia for Information." *US News and World Report*, September 12. Accessed May 17, 2015. www.usnews.com/news/national/articles/2008/09/12/spy-agencies-turn-to -newspapers-npr-and-wikipedia-for-information.

Kirkhorn, Michael J. 1999. "The Cold War Generation of Patriotic Journalists." *Nieman Reports* 53, no. 3: 71–73. Accessed April 10, 2015. http://niemanreports.org /articles/the-cold-war-generation-of-patriotic-journalists.

Kissinger, Henry. 1957. *Nuclear Weapons and Foreign Policy*. New York: Harper and Brothers.

———. (1994) 2012. *Diplomacy*. New York: Simon and Schuster.

Klein, Peter. 2014. "*The Interview* Reinforces a Negative View of US Journalists." *Columbia Journalism Review*, December 30. Accessed March 3, 2015. www.cjr .org/the_kicker/the_interview_negative.php.

Kofman, Michael, and Matthew Rojansky. 2015. "A Closer Look at Russia's 'Hybrid War.'" *Kennan Cable*, no. 7. Accessed May 7, 2016. www.wilsoncenter.org/sites /default/files/7-KENNAN%20CABLE-ROJANSKY%20KOFMAN.pdf.

Kounalakis, Eleni. 2015. *Madam Ambassador: Three Years of Diplomacy, Dinner Parties, and Democracy in Budapest*. New York: New Press.

Kounalakis, Markos. 2014a. "The Risky Business of a Foreign Correspondent." *Sacramento Bee*, September 7. Accessed May 3, 2015. www.sacbee.com/opinion /op-ed/article2608825.html.

———. 2014b. "The Conversation: America's International Broadcasters Are Losing the Air Wars." *Sacramento Bee*, June 22. Accessed May 3, 2015. www.sacbee.com /opinion/the-conversation/article2601683.html.

———. 2015a. "The Press and Pressure: A Critical Discourse Analysis of the Promotion of 'Responsibility to Protect' or 'Sovereignty' Narratives in the Ongoing Syrian Crisis." *Brazilian Journalism Research* 11, no. 1: 44–61. Accessed May 6, 2016. http://bjr.sbpjor.org.br/bjr/article/view/805.

———. 2015b. "The Feminist Was a Spook | The Sacramento Bee." *Sacramento Bee*, October 23. Accessed May 7, 2016. www.sacbee.com/opinion/op-ed/markos -kounalakis/article40988637.html.

Kounalakis, Markos, and Andras Simonyi. 2011. *The Hard Truth about Soft Power*. Los Angeles: Figueroa Press. Accessed January 9, 2018. https://uscpublic diplomacy.org/sites/uscpublicdiplomacy.org/files/useruploads/u35361 /2011%20Paper%205.pdf.

Kovach, Bill. 2002. "Commentary: Journalism and Patriotism." *Center for Public Integrity*, August 7. Accessed April 10, 2015. www.publicintegrity.org/2002/08 /07/3175/commentary-journalism-and-patriotism.

Kovach, Bill, and Tom Rosenstiel. 2014. *The Elements of Journalism: What Newspeople Should Know and the Public Should Expect*. New York: Three Rivers.

Kraut, Robert E., and Donald B. Poe. 1980. "Behavioral Roots of Person Perception: The Deception Judgments of Customs Inspectors and Laymen." *Journal of Personality and Social Psychology* 39, no. 5: 784–98. Accessed May 1, 2015. doi:10 .1037/0022-3514.39.5.784.

Kumar, Priya. 2011a. "Foreign Correspondents: Who Covers What." *American Journalism Review*, December/January. Accessed October 17, 2012. www.ajr.org/article.asp?id=4997.

———. 2011b. "Backpack Journalism Overseas." *American Journalism Review*, December/January. Accessed February 8, 2013. www.ajr.org/article.asp?id=4986.

Kurlantzick, Joshua. 2007. *Charm Offensive: How China's Soft Power Is Transforming the World*. New Haven, CT: Yale University Press.

Lai, Carol P. 2007. *Media in Hong Kong: Press Freedom and Political Change, 1967–2005*. Abingdon: Routledge.

Lang, A. 2000. "The Limited Capacity Model of Mediated Message Processing." *Journal of Communication* 50, no. 1: 46–70. Accessed April 19, 2015. doi:10.1111/j.1460-2466.2000.tb02833.x.

Larsen, Solana. 2010. "Should Local Voices Bring Us Foreign News?" *Nieman Reports* 64, no. 3: 14–15. Accessed April 10, 2014. http://niemanreports.org/articles/should-local-voices-bring-us-foreign-news.

Larson, James F. 2004. *The Internet and Foreign Policy*. Headline Series 325. New York: Foreign Policy Association.

Le, Elisabeth. 2006. *The Spiral of "Anti-Other Rhetoric": Discourses of Identity and the International Media Echo*. Amsterdam: John Benjamins.

Lenin, V. I. (1926) 1973. "To N. P. Gorbunov." In *Collected Works*, edited by Robert Daglish, translated by Andrew Rothstein, vol. 35, 473. Moscow: Progress. Accessed May 1, 2015. www.marx2mao.com/PDFs/Lenin%20CW-Vol.%2035.pdf.

Leonard, Mark. 2002. "Diplomacy by Other Means." *Foreign Policy*, no. 132 (September): 48–56. Accessed April 19, 2015. doi:10.2307/3183455.

Levendusky, Matthew S. 2013. "Why Do Partisan Media Polarize Viewers?" *American Journal of Political Science* 57, no. 3: 611–23. Accessed May 14, 2015. doi:10.1111/ajps.12008.

Levie, Howard S. 1961. "Prisoners of War and the Protecting Power." *American Journal of International Law* 55, no. 2: 374–97. Accessed April 9, 2015. doi:10.2307/2196124.

LeVine, Mark. 2012. "Scholars and Spies: A Disastrous Combination." *Al Jazeera English*, December 5. Accessed April 23, 2015. www.aljazeera.com/indepth/opinion/2012/12/201212475854134641.html.

Levy, Jack S. 2002. "Qualitative Methods in International Relations." In *Millennial Reflections on International Studies*, edited by Michael Brecher and Frank P. Harvey, 432–54. Ann Arbor: University of Michigan Press.

Li, Jing, and Andrea Chen. 2014. "Mainland Media Regulator Bans Journalists from Sharing Information." *South China Morning Post*, July 9.

Lichter, S. Robert, Stanley Rothman, and Linda S. Lichter. 1990. *The Media Elite: America's New Power Brokers*. Winter Park, FL: Hastings House.

Lilleker, Darren G. 2003. "Interviewing the Political Elite: Navigating a Potential Minefield." *Politics* 23, no. 3: 207–214. Accessed March 11, 2013. doi:10.1111 /1467-9256.00198.

Livingston, S. 1997. *Clarifying the CNN Effect: An Examination of Media Effects according to Type of Military Intervention*. Joan Shorenstein Center on the Press, Politics and Public Policy, John F. Kennedy School of Government, Harvard University. Accessed February 8, 2013. http://tamilnation.co/media/CNN effect.pdf.

Loane, Jabez W., IV. 1965. "Treason and Aiding the Enemy." *Military Law Review* 30: 43.

Loeb, Vernon. 2001. "Ex-Spy Says Expulsions Won't Slow Russia's Snooping." *Houston Chronicle*, April 2. Accessed April 26, 2015. www.chron.com/news/nation -world/article/Ex-spy-says-expulsions-won-t-slow-Russia-s-2015703.php.

Louw, Eric. 2010. *The Media and Political Process*. 2d ed. Los Angeles: SAGE.

Lukes, S. 2005. "Power and the Battle for Hearts and Minds." *Millennium* 33, no. 3: 477–93. Accessed June 4, 2013. doi:10.1177/03058298050330031201.

Lund, Michael. 2001. "A Toolbox for Responding to Conflicts and Building Peace." In *Peacebuilding: A Field Guide*, edited by Luc Reychler and Thania Paffenholz, 16–20. Boulder, CO: Lynne Rienner.

Luo, Ya. 2011. "Former Chinese Diplomat: Xinhua Part of Spy Network." *Epoch Times*, September 27. Accessed October 7, 2012. www.theepochtimes.com/n3 /1493656-former-chinese-diplomat-xinhua-part-of-spy-network.

MacLeod, Scott. 2001. "The Life and Death of Kevin Carter." *Time*, June 24. Accessed May 2, 2015. http://content.time.com/time/magazine/article/0,9171 ,165071,00.html.

Maguire, Miles. 2017. "Embedding Journalists Shape Iraq News Story." *Newspaper Research Journal* 38, no. 1: 8–18. Accessed December 27, 2017. https://doi.org /10.1177/0739532917696104.

Mansfield, Mark. 2010. "Spinning Intelligence: Why Intelligence Needs the Media, Why the Media Needs Intelligence." *Studies in Intelligence* 54, no. 1. Accessed May 3, 2015. https://www.cia.gov/library/center-for-the-study-of-intelligence /csi-publications/csi-studies/studies/volume-54-number-1/spinning -intelligence-why-intelligence-needs-the.html.

Maoz, Zeev. 2002. "Case Study Methodology in International Studies: From Storytelling to Hypothesis Testing." In *Evaluating Methodology in International Studies*, edited by P. Harvey and M. Brecher, 161–86. Ann Arbor: University of Michigan Press.

Markon, Jerry. 2010. "FBI Arrests 10 Accused of Working as Russian Spies." *Washington Post*, June 29, sec. Politics. Accessed April 26, 2015. www.washingtonpost.com/wp-dyn/content/article/2010/06/28/AR2010062805227.html.

Marsh, Vivien. 2016. "Mixed Messages, Partial Pictures? Discourses under Construction in CCTV's Africa Live Compared with the BBC." *Chinese Journal of Communication* 9, no. 1: 56–70. Accessed December 29, 2017. https://doi.org/10.1080/17544750.2015.1105269.

———. 2017. "Small Acts of Journalism: Professionalism and Integrity in CCTV's English-Language News." *China Policy Institute: Analysis* (blog), May 3. Accessed December 29, 2017. https://cpianalysis.org/2017/05/03/small-acts-of-journalism-professionalism-and-integrity-in-cctvs-english-language-news.

Martinson, Jane. 2015. "The Virtues of Vice: How Punk Magazine Was Transformed into Media Giant." *Guardian*, January 1. Accessed May 7, 2016. www.theguardian.com/media/2015/jan/01/virtues-of-vice-magazine-transformed-into-global-giant.

Marton, Kati. 2009. *Enemies of the People: My Family's Journey to America*. New York: Simon and Schuster.

———. 2011. "The Weapons of Diplomacy, and the Human Factor." *New York Times*, April 19. Accessed April 19, 2015. www.nytimes.com/2011/04/20/opinion/20iht-edmarton20.html.

Matelski, M. 1995. *Vatican Radio: Propagation by the Airwaves*. Westport, CT: Praeger.

Matthews, Christopher M., and Nicole Hong. 2015. "U.S. Charges Russian Banker in Spy Case." *Wall Street Journal*, January 26, sec. US. Accessed January 10, 2018. www.wsj.com/articles/u-s-accuses-three-of-spying-for-russia-1422303712.

Mattis, Peter. 2012. "The Analytic Challenge of Understanding Chinese Intelligence Services." *Studies in Intelligence* 56, no. 3: 50.

McCombs, Maxwell. 2005. "A Look at Agenda-Setting: Past, Present and Future." *Journalism Studies* 6, no. 4: 543–57. Accessed March 26, 2015. doi:10.1080/14616700500250438.

McQuail, Denis. 2013. *Journalism and Society*. Los Angeles: SAGE.

Melman, Yossi. 2010. "Respected Danish Journalist Admits 'I Was a Mossad Agent.'" *Haaretz.com*, March 4. Accessed May 5, 2015. www.haaretz.com/print-edition/features/respected-danish-journalist-admits-i-was-a-mossad-agent-1.264127.

Meraz, Sharon Melissa. 2007. "The Networked Political Blogosphere and Mass Media: Understanding How Agendas Are Formed, Framed, and Transferred in the Emerging New Media Environment." Austin: University of Texas at Austin.

———. 2011. "Using Time Series Analysis to Measure Intermedia Agenda-Setting Influence in Traditional Media and Political Blog Networks." *Journalism and*

Mass Communication Quarterly 88, no. 1: 176–94. Accessed May 2, 2015. doi:10.1177/107769901108800110.

Messner, Marcus, and Marcia Watson Distaso. 2008. "The Source Cycle." *Journalism Studies* 9, no. 3: 447–63. Accessed May 2, 2015. doi:10.1080/146167008019 99287.

Midtbø, Tor, Stefaan Walgrave, Peter Van Aelst, and Dag Arne Christensen. 2014. "Do the Media Set the Agenda of Parliament or Is It the Other Way Around? Agenda Interactions between MPs and Mass Media." In *Representing the People: A Survey among Members of Statewide and Substate Parliaments*, edited by Kris Deschouwer and Sam Depauw, 188–208. Oxford: Oxford University Press.

Miel, Persephone, and Robert Faris. 2008. "A Typology for Media Organizations." In *Media Re:Public*. Berkman Center for Internet and Society at Harvard University. Accessed May 1, 2015. https://cyber.law.harvard.edu/sites/cyber.law .harvard.edu/files/Typologies_MR.pdf.

Mkhoyan, Anna. 2017. "Soft Power, Russia and the Former Soviet States: A Case Study of Russian Language and Education in Armenia." *International Journal of Cultural Policy* 23, no. 6: 690–704. Accessed December 23, 2017. https://doi.org /10.1080/10286632.2016.1251426.

Moos, Felix, Richard Fardon, and Hugh Gusterson. 2005. "Anthropologists as Spies." *Anthropology Today* 21, no. 3: 25–26. Accessed April 23, 2015. doi:10.1111 /j.0268-540X.2005.00358.x.

Morello, Carol, Karen DeYoung, William Branigin, and Joby Warrick. 2016. "Plane Leaves Iran with Post Reporter, Other Americans in Swap." *Washington Post*, January 17. Accessed May 9, 2016. https://www.washingtonpost.com/world /iran-releases-post-correspondent-jason-rezaian-iranian-reports-say/2016/01 /16/e8ee7858-ba38-11e5-829c-26ffb874a18d_story.html.

Morozov, Evgeny. 2009. "Iran: Downside to the 'Twitter Revolution.'" *Dissent* 56, no. 4: 10–14.

Morris, Jonathan S. 2005. "The Fox News Factor." *Harvard International Journal of Press/Politics* 10, no. 3: 56–79. Accessed May 14, 2015. doi:10.1177 /1081180X05279264.

Mukherjee, Rohan. 2014. "The False Promise of India's Soft Power." *Geopolitics, History, and International Relations* 6, no. 1: 46–62.

Mullin, Benjamin. 2015. "McClatchy to Shutter Foreign Bureaus in Reorganization of D.C. Operation." *Poynter*, October 12. Accessed May 8, 2016. www.poyn ter.org/2015/mcclatchy-to-shutter-foreign-bureaus-in-reorganization-of-d-c -operation/378166/.

Mullins, Brody. 2015. "Google Makes Most of Close Ties to White House." *Wall Street Journal*, March 25, sec. Tech. Accessed May 5, 2015. www.wsj.com/articles /google-makes-most-of-close-ties-to-white-house-1427242076.

Murtha, John P. 2010. *From Vietnam to 9/11: On the Front Lines of National Security.* University Park: Pennsylvania State University Press.

Mustafi, Sambuddha Mitra. 2012. "Sino the Times: Can China's Billions Buy Media Credibility?" *Columbia Journalism Review* 51, no. 1 (May/June): 19. Accessed February 4, 2013. www.cjr.org/feature/sino_the_times.php.

National Intelligence Council. 2017. *Intelligence Community Assessment: Assessing Russian Activities and Intentions in Recent US Elections.* ICA 2017-01D. 2017. Accessed December 28, 2017. https://www.dni.gov/files/documents/ICA_2017_01.pdf.

Naureckas, Jim. 1991. "Gulf War Coverage: The Worst Censorship Was at Home." *Fairness and Accuracy in Reporting*, April. Accessed January 8, 2018. https://fair.org/extra/gulf-war-coverage.

Naveh, Chanan. 2002. "The Role of the Media in Foreign Policy Decision-Making: A Theoretical Framework." *Conflict and Communication Online* 1, no. 2: 1–14. Accessed October 17, 2012. www.cco.regener-online.de/2002_2/pdf_2002_2/naveh.pdf.

Nelson, Anne. 2013. *CCTV's International Expansion: China's Grand Strategy for Media?* Center for International Media Assistance. Accessed May 7, 2016. www.cima.ned.org/wp-content/uploads/2015/02/CIMA-China%20Anne%20Nelson_0.pdf.

Nelson, Michael. 1997. *War of the Black Heavens: The Battles of Western Broadcasting in the Cold War.* Syracuse, NY: Syracuse University Press.

Nesbitt-Larking, Paul. 2007. *Politics, Society, and the Media.* Toronto: University of Toronto Press.

Nichols, John Spicer. 1984. "Wasting the Propaganda Dollar." *Foreign Policy*, no. 56: 129. Accessed May 12, 2013. doi:10.2307/1148478.

Nicholson, Nigel. 1998. "How Hardwired Is Human Behavior." *Harvard Business Review* (August): 135–47.

Nieman Journalism Lab. 2009. "NGOs and the News." *Nieman Lab.* Accessed May 4, 2015. www.niemanlab.org/ngo/.

Nisbet, Erik C., Matthew C. Nisbet, Dietram A. Scheufele, and James E. Shanahan. 2004. "Public Diplomacy, Television News, and Muslim Opinion." *Harvard International Journal of Press/Politics* 9, no. 2: 11–37. Accessed March 11, 2014. doi:10.1177/1081180X04263459.

Nothias, Toussaint. 2016. "How Western Journalists Actually Write about Africa: Re-assessing the Myth of Representations of Africa." *Journalism Studies*, 1–22. Accessed December 28, 2017. https://doi.org/https://doi.org/10.1080/1461670X.2016.1262748.

Nye, Joseph S. 1990a. *Bound to Lead: The Changing Nature of American Power.* New York: Basic Books.

————. 1990b. "The Changing Nature of World Power." *Political Science Quarterly* 105, no. 2: 177–92. Accessed May 12 2015. doi:10.2307/2151022.

————. 2004. *Soft Power: The Means to Success in World Politics.* New York: Public Affairs.

————. 2008. "Public Diplomacy and Soft Power." *Annals of the American Academy of Political and Social Science* 616, no. 1: 94–109. Accessed February 12, 2013. doi:10.1177/0002716207311699.

————. 2009. "Smart Power." *New Perspectives Quarterly* 26, no. 2: 7–9. Accessed May 30, 2013. doi:10.1111/j.1540-5842.2009.01057.x.

————. 2011. *The Future of Power.* New York: PublicAffairs.

Oğuzlu, Tarik. 2007. "Soft Power in Turkish Foreign Policy." *Australian Journal of International Affairs* 61, no. 1: 81–97. Accessed March 11, 2014. doi:10.1080/10357710601142518.

————. 2013. "The Gezi Park Protests and Its Impact on Turkey's Soft-Power Abroad." *Middle Eastern Analysis / Ortadogu Analiz* 5, no. 55: 10–15.

Okrent, Daniel. 2004. "Paper of Record? No Way, No Reason, No Thanks." *New York Times*, April 25. Accessed May 7, 2015. www.nytimes.com/2004/04/25/weekinreview/the-public-editor-paper-of-record-no-way-no-reason-no-thanks.html.

Olander, Eric. 2015a. "[AUDIO] China's Expanding Military Presence in Africa." *China Africa Project*, July 1. Accessed May 7, 2016. www.chinaafricaproject.com/podcast-china-military-africa-david-shinn.

————. 2015b. "[AUDIO] The China Economy: What Lessons for Africa?" *China Africa Project*, August 29. Accessed May 7, 2016. www.chinaafricaproject.com/podcast-china-africa-economy-lessons-daouda-cisse/.

————. 2016. "[AUDIO] The Long Arm of Chinese Law Reaches All the Way to Kenya." *China Africa Project*, April 20. Accessed May 7, 2016. www.chinaafricaproject.com/audio-long-arm-chinese-law-reaches-way-kenya/.

Otmazgin, Nissim Kadosh. 2008. "Contesting Soft Power: Japanese Popular Culture in East and Southeast Asia." *International Relations of the Asia-Pacific* 8, no. 1: 73–101. Accessed March 11, 2014. doi:10.1093/irap/lcm009.

Ott, Brian L. 2017. "The Age of Twitter: Donald J. Trump and the Politics of Debasement." *Critical Studies in Media Communication* 34, no. 1: 59–68. Accessed December 23, 2017. https://doi.org/10.1080/15295036.2016.1266686.

Otto, Florian, and Christoph O. Meyer. 2012. "Missing the Story? Changes in Foreign News Reporting and Their Implications for Conflict Prevention." *Media, War and Conflict* 5, no. 3: 205–21. Accessed February 8, 2013. doi:10.1177/1750635212458621.

Painter, James. 2008. *Counter-Hegemonic News: A Case Study of Al-Jazeera English and Telesûr.* Reuters Institute for the Study of Journalism, University of Oxford.

Accessed May 11, 2015. http://reutersinstitute.politics.ox.ac.uk/publication /counter-hegemonic-news.

Paradise, James F. 2009. "China and International Harmony: The Role of Confucius Institutes in Bolstering Beijing's Soft Power." Accessed March 11, 2014. doi:10.1525/as.2009.49.4.647.

Pareene, Alex. 2013. "The Presidential Hack List: Ranking Barack Obama's Favorite Columnists." *Salon,* December 23. Accessed April 8, 2015. www.salon.com /2013/12/23/the_presidential_hack_list_ranking_barack_obamas_favorite _columnists.

Peksen, Dursun, Timothy M. Peterson, and A. Cooper Drury. 2014. "Media-Driven Humanitarianism? News Media Coverage of Human Rights Abuses and the Use of Economic Sanctions." *International Studies Quarterly* 58, no. 4: 855–66. Accessed December 27, 2017. https://doi.org/10.1111/isqu.12136.

Pesek, William. 2012. "Billionaire Princelings Ruin a Chinese Vision." *Bloomberg View,* December 27. Accessed May 6, 2016. www.bloombergview.com/articles /2012-12-27/billionaire-princelings-ruin-a-chinese-vision.

Philipson, Alice. 2013. "BBC's Africa Funded by China." *Telegraph,* January 25. Accessed May 22, 2015. www.telegraph.co.uk/culture/tvandradio/bbc/98270 96/BBCs-Africa-funded-by-China.html.

Pinghui, Zhuang. 2014. "Cai Mingzhao to Head Xinhua News Agency as China Focuses on Party Ideology in Media." *South China Morning Post,* December 31. Accessed May 16, 2015. www.scmp.com/news/china/article/1672049 /cai-mingzhao-head-xinhua-news-agency-china-focuses-party-ideology -media.

Plunkett, John. 2015. "World Service Cuts Will Reduce UK's Global 'Soft Power,' BBC Report Warns." *Guardian,* January 28, sec. Media. Accessed December 21, 2017. www.theguardian.com/media/2015/jan/28/bbc-world-service-cuts-uk -global-soft-power.

Power, Samantha. 2003. *"A Problem from Hell": America and the Age of Genocide.* New York: Basic Books.

Powers, Matthew. 2015. "The New Boots on the Ground: NGOs in the Changing Landscape of International News." *Journalism* 17, no. 4: 401–16. Accessed December 21, 2017. https://doi.org/10.1177/1464884914568077.

Powers, Shawn. 2009. "The Geopolitics of the News: The Case of the Al Jazeera Network." Accessed April 19, 2015. https://www.academia.edu/556090/The _Geopolitics_of_the_News_The_Case_of_the_Al_Jazeera_Network.

Price, David. 2000. "Anthropologists as Spies." *Nation,* November 2. Accessed May 1, 2015. www.thenation.com/article/anthropologists-spies.

Price, Monroe, and Daniel Dayan. 2008. *Owning the Olympics: Narratives of the New China.* Ann Arbor: University of Michigan Press.

Price, Monroe, Libby Morgan, and Kristina Klinkforth. 2009. "NGOs as News-makers: A New Series on the Evolving News Ecosystem." *Nieman Lab*, November 9. Accessed May 7, 2016. www.niemanlab.org/2009/11/ngos-as-news makers-a-new-series-on-the-evolving-news-ecosystem.

Pritchard, David. 1992. "The News Media and Public Policy Agendas." In *Public Opinion, the Press and Public Policy*, edited by J. David Kennamer, 103–12. Westport, CT: Praeger.

Rauhala, Emily. 2016. "China Moves to Sidestep Panama Papers Story." *Washington Post*, April 5, sec. WorldViews. Accessed December 29, 2017. https://www.wash ingtonpost.com/news/worldviews/wp/2016/04/05/china-moves-to-sidestep -panama-papers-story/.

Rawnsley, Gary D. 2015. "To Know Us Is to Love Us: Public Diplomacy and International Broadcasting in Contemporary Russia and China." *Politics* 35, nos. 3–4: 273–86. Accessed December 23, 2017. https://doi.org/10.1111/1467-9256 .12104.

Read, Russ. 2016. "Who Are the Seven Iranians Released in Exchange for the U.S. Prisoners?" *Daily Caller*, January 16. Accessed May 9, 2016. http://dailycaller .com/2016/01/16/who-are-the-seven-iranians-released-in-exchange-for-the -u-s-prisoners.

Reese, Stephen, and Lucig Danielian. 1989. "Intermedia Influence and the Drug Issue: Converging on Cocaine." In *Communication Campaigns about Drugs: Government, Media, and the Public*, edited by Pamela J. Shoemaker, 29–46. New York: Routledge.

Reich, Zvi. 2008. "How Citizens Create News Stories." *Journalism Studies* 9, no. 5: 739–58. Accessed November 27, 2013. doi:10.1080/14616700802207748.

Reporters Committee for Freedom of the Press. 2011. "2. Others, Including Non-Traditional News Gatherers." *Reporters Committee for Freedom of the Press*, October 12. Accessed May 4, 2016. www.rcfp.org/1st-cir-privilege-compendium/2 -others-including-non-traditional-news-gatherers.

Reporters without Borders. 2005. "Xinhua: The World's Biggest Propaganda Agency." *Reporters without Borders*. Accessed May 8, 2016. https://rsf.org/en /reports/xinhua-worlds-biggest-propaganda-agency.

Ritchie, Jane, Jane Lewis, Gilliam Elam, Rosalind Tennant, and Nilufer Rahim. 2014. "Designing and Selecting Samples." In *Qualitative Research Practice: A Guide for Social Science Students*, edited by Jane Ritchie, Jane Lewis, Carol McNaughton Nicholls, and Rachel Ormston, 2d ed., 111–46. London: Sage.

Roberts, Jeff John. 2016. "The Real Reason Mark Zuckerberg Won't Admit Facebook Is a Media Company." *Fortune*, November 14. Accessed January 11, 2018. http://fortune.com/2016/11/14/facebook-zuckerberg-media.

Roberts, Marilyn, and Maxwell McCombs. 1994. "Agenda Setting and Political Advertising: Origins of the News Agenda." *Political Communication* 11, no. 3: 249–62. Accessed May 2, 2015. doi:10.1080/10584609.1994.9963030.

Robinson, Piers. 2001. "Theorizing the Influence of Media on World Politics Models of Media Influence on Foreign Policy." *European Journal of Communication* 16, no. 4: 523–44. Accessed February 23, 2013. doi:10.1177/0267323101016004005.

———. 2002. *The CNN Effect: The Myth of News, Foreign Policy and Intervention.* London: Routledge.

———. 2011. "The CNN Effect Reconsidered: Mapping a Research Agenda for the Future." *Media, War and Conflict* 4, no. 1: 3–11. Accessed October 17, 2012. doi:10.1177/1750635210397434.

Rohrabacher, Dana. 2013. "Under Cover." *Foreign Policy*, January 8. Accessed May 22, 2015. http://foreignpolicy.com/2013/01/08/under-cover.

Rothmeyer, Karen. 2011. "Hiding the Real Africa." *Columbia Journalism Review.* Accessed May 7, 2016. www.cjr.org/reports/hiding_the_real_africa.php.

Rowling, Charles M., Penelope Sheets, and Timothy M. Jones. 2015. "American Atrocity Revisited: National Identity, Cascading Frames, and the My Lai Massacre." *Political Communication* 32, no. 2: 310–30. Accessed May 9, 2016. doi:10.1080/10584609.2014.944323.

Russell, Frank S. 1999. *Information Gathering in Classical Greece.* Ann Arbor: University of Michigan Press.

Rutenberg, Jim. 2017. "RT, Sputnik and Russia's New Theory of War." *New York Times*, September 13, sec. Magazine. Accessed December 31, 2017. https://www.nytimes.com/2017/09/13/magazine/rt-sputnik-and-russias-new-theory-of-war.html.

Rutland, Peter, and Andrei Kazantsev. 2016. "The Limits of Russia's 'Soft Power.'" *Journal of Political Power* 9, no. 3: 395–413. Accessed December 23, 2017. https://doi.org/10.1080/2158379X.2016.1232287.

Sambrook, Richard. 2010. *Are Foreign Correspondents Redundant? The Changing Face of International News.* RISJ Challenges. Oxford: Reuters Institute for the Study of Journalism. Accessed February 6, 2013. https://reutersinstitute.politics.ox.ac.uk/our-research/are-foreign-correspondents-redundant.

Samuel-Azran, Tal. 2013. "Al-Jazeera, Qatar, and New Tactics in State-Sponsored Media Diplomacy." *American Behavioral Scientist* 57, no. 9: 1293–1311. Accessed December 27, 2017. https://doi.org/10.1177/0002764213487736.

Samuel-Azran, Tal, Inbal Assaf, Annie Salem, Loreen Wahabe, and Nadine Halabi. 2016. "Is There a Qatari–Al-Jazeera Nexus? Coverage of the 2022 FIFA World Cup Controversy by Al-Jazeera versus Sky News, CNNI and ITV." *Global Media and Communication* 12, no. 3: 195–209. Accessed December 27, 2017. https:// doi.org/10.1177/1742766516676208.

Samuel-Azran, Tal, and Naama Pecht. 2014. "Is There an Al-Jazeera–Qatari Nexus? A Study of Al-Jazeera's Online Reporting throughout the Qatari–Saudi Conflict." *Media, War and Conflict* 7, no. 2: 218–32. Accessed December 27, 2017. https://doi.org/10.1177/1750635214530207.

Samuels, David. 2016. "The Aspiring Novelist Who Became Obama's Foreign-Policy Guru." *New York Times*, May 5. Accessed May 9, 2016. www.nytimes.com/2016 /05/08/magazine/the-aspiring-novelist-who-became-obamas-foreign-policy -guru.html.

Sarbin, Theodore R., Ralph M. Carney, and Carson Eoyang. 1994. *Citizen Espionage: Studies in Trust and Betrayal*. Westport, CT: Greenwood Publishing.

Satow, Ernest Mason. 2009. *Satow's Diplomatic Practice*. Edited by Ivor Roberts. 6th ed. Oxford: Oxford University Press.

Savage, Charlie, Edward Wyatt, and Peter Baker. 2013. "U.S. Confirms That It Gathers Online Data Overseas." *New York Times*, June 6. Accessed January 10, 2018. www.nytimes.com/2013/06/07/us/nsa-verizon-calls.html.

Schattschneider, Elmer E. 1960. *The Semi-Sovereign People: A Realist's View of Democracy in America*. New York: Holt, Rinehart and Winston.

Scheufele, Dietram A., and David Tewksbury. 2007. "Framing, Agenda Setting, and Priming: The Evolution of Three Media Effects Models." *Journal of Communication* 57, no. 1: 9–20. Accessed March 13, 2014. doi:10.1111/j.0021-9916 .2007.00326.x.

Schudson, Michael. 2002. "The News Media as Political Institutions." *Annual Review of Political Science* 5, no. 1: 249–69. Accessed May 16, 2015. doi:10.1146 /annurev.polisci.5.111201.115816.

Sevenans, Julie, Stefaan Walgrave, and Debby Vos. 2015. "Political Elites' Media Responsiveness and Their Individual Political Goals: A Study of National Politicians in Belgium." *Research and Politics* 2, no. 3. Accessed December 27, 2017. https://doi.org/10.1177/2053168015593307.

Shafer, Jack. 2007. "Hail to the Return of Motherland-Protecting Propaganda!" *Slate*, August 30. Accessed May 16, 2015. www.slate.com/articles/news_and _politics/press_box/2007/08/hail_to_the_return_of_motherlandprotect ing_propaganda.html.

———. 2010. "The Journalist as Spy." *Slate*, September 20. Accessed May 3, 2015. www.slate.com/articles/news_and_politics/press_box/2010/09/the _journalist_as_spy.html.

Shambaugh, David. 2013. *China Goes Global: The Partial Power*. Oxford: Oxford University Press.

Shane, Daniel. 2017. "U.S. Panel Accuses Chinese Journalists of Spying for Beijing." *CNNMoney*, November 16. Accessed December 29, 2017. http://money.cnn .com/2017/11/16/media/chinese-media-us-foreign-agents/index.html.

Shane, Scott, and Benjamin Weiser. 2010. "Spying Suspects Seemed Short on Secrets." *New York Times*, June 29, sec. World/Europe. Accessed May 8, 2016. www.nytimes.com/2010/06/30/world/europe/30spy.html.

Shaw, Lucas, and Christopher Palmeri. 2015. "Disney Doubles Investment in Vice Media to $400 Million." *Bloomberg.com*, December 8. Accessed May 7, 2016. www.bloomberg.com/news/articles/2015-12-08/disney-said-to-double-invest ment-in-vice-media-to-400-million.

Sheafer, Tamir, Shaul R. Shenhav, Janet Takens, and Wouter van Atteveldt. 2014. "Relative Political and Value Proximity in Mediated Public Diplomacy: The Effect of State-Level Homophily on International Frame Building." *Political Communication* 31, no. 1: 149–67. Accessed March 13, 2013. doi:10.1080/1058 4609.2013.799107.

Shek, Colin. 2013. "Chinese Media Expands Africa Presence." *Al Jazeera*, January 24. Accessed May 7, 2016. www.aljazeera.com/indepth/features/2013/01/2013 12071929822435.html.

Shotwell, John M. 1991. "The Fourth Estate as a Force Multiplier." *Marine Corps Gazette* 75, no. 7. Accessed February 18, 2018. https://www.mca-marines.org /gazette/1991/07/fourth-estate-force-multiplier.

Shulsky, Abram N., and Gary James Schmitt. 2002. *Silent Warfare: Understanding the World of Intelligence*. Lincoln, NE: Potomac Books.

Shuster, Simon. 2015. "Inside Putin's Media Machine." *Time*, March 5. Accessed May 8, 2016. http://time.com/rt-putin/.

Simon, Zoltan. 2017. "Soros's Native Hungary Approves Crackdown on Foreign-Funded NGOs." *Bloomberg*, June 13. Accessed December 28, 2017. https://www .bloomberg.com/news/articles/2017-06-13/soros-s-native-hungary-approves -crackdown-on-foreign-funded-ngos.

Smolkin, Rachel. 2006. "Off the Sidelines." *American Journalism Review*, January. Accessed April 8, 2015. http://ajrarchive.org/Article.asp?id=3999.

Sparks, Colin. 2015. "China, Soft Power and Imperialism." In *Routledge Handbook of Chinese Media*, edited by Gary D. Rawnsley and Ming-yeh T. Rawnsley, 27–46. London: Routledge.

Spyksma, Hannah. 2017. "Unintentional Journalists." *Journalism Studies*, August 10, 1–21. Accessed December 27, 2017. https://doi.org/10.1080/1461670X.2017 .1351885.

StarTimes. "Corporate Responsibility." 2016. *StarTimes*. Accessed May 10. http://en .startimes.com.cn/corporateresponsibility/index.htm.

Stavisky, Samuel E. 1999. *Marine Combat Correspondent: World War II in the Pacific.* New York: Ivy Books.

Steele, Robert David. 2007. "Open Source Intelligence." In *Handbook of Intelligence Studies,* edited by Loch K. Johnson, 129–47. London: Routledge.

Stratfor. 2015. "China Flaunts Its Missile Arsenal." *Stratfor Worldview,* September 5. Accessed May 7, 2016. https://www.stratfor.com/analysis/china-flaunts-its-missile-arsenal.

Street, Nancy, and Marilyn Matelski. 1997. *Messages from the Underground : Transnational Radio in Resistance and in Solidarity.* Westport, CT: Praeger.

Stubbs, Jack, and Ginger Gibson. 2017. "Russia's RT America Registers as 'Foreign Agent' in U.S." *Reuters,* November 13. Accessed December 27, 2017. https://www.reuters.com/article/us-russia-usa-media-restrictions-rt/russias-rt-registers-as-foreign-agent-in-usa-editor-idUSKBN1DD25B.

Sullivan, Margaret. 2014. "When the Government Says, 'Shhh!'" *New York Times,* December 20. Accessed December 28, 2017. www.nytimes.com/2014/12/21/public-editor/when-the-government-says-shhh.html.

Sundaram, Anjan. 2014a. *Stringer: A Reporter's Journey in the Congo.* New York: Knopf Doubleday.

———. 2014b. "We're Missing the Story: The Media's Retreat from Foreign Reporting." *New York Times,* July 25. Accessed May 17, 2015. www.nytimes.com/2014/07/27/opinion/sunday/the-medias-retreat-from-foreign-reporting.html.

Sun Tzu (Sunzi). 2002. *The Art of War.* North Chelmsford, MA: Courier Corporation.

Sweetser, Kaye D., Guy J. Golan, and Wayne Wanta. 2008. "Intermedia Agenda Setting in Television, Advertising, and Blogs during the 2004 Election." *Mass Communication and Society* 11, no. 2: 197–216. Accessed May 2, 2015. doi:10.1080/15205430701590267.

Symon, Paul B., and Arzan Tarapore. 2015. "Defense Intelligence Analysis in the Age of Big Data." *Joint Force Quarterly,* October. Accessed May 10, 2016. http://ndupress.ndu.edu/Portals/68/Documents/jfq/jfq-79/jfq-79_4-11_Symon-Tarapore.pdf.

Taibbi, Matt. 2015. "Thomas Friedman Said Something Awesome at Davos: T-Shirt Contest!" *Rolling Stone,* January 23. Accessed May 7, 2016. www.rollingstone.com/politics/news/thomas-friedman-said-something-awesome-at-davos-t-shirt-contest-20150123.

Taibi, Catherine. 2014. "CNN Reporter Recounts 'Terrifying' Rescue In Iraq." *Huffington Post,* August 11. Accessed April 9, 2015. www.huffingtonpost.com/2014/08/11/cnn-reporter-isis-rescue-helicopter-iraq_n_5669325.html.

Takeshita, Toshio. 2006. "Current Critical Problems in Agenda-Setting Research." *International Journal of Public Opinion Research* 18, no. 3: 275–96. Accessed May 2, 2015. doi:10.1093/ijpor/edh104.

Tansey, Oisín. 2007. "Process Tracing and Elite Interviewing: A Case for Non-Probability Sampling." *PS: Political Science and Politics* 40, no. 4: 765–72. Accessed August 26, 2015. doi:10.1017/S1049096507071211.

Taylor, Peter. 2013. "Iraq War: The Greatest Intelligence Failure in Living Memory." *Telegraph*, March 18. Accessed May 3, 2015. www.telegraph.co.uk/news/world news/middleeast/iraq/9937516/Iraq-war-the-greatest-intelligence-failure-in -living-memory.html.

Thies, Cameron G. 2002. "A Pragmatic Guide to Qualitative Historical Analysis in the Study of International Relations." *International Studies Perspectives* 3, no. 4: 351–72. Accessed March 11, 2013. doi:10.1111/1528-3577.t01-1-00099.

Thomas, Gary. 2013. "Mission Impossible." *Columbia Journalism Review*. Accessed November 24, 2015. www.cjr.org/feature/mission_impossible.php.

Thorsen, Einar, and Stuart Allan, eds. 2014. *Citizen Journalism: Global Perspectives.* Vol. 2. New York: Peter Lang.

Thussu, Daya Kishan. 2013. *Communicating India's Soft Power: Buddha to Bollywood.* Palgrave Macmillan Series in Global Public Diplomacy. New York: Palgrave Macmillan.

———. 2014. *De-Americanizing Soft Power Discourse?* CPD Perspectives on Public Diplomacy. Los Angeles: Figueroa. Accessed December 23, 2017. https://usc publicdiplomacy.org/sites/uscpublicdiplomacy.org/files/useruploads/u20150 /CPDPerspectives2_2014_SoftPower.pdf.

———. 2016. "The Soft Power of Popular Cinema: The Case of India." *Journal of Political Power* 9, no. 3: 415–29. Accessed December 23, 2017. https://doi.org /10.1080/2158379X.2016.1232288.

Times of Israel Staff. 2016. "After Contentious Debate, Knesset Passes NGO Law." *Times of Israel*, July 12. Accessed December 28, 2017. www.timesofisrael.com /after-hours-of-debate-controversial-ngo-bill-passes-into-law/.

Trudolyubov, Maxim. 2016. "Russia's Hybrid War." *New York Times*, February 24. Accessed May 10, 2016. www.nytimes.com/2016/02/25/opinion/russias -hybrid-war.html.

Tryhorn, Chris. 2013. "BBC Is in a 'Soft Power' Battle with International Broadcast-ers." *Guardian*, November 13. Accessed May 19, 2015. www.theguardian.com /media/media-blog/2013/nov/13/bbc-broadcasters-tony-hall-worldwide -audience-cctv-al-jazeera.

Tuch, Hans N. 1990. *Communicating with the World: U.S. Public Diplomacy Overseas.* New York: Palgrave Macmillan.

Tumber, Howard, and Frank Webster. 2006. *Journalists under Fire: Information War and Journalistic Practices.* London: SAGE.

Ulfkotte, Udo. 2014. *Gekaufte Journalisten: Wie Politiker, Geheimdienste und Hochfinanz Deutschlands Massenmedien lenken.* Rottenburg: Kopp Verlag.

Upano, Alicia. 2003. "Will a History of Government Using Journalists Repeat Itself under the Department of Homeland Security?" *News Media and the Law.* Accessed March 3, 2015. www.rcfp.org/browse-media-law-resources/news -media-law/news-media-and-law-winter-2003/will-history-government-usi.

US-China Economic and Security Review Commission. 2017. *Report to Congress of the U.S.-China Economic and Security Review Commission.* Washington, DC: US Government Printing Office. www.uscc.gov/sites/default/files/annual_reports /2017_Annual_Report_to_Congress.pdf.

Utley, Garrick. 1997. "The Shrinking of Foreign News: From Broadcast to Narrowcast." *Foreign Affairs* 76, no. 3: 2–10. Accessed February 18, 2018. https://doi.org /10.2307/20047932.

Vargo, Chris J., and Lei Guo. 2017. "Networks, Big Data, and Intermedia Agenda Setting: An Analysis of Traditional, Partisan, and Emerging Online U.S. News." *Journalism and Mass Communication Quarterly* 94, no. 4: 1031–55. Accessed December 23, 2017. https://doi.org/10.1177/1077699016679976.

Vlassis, Antonios. 2016. "Soft Power, Global Governance of Cultural Industries and Rising Powers: The Case of China." *International Journal of Cultural Policy* 22, no. 4: 481–96. Accessed December 22, 2017. https://doi.org/10.1080/102866 32.2014.1002487.

Voci, Paola, and Luo Hui, eds. 2018. *Screening China's Soft Power.* New York: Routledge.

Walgrave, Stefaan, and Peter Van Aelst. 2006. "The Contingency of the Mass Media's Political Agenda Setting Power: Toward a Preliminary Theory." *Journal of Communication* 56, no. 1: 88–109. Accessed March 16, 2015. doi:10.1111/j.1460 -2466.2006.00005.x.

Wallsten, Kevin. 2007. "Agenda Setting and the Blogosphere: An Analysis of the Relationship between Mainstream Media and Political Blogs." *Review of Policy Research* 24, no. 6: 567–87. Accessed May 2, 2015. doi:10.1111/j.1541-1338.2007 .00300.x.

Wan, William. 2015. "China Raids NGO Offices in Latest Sign of Crackdown on Dissent." *Washington Post*, March 26. Accessed January 10, 2018. www.wash ingtonpost.com/world/china-raids-ngo-offices-in-latest-sign-of-crackdown -on-dissent/2015/03/26/4badeaac-d3b0-11e4-ab77-9646eea6a4c7_story .html.

Wanta, Wayne, Guy Golan, and Cheolhan Lee. 2004. "Agenda Setting and International News: Media Influence on Public Perceptions of Foreign Nations." *Jour-*

nalism and Mass Communication Quarterly 81, no. 2: 364–77. Accessed October 7, 2012. doi:10.1177/107769900408100209.

Wasburn, Philo C. 1997. "Review of *Radio Wars: Truth, Propaganda and the Struggle for Radio Australia* by Errol Hodge; *Radio Diplomacy and Propaganda: The BBC and VOA in International Politics, 1956–64* by Gary D. Rawnsley." *American Historical Review* 102, no. 4: 1210–12. Accessed May 21, 2013. doi:10.2307 /2170746.

Watanabe, Yasushi, and David L. McConnell. 2008. *Soft Power Superpowers: Cultural and National Assets of Japan and the United States.* Armonk, NY: M. E. Sharpe.

Weaver, David H. 2007. "Thoughts on Agenda Setting, Framing, and Priming." *Journal of Communication* 57, no. 1: 142–47. Accessed March 12, 2014. doi:10.1111/j .1460-2466.2006.00333.x.

Weimann, Gabriel, and Hans-Bernd Brosius. 2016. "A New Agenda for Agenda-Setting Research in the Digital Era." In *Political Communication in the Online World: Theoretical Approaches and Research Desgins,* edited by Gerhard Vowe and Philipp Henn, 26–44. Routledge Research in Political Communication. New York: Routledge.

Wekesa, Bob. 2014a. "No Need to Fear Chinese Media in Africa." *Business Day,* March 11. Accessed May 10, 2016. www.bdlive.co.za/opinion/2014/03/11/no -need-to-fear-chinese-media-in-africa.

———. 2014b. "An Analysis of China Central Television's Talk Africa Debate Show." Paper presented at the China and Africa Media, Communications and Public Diplomacy conference, September 10–11, 2014, Beijing. Accessed May 10, 2016. www.cmi.no/file/2917-.pdf.

Wekesa, Bob, and Yanqiu Zhang. 2014. *Live, Talk, Faces: An Analysis of CCTV's Adaptation to the African Media Market.* Stellenbosch: Universiteit Stellenbosch.

Whitehurst, Clinton H., Jr. 1965. "The Merchant Marine Act of 1936: An Operational Subsidy in Retrospect." *Journal of Law and Economics* 8 (October): 223–42. Accessed April 8, 2015. www.jstor.org/stable/724791.

Wilford, Hugh. 2009. *The Mighty Wurlitzer: How the CIA Played America.* Cambridge, MA: Harvard University Press.

Williams, Carol J. 1992. "Balkan War Rape Victims: Traumatized and Ignored." *Los Angeles Times,* November 30. Accessed May 2, 2015. http://articles.latimes.com /1992-11-30/news/mn-984_1_refugee-camp.

———. 1996. "Russian Security Service Expels U.S. Businessman as Spy." *Los Angeles Times,* May 13. Accessed January 10, 2018. http://articles.latimes.com/1996 -05-13/news/mn-3658_1_russian-federal-security-service.

Wilson, Jeanne L. 2015a. "Russia and China Respond to Soft Power: Interpretation and Readaptation of a Western Construct." *Politics* 35, nos. 3–4: 287–300. Accessed December 11, 2015. doi:10.1111/1467-9256.12095.

————. 2015b. "Soft Power: A Comparison of Discourse and Practice in Russia and China." *Europe-Asia Studies* 67, no. 8: 1171–1202. Accessed December 23, 2017. https://doi.org/10.1080/09668136.2015.1078108.

Wilson, Valerie Plame. 2012. *Fair Game: My Life as a Spy, My Betrayal by the White House.* New York: Simon and Schuster.

Winks, Robin W. 1996. *Cloak and Gown: Scholars in the Secret War, 1939–1961.* New Haven, CT: Yale University Press.

Wong, Edward. 2016. "Clampdown in China Restricts 7,000 Foreign Organizations." *New York Times,* April 28. Accessed May 7, 2016. www.nytimes.com/2016/04/29/world/asia/china-foreign-ngo-law.html?_r=1.

Woodward, Bob. 2002. *Bush at War.* New York: Simon and Schuster.

Wright, Katherine. 2015. "A Quiet Revolution: The Moral Economies Shaping Journalists' Use of NGO-Provided Multimedia in Mainstream News about Africa." PhD diss., University of London. Accessed May 2, 2016. http://research.gold.ac.uk/11854.

Wu, H. Denis, and John Maxwell Hamilton. 2004. "US Foreign Correspondents Changes and Continuity at the Turn of the Century." *Gazette* 66, no. 6: 517–32. Accessed February 5, 2013. doi:10.1177/0016549204047574.

Xinhua. 2011. "Xinhua Mobile Newspaper Delivers Soft-Launch in Kenya." *Xinhua,* April 19. Accessed February 18, 2018. www.focac.org/eng/zfgx/t816730.htm.

Xinrui, Song. 2013. "China Opens Its First African Media Research Institute [Translation]." *China Africa Project,* January 9. Accessed May 10, 2016. www.chinaafricaproject.com/201301chinas-first-institute-for-african-media-research-established-at-the-communication-university-of-china.

Yglesias, Matthew. 2013. "How to Revive Airline Competition." *Slate,* August 14. Accessed April 9, 2015. www.slate.com/articles/health_and_science/transportation/2013/08/cabotage_will_revive_airline_competition_foreign_airlines_should_be_able.html.

York, Geoffrey. 2013. "Why China Is Making a Big Play to Control Africa's Media." *Globe and Mail,* September 11. Accessed May 7, 2016. www.theglobeandmail.com/news/world/media-agenda-china-buys-newsrooms-influence-in-africa/article14269323.

Yörük, Zafer, and Pantelis Vatikiotis. 2013. "Soft Power or Illusion of Hegemony: The Case of the Turkish Soap Opera 'Colonialism.'" *International Journal of Communication* 7: 2361–85. Accessed December 23, 2017. https://insidestory.gr/sites/default/files/1880-9797-1-pb_2.pdf.

Young, Doug. 2013. *The Party Line: How The Media Dictates Public Opinion in Modern China.* Singapore: John Wiley & Sons.

Zavadski, Katie. 2015. "Putin's Propaganda TV Lies about Its Popularity." *Daily Beast*, September 17. Accessed May 9, 2016. www.thedailybeast.com/articles /2015/09/17/putin-s-propaganda-tv-lies-about-ratings.html.

Zengerle, Jason. 2013. "The Journalist Diplomat." *New York Magazine*, June 15. Accessed April 14, 2015. http://nymag.com/news/intelligencer/samantha -powers-2013-6.

Zhang, Guozuo. 2017. *Research Outline for China's Cultural Soft Power.* Research Series on the Chinese Dream and China's Development Path. Singapore: Springer.

Zhang, Xiaoling. 2010. "Chinese State Media Going Global." *East Asian Policy* 2, no. 1: 42–50. Accessed February 18, 2018. www.eai.nus.edu.sg/publications /files/BB488.pdf.

Zhang, Xiaoling, Herman Wasserman, and Winston Mano, eds. 2016. *China's Media and Soft Power in Africa: Promotion and Perceptions.* Palgrave Series in Asia and Pacific Studies. New York: Palgrave Macmillan.

Zhang, Yanqiu. 2014. "Understand China's Media in Africa from the Perspective of Constructive Journalism." Paper presented at the China and Africa Media, Communications and Public Diplomacy conference, September 10–11, 2014, Beijing. Accessed May 10, 2016. www.cmi.no/file/2922-.pdf.

Zhang, Yanqui, and Simon Matingwina. 2016. "Constructive Journalism: A New Journalistic Paradigm of Chinese Media in Africa." In *China's Media and Soft Power in Africa,* edited by Xiaoling Zhang, Herman Wasserman, and Winston Mano, 93–105. Palgrave Series in Asia and Pacific Studies. New York: Palgrave Macmillan.

ABOUT THE AUTHOR

MARKOS KOUNALAKIS, PhD, is an author, publisher, journalist, and scholar. During the 1980s and 1990s, Dr. Kounalakis worked as a foreign correspondent, covering wars and revolutions for *Newsweek* and as the NBC-Mutual News Moscow correspondent. He reported on the fall of the Berlin Wall and lived in the Soviet Union during its collapse. His assignments included the overthrow of Communism in East Germany, Czechoslovakia, Hungary, Romania, and Bulgaria. He reported on the Soviet war in Afghanistan and the outbreak of ethnic strife and war in Yugoslavia. He was based in Rome and Vienna, and ran *Newsweek*'s Prague bureau. Dr. Kounalakis became president and publisher of the *Washington Monthly* magazine and the chairman of Internews.

Dr. Kounalakis is currently a Central European University senior fellow at the Center for Media, Data and Society and a visiting fellow at the Hoover Institution. He writes a regular McClatchy syndicated foreign affairs column. He is a presidentially appointed member of the Fulbright Foreign Scholarship Board and a board member at USC's Annenberg School for Communication and Journalism, USC's Center on Public Diplomacy, and at America Abroad Media. He lives in San Francisco with his wife, Ambassador Eleni Kounalakis, and their two boys, Neo and Eon.

INDEX

academia, 7
  data on, 110
  foreign researchers in, 94
  intelligence system and, 95
  media studies in, 22
access, 5, 68, 70–71
  citizen journalism and, 96
  credibility and, 78, 98–100
  denial of, 159
  NGOs and, 107
  for noninstitutional journalists,
    31–32, 99–100
  to policymakers, 53
  privilege and, 35, 123
actors, 22, 35, 39, 134, 176
advocacy, 56
Afghanistan, 86
  IMV and, 103
  Soviet Union and, ix–xi, 122
Africa, 70–71
  Chinese GNNs in, 132, 137
  local journalists in, 74n103
  NGOs and, 106, 106n77
African Communication Research
    Center, 138
African Media Research Center,
    137
agenda setting, 24, 24n15, 31, 40
aggregation, 96, 110
AJ. *See* Al Jazeera
*AJR. See American Journalism
    Review*
ambassadors, 117

AMCOMLIB. *See* American
    Committee for Liberation
America Now, 144
American Committee for Liberation
    (AMCOMLIB), 93
American Journalism Review (AJR),
    10, 55
  survey with Kumar and, 17n48
Annan, Kofi, 141
anonymity, 3, 155
Arafat, Yasser, 118
Aristide, Jean-Bertrand, 165, 166
Armenia, 171
The Art of War (Tzu), 81
Assange, Julian, 115
assassination, 109
Athenaeum literary magazine, 43
attention, 29, 32
attitudes, 71–74, 163
audience, 14n42
  dependence of, 24
  as international, 4
  presentation to, 136
  pursuit of, 7
Avdoshin, Evgeny, 146
Azerbaijan, 172
Azran, Samuel, 50

Baker, Ray Stannard, 45
bartering, 118
Bazell, Bob, 136
BBC. *See* British Broadcast
    Corporation

BBC World Service, 102
BBG. *See* Broadcast Board of
    Governors
Begin, Menachem, 57
Bennett, Andrew, 173
Berringer, Felicity, 115
Black, Shirley Temple, 117, 119
bloggers, 99
blogosphere, 73
Bloomberg News, 16
Boas, Franz, 7n18
Bonsal, Stephen, 43, 43n14
*Born to Spy: Recollections of a CIA
    Case Officer* (Goodrich, A.),
    109
Bourrie, Mark, 148
Brazilian Journalism Research Journal,
    154
British Broadcast Corporation (BBC),
    11, 50n29, 102
broadcast, 1, 26
Broadcast Board of Governors (BBG),
    2, 129, 129n16
Brown, Al, 97
Bukashkin, Andrey, 128
Bulgaria, xii
Burt, Richard R., 47
Burundi, 141
Buryakov, Evgeny, 151, 152
Bush, George W., 76

Cai Mingzhao, 147
capacities, 18, 158
    as diminished, 126
    increase of, 94, 104
    service and, 170
    states and, 37
Carney, Jay, 46n23
Carter, Jimmy, 168
cascading activation model, 34–35

case study, 3, 4, 174–75
    See also studies
CBS News, 58
CCP. *See* Chinese Communist Party
Cédras, Raoul, 166
censorship, 60, 112, 112n94, 144
Central Intelligence Agency (CIA),
    84, 172
    RFE/RL, 92–93, 92n27, 101
CGTN/X. *See* China Global
    Television Network
Chen Yonglin, 149
China, 106, 130
    Africa and GNNs in, 132, 137
    CGTN/X in, xvi, 2
    diplomacy and, 135–45
    Film Bureau in, 132
    GNNs and, 14, 44, 131f
    NGOs and, 14n34, 134
    soft power of, 142
China Daily, 52, 143
China Global Television Network
    (CGTN/X), xv, 142
    in China, xvi, 2
    growth of, 11
    intelligence links and, 20
China Youth Daily, 148
China-Africa Reporting Project, 143
ChinAfrica magazine, 138
Chinese Communist Party (CCP),
    16, 131
Chinese Ministry of State Security
    (MSS), 150
Chinese Radio International Service
    (CRIS), 132
Chirol, Valentine, 42, 42n12
CIA. *See* Central Intelligence Agency
citizen journalism, 8, 63, 68, 96–98
Clinton, Hillary, xvi, 82n4
cloak and gown, 93–96, 94n35

CNN, 55
　on First Iraq War, 29
　Trump and, 51
Cohen, Bernard C., 22
Cohen, Y., 27n38
Cold War, 9, 84, 87, 91
Cole, Juan, 67
collaboration, 114–15
Columbia Journalism Review, 11
Combat Correspondent Corps, 60
communication studies, 24
community, 123
conflict, 19, 158n8
　intervention in, 33, 155
　safety during, 88
　stalling of, 170
Confucius Institute, 143
consultants, 130
consumption, 85
content, 65
context, 41
corporate entities, 103–5
counternarratives, 154
Craft of Intelligence (Dulles), 81
credentials, 172
credibility, 29–30, 161
　access and, 78, 98–100
CRIS. *See* Chinese Radio International
　Service
Cronkite, Walter, 57–58
Cross Talk with Peter Lavelle, 77
Crowley, P. J., 76
Cuban missile crisis, 168, 171
cultural congruence, 35
Cyprus, 44
Czechoslovakia, 64, 118, 171

data, 8, 15
　aggregation of, 110
　analysis structure for, 37

as ancillary, 85, 88
IMV collection of, 89
interpretation of, 19
journalists and, 65, 113–14
metadata as, 161
as unique, 107
uses for, 87
Dean's Hotel, x
decision-making, 69
demographics, 32
Department of Defense, US, 86
desire, 73
digital diplomacy, 27n34
digital media, 36n79
diplomacy, 12, 28
　China and, 135–45
　foreign correspondents and, 153
　GNNs and, 13–14, 48t, 74–77
　hard power and, 16, 41
　institutions and, 48–49
　intelligence gathering and, 65,
　　78–79, 82
　literature and, 27
　non-Western GNNs and, 125–52,
　　159
　obligation and, 59–63
　Russia and, 145–47
　soft power as, 40–41
　state power and Western GNNs as,
　　39–79
　See also specific types of diplomacy
Diplomat without Portfolio (Fritzinger),
　42
diplomats, 54
discourse, 8
Doctors without Borders, 66
documentaries, 98
documents, 92–93, 127
Drury, Barbara, 144
Dulles, Allen, 81

Eftimiades, Nicholas, 129
election, 127
elites, 34
    interviews with, 175–78
Elman, Colin, 173
embassy, 64, 75, 87
    attacks on, 119
    community at, 123
    information sharing at, 117, 120
    news bureau as, 78, 160
engagement, 19
English-language service, 4
Entman, Robert M., 34–35
Epoch Times, 149
espionage, 90n13, 91–92
    arrest for, 101, 156
    Russia and, 150–51
    Xinhua News Agency and, 149
ethics, 171
ethnography, 174
Euan-Smith, Charles, 43
exile, 166
expatriates, 123
external perception, 49–52

Face the Nation, 76
fact, 30, 64
fake news, 51
Famularo, Julia, 53
FARA. *See* Foreign Agents Registration
    Act
fear, 73, 169
Fingar, Thomas, 104–5, 178
FOCAC. *See* Forum on China-Africa
    cooperation
foreign affairs, 18
Foreign Agents Registration Act
    (FARA), 38, 51–52, 148
foreign bureaus, 162
    closure of, xv, 10, 17, 160

as embassy, 78, 160
    Xinhua and, 135
foreign correspondents, x–xii, 87
    Bonsal as, 43
    career as, 155, 155n3
    as de facto ambassadors, 78
    decrease of, xv, 10, 17
    role of, 153
formal diplomacy, 42–49
Forum on China-Africa cooperation
    (FOCAC), 137–38
Fox News, 51
framing, 33
Fresno State University, 66
Friedman, Thomas, 76–77
Fritzinger, Linda, 42
functions, 40, 48t
    hard power as, 157
    as parallel, 74–77
funding, 94, 134
    for BBC, 102
    military for, 95
    Vice and, 98, 98n49
Furlong, Michael D., 103

al-Gaddafi, Saif al Islam, 69
gatekeepers, 29
    GNNs as, 30
Gekaufte Journalisten (Ulfkotte), 90,
    90n14, 116
geography, xii
geopolitics, 15
    GNNS and, 70
    international media and, 39–40
    power and, 18
GIJN. *See* Global Investigative
    Journalist Network
Gilboa, Eytan, 22, 27, 36
Global Investigative Journalist
    Network (GIJN), 6

global news networks (GNNs),
xv–xvi
China and, 14, 44, 131f
definition and typology of, 3–9
degradation of, 162
diplomacy and, 13–14, 48t, 74–77
framework for, 5n9
as gatekeepers, 30
geopolitics and, 70
hard power and, 13–14, 19, 36–38,
157
infrastructure as, xvii
intelligence flow and, 37f
intelligence gathering and, 20
intermediaries as, 56
landscape changes for, 9–16
newsgathering and, 37
as nonstate-run, 53
power and, 12
resources as, 162
Russia and, 44
soft power of, 2–3, 2n6, 21, 23–36
state power and, 21–38
GNNs. See global news networks
Goodrich, Austin, 108–9
Goodrich, Mona, 109
Google News, 161
government, xi, 59, 62
Greece, 91
Guitchounts, Olga, 146
Gulf Wars, 29, 136

Haiti, 19
coup in, 165–68
Port-au-Prince in, 58–59
Hamilton, John Maxwell, 17, 18
Hamilton, Lee, 167, 169
hard power, 12
diplomacy as, 16, 41
functions as, 157

GNNs as, 13–14, 19, 36–38, 157
loss of, 126
Harvard University, 94
Havel, Václav, 64
Hemingway, Ernest, 149
historians, 54, 60
history, 101, 108
Holbrooke, Richard, 47
HRW. See Human Rights Watch
human intelligence (HUMINT), 104,
105
Human Rights Watch (HRW), 6
humanitarian diplomacy, 55
humanitarian organizations, 67
HUMINT. See human intelligence
Hungary, 44
media laws in, 45

ICC. See International Criminal Court
ideal types, 48, 110t
ideology, 154
IFAW. See International Fund for
Animal Welfare
IMV. See International Media Ventures
incentive, 58
independent journalists, x
influence, xvii
public discourse and, 8
soft power of, 40
on standards, 139
informal diplomacy, 49–52, 57–59
information, xv, 56, 158
bartering with, 118
as confidential, 20
exchange of, 64–65
IMV for, 86
intake of, 97
networks to gather, 68
in notebooks, 116, 116n107
sensitivity of, 62

information (*continued*)
    sharing of, 117, 120
    sources of, 24
    vacuum of, 126
    withholding of, 112
information revolution, 29
information sovereignty, 101
Informed Comment blog, 67
infrastructure
    capital cities for, 144
    GNNs and, xvii
INGOs. *See* international nongovern-
    mental organizations
institutions, 10
    as brand-name, 66
    diplomacy and, 48–49
    intelligence gathering and, 111–12
    products by, 97
integrity, 68, 170
intelligence
    academia and, 95
    material capacity of, 90–93
intelligence analysts, 111
intelligence gathering, 14, 158
    corporate entities and, 103–5
    diplomacy and, 65, 78–79, 82
    foreign correspondents and, 153
    as formal, 100–103
    GNNs and, 20
    INGOs and, 105–7
    institutions and, 111–12
    NOCs, 107
    non-Western GNNs and, 125–52
    personnel and, 107–11, 113–23
    state power and Western GNNs
        for, 81–123
    types of, 84t
Intelligence Threat Handbook (US
    government), 129, 129n18, 150

intermediaries
    GNNs as, 56
    governments and, 59
International Criminal Court (ICC),
    140
International Fund for Animal Welfare
    (IFAW), 134
international media, 39–40
International Media Ventures (IMV),
    84
    Afghanistan and, 103
    data collection by, 89
    Department of Defense and, 86
international nongovernmental organi-
    zations (INGOs), 5, 5n10, 82
    intelligence gathering and, 105–7
international relations, 22, 25
    literature on, 36
    soft power and, 26
International Reporting Project (IRP),
    6n13
international studies, 104
internet, 7, 61
intersectional diplomatic functions,
    63–70
interviews, 31, 61, 73, 120
    with elites, 175–78
    journalists, 89
    with Phillips, 165–72
    presidents for, 141
intimidation tactics, 159
Ioffe, Julia, 150–51, 151n93
Iran, 75, 156
Iraq, 29, 86
Iron Curtain, xii
IRP. *See* International Reporting
    Project
Ismayilova, Khadija, 156
Israel, 109

issues, 33
ITAR-TASS news agency, 151, 152
ivory, 134
Izetbegovic, Alija, 47

Jawoko, Kennedy, 71, 140, 174
Al Jazeera (AJ), 2, 11, 142
    on Gulf War, 29
Al Jazeera America, 77
Al Jazeera Arabic, 50
Jenner, Eric, 17
Jervis, Robert, 92
Jones Act/Merchant Marine Act, US,
    51n36
journalism profession, xvi, 157
    criticism of, 55
    ethics of, 171
    performance as, 83, 153
    role of, 39, 39n1
journalists, 28, 163, 172
    collaboration with, 114–15
    Combat Correspondent Corps
        for, 60
    data for, 65, 113–14
    diplomats and, 54
    interviews with, 89
    notebooks of, 116, 116n107
    perspective of, 72
    propaganda and, 149
A Journalist's Diplomatic Mission
    (Baker), 45

Kalugin, Oleg, 151
Kasyanov, Mikhail, 149
Keller, Bill, 115
Kennan Institute, 127, 127n7
Kennedy, John F., 161
Kenya, 72, 136, 140
Kenyatta, Uhuru, 140

kidnapping, 75
Kim Jong-un, 88
King, Nathan, 76
Kiselyov, Dmitry, 147
Kissinger, Henry, 41n8
Kojm, Chris, 167
Koppel, Ted, 75
Kounalakis, Markos, x–xi
    Phillips interview with, 165–72
Krasnoff, Lindsay, 54
Kumar, Priya, 17
    AJR and, 17n48
Kuwait, 29

bin Laden, Osama, 28
Larson, James F., 41
Laufer, Peter, ix–xiii, 122
Lenin, V. I., 1, 1n1
Libya, 33, 69
license plates, 119
literature, 5, 12, 25
    on diplomacy, 27
    on international relations, 36
Liu, Guangyuan, 139
Los Angeles Times, 113
Lothrop, Samuel, 7n18
Lukes, S., 23
Lunev, Stanislav, 152

M16 foreign intelligence service, 102,
    102n59
Marconi, Guglielmo, 1
The Marine Corps, 60
marketplace, 131f
Marsh, Vivien, 136, 136n41
Marshall, Joshua Michael, 99n53
Marton, Kati, 47, 47n26
Massoud, Ahmad Shah, 109
material capacity, 90–93

material resources, 14, 20
MBN. *See* Middle East Broadcasting
  Network
McClatchy newspaper company, 10,
  160
McCombs, Maxwell, 30
media
  diplomacy with, 27
  policymaking and, 34, 41–42
  relationships and, 138
media diplomacy, 27n38
media studies, 22
media-broker diplomacy, 28
Meet the Press, 76
Merkel, Angela, 99
metadata, 161
methodology, 173–78
Meyer, Christoph O., 8n22
Middle East Broadcasting Network
  (MBN), 49
*The Mighty Wurlitzer: How the CIA
  Played America* (Wilford), 84
military, 61, 95
minefields, x
Minerva Project, 95
mines, 122
monopoly, 9, 23
Morse code, 1
MSS. *See* Chinese Ministry of State
  Security
Mueke, Jonathan, 142
multilingual service, 128

Nagujja, Christine, 143
narratives, 30, 139
  China rising as, 154
  nationalism as, 51n35
  negativity and, 140
national alignment, 71–74

National Intelligence Council, 104
national service, 52
nationalism, 51n35
NBC News, ix
Ndebu, Newton, 139, 141–42
Near v. Minnesota, 60
neican, 130
new media, 25
New York Herald, 43
New York Times, xii, 16, 47
  online, 31
  response to, 100
news correspondents, ix–xii
newsgathering
  Chinese institutions and, 130
  GNNs and, 37
  operations for, 10
Newsweek, 62
NGOs. *See* nongovernmental
  organizations
NHK Cosmomedia, 52
Nieman Lab at Harvard University, 94
Nightline, 75n109
Nkrunziza, Pierre, 141
NOCs. *See* nonofficial cover agents
nongovernmental organizations
  (NGOs), 6
  Africa and, 106, 106n77
  China and, 134, 134n34
  data on, 110
  importance of, 105
  See also international nongovern-
    mental organizations
noninstitutional journalists, 31–32
  access for, 99–100
nonjournalistic institutions, 5
nonofficial cover agents (NOCs), 91
  intelligence gathering for, 107
nonprofit organizations, 6

nonstate foreign correspondents, x
non-Western NGOs, 133–35
non-Western type III GNNs, 82, 158
    diplomacy and intelligence
        gathering for, 125–52, 159
North Korea, 88, 156
notebook, 116, 116n107
nuclear weapons, 63, 120
Nuland, Victoria, 126, 126n3
Nunn, Sam, 168
Nye, Joseph S., 23

Obama, Barack, 46, 162
Obasanjo, Olusegun, 141
obligation, 59–63
Office of Strategic Services (OSS),
    93
online media, 31
open-source intelligence (OSINT),
    67, 83, 112–13
Operation Uphold Democracy, 165
opinion, 56
organizations, 131f, 132
Orville Schell, xvi
Orwell, George, 108
OSINT. *See* open-source intelligence
OSS. *See* Office of Strategic Services
Otto, Florian, 8n22
Overseas Press Club, 54
ownership, 67

Pakistan, ix, 122
Pan Am flight 103, 118
Paris Peace Conference, 45
participant observation, 174
patriotic empathy, 72
PDB. *See* presidential daily brief
Pelton, Robert, Young, 103
Pentagon, 103

People's Daily, 148
People's Republic of China (PRC),
    20, 135
    soft power of, 25
    Taiwan and, 137n43
perception conflict, 50
performance
    citizen journalism and, 96
    practices and, 21, 157
    presence and, 26
    profession and, 83, 153
personnel, 107–11, 113–23
perspective, 18, 34, 72
Phillips, Terry, 58–59, 88
    interview with, 165–72
photographers, 88
plausible deniability, 56, 160
pledge of allegiance, xii
poaching, 134
policy talk show format, 76
policymakers, 69, 162
    access to, 53
policymaking, 26, 111
    lack of reach to, 32
    media and, 34, 41–42
    soft power and, 133
political science, 24
popularity, 13
Powell, Colin, 168
power, xv, 160
    actors positions and, 35
    geopolitics and, 18
    GNNs and, 12, 15, 21–38
    political agendas and, 24
    relativity of, 66
    types of, xvi
    See also specific types of power
Power, Samantha, 46
Powers, Shawn, 39

practices, 20, 60, 158
  foreshadowing of, 45
  of non-Western GNNs, 125
  as obscure, 159
  performance and, 21, 157
  standards and, 102, 102n64
  support as, 155
  of USSR, 147
Prague, 64, 101, 117
PRC. *See* People's Republic of China
prepublication censorship, 112,
  112n94
presence, 26
presidential daily brief (PDB), 85,
  86–87, 114
presidents, 141
print media, 4n7
private actors, 28
privilege, 35, 123
A Problem from Hell (Power), 46
products, 38, 85
  institutions and, 97
  reliance on, 125
propaganda, 15n43
  Cold War and, 84
  implementation of, 133
  journalists and, 149
  Kremlin and, 128
protecting power, 44
protection, 155
psychology operations (PSYOPS),
  103
public opinion
  framing and, 33
  Russia and, 126
Pulitzer Center on Crisis Reporting,
  6n13
Putin, Vladimir, 53, 127

Qatar, 50

Radio Free Asia (RFA), 49
Radio Free Europe/Radio Liberty
  (RFE/RL), 49
  CIA and, 92–93, 92n27, 101
  research and observation at, 174
Radio Sweden, 108–9
Rather, Dan, 136, 167, 168
RBTH. *See* Russia beyond the
  Headlines
Red Crescent, 66
The Red Cross, 66
red mercury, 120, 120n114, *121*
relationships
  data on, 107
  media and, 138
  state and non-Western GNNs in,
  129–33, 145
relevance, 16–19, 153
reporters. *See* journalists
Reporters without Borders, 148
reporting, 61, 89
representation, 51, 62
request for proposal (RFP), 4
research, 83, 137, 173, 174
resources
  diminution of, 68, 161
  GNNs as, 162
  material resources as, 14, 20
Rezaian, Jason, 92, 156
RFA. *See* Radio Free Asia
RFE/RL. *See* Radio Free Europe/
  Radio Liberty
RFP. *See* request for proposal
Rhodes, Ben, 162–63
Rice, Condoleezza, 115
Robinson, Piers, 36
Rossiyskaya Gazeta, 146
RT. *See* Russia Today
Russia, 106, 106n76
  diplomacy and, 145–47

espionage and, 150–51
GNNs and, 44
public opinion and, 126
Ukraine and, 127
Russia beyond the Headlines (RBTH), 146
Russia Foreign Intelligence Service (SVR), 151
Russia Today (RT), xv, 2, 61n68
ambition of, 128
image of, 77
military and, 61
YouTube and, 11, 128
Ruto, William, 140

Sadat, Anwar, 57
satellite bureaus, 73
Save the Children, 69
Scali, John, 57, 63
Schultz, George P., 114, 178
scrutiny, 23
security studies, 81
self-perception, 52–57
Semtex, 118, *119*, 171
sensationalism, 32
sentiment, 72
Shafer, Jack, 89n11
shortwave radio, 1
signals of intelligence (SIGINT), 104
smart power
analysis framework as, 13
Clinton and, 82n4
soft power and, xvi, 25, 28
Smolkin, Rachel, 55
Snowden, Edward, 90n13, 112n94
Social Science Research Council, 95
soft power, 12, 12n35
agenda setting as, 40
China and, 142

diplomacy as, 40–41
of GNNs, 2–3, 2n6, 21, 23–36
international relations and, 26
policy and, 133
smart power and, xvi, 25, 28
sovereignty, 1
Soviet Union (USSR)
Afghanistan and, ix–xi, 122
practices of, 147
Sporyshev, Igor, 151
standards
compliance with, 146
influence on, 139
practices and, 102, 102n64
START I. *See* Strategic Arms Reduction Treaty
state, 163
capacities of, 37
GNNs and, 3, 4, 13, 15
intelligence gathering and Western GNNs for, 81–123
journalism value to, 67
non-Western GNNs and, 129–33, 145
relationships, 85
Western GNNs and power of, 39–79
statecraft, 15, 43
state-sponsored reporters, xi
Stavisky, Sam, 60
Steinem, Gloria, 108
Stephanopoulos, George, 75–76
Strategic Arms Reduction Treaty (START I), 47
structural exigency, 83
studies, 33, 33n64, 94, 96n42
SVR. *See* Russia Foreign Intelligence Service
sympathy, 73
Syria, 33, 72, 154, 155

Taiwan, 137, 137n34, 144, 159
Talk Africa show, 140
Talking Points Memo blog (TPM), 99n53
Taubman, Phil, 115
technology, 1, 150
telephone, xi
television, 10, 58
terrorist attacks, 119
theory, 22, 34
This Week, 76
Thomas, Gary, 50
Thucydides, 60, 81n2
Tibet, 144
TIME magazine, 62
TPM. *See Talking Points Memo* blog
transnational media, 21
transparency, 108
Trump, Donald, 51, 97, 126, 162
Tudjman, Franjo, 87
typology, 3t, 4n8
    of GNN-state relationships, 9t

Ukraine, 61, 127
Ulfkotte, Udo, 90n 14, 116
underwriting, 102
United Nations, 46, 166
University of Nairobi, 143
University of Oregon, xiii
University of Southern California, 150
University of Witwatersrand, 143
USSR. *See* Soviet Union

values, 17
Velvet Revolution, 117, 118
Vice News, 69, 97–98, 98n49
Voice of America (VOA), 49, 174

Walt Disney Company, 98n49
Wasemu, Moses, 142
Washington Post, 92, 156
Wekesa, Bob, 139–40
Western democratic states, xvii
Western GNNs
    intelligence gathering and, 81–123
    state power and diplomacy as, 39–79
Western institutions, xv
white papers, 7, 83
Wilford, Hugh, 84, 85
Williams, Carol, 113
Wilson, Valerie Plame, 91n17, 116, 116n107
Wilson, Woodrow, 45
Wisner, Frank, 93
Wolfowitz, Paul, 107
Woodward, Bob, 114
Wu, Denis H., 18

Xerxes, 91
Xi Jinping, 53
Xinhua News Agency, 70, 130, 131f
    Bourrie and, 148
    espionage and, 149
    foreign bureaus for, 135
    Google News and, 161

Yarim-Agaev, Yuri, 149, 149n87
Yazidis, 55
Young, Doug, 129–30
YouTube, 11, 128, 146

Zengerle, Jason, 46
Zhang, Yanqui, 71, 137
Zheng, Wang, 143